Reclaiming Class

Women, Poverty, and the Promise of
Higher Education in America

In the series

TEACHING/LEARNING SOCIAL JUSTICE

edited by Lee Anne Bell

Reclaiming Class

Women, Poverty, and the Promise of Higher Education in America

Edited by
VIVYAN C. ADAIR AND
SANDRA L. DAHLBERG

TEMPLE UNIVERSITY PRESS
Philadelphia

Temple University Press, Philadelphia 19122
Copyright © 2003 by Temple University
All rights reserved
Published 2003
Printed in the United States of America

Library of Congress Cataloging-in-Publication Data

Reclaiming class : women, poverty, and the promise of higher education in
America / edited by Vivyan C. Adair and Sandra L. Dahlberg.
     p.   cm. — (Teaching/learning social justice)
     Includes bibliographical references.
     ISBN 1-59213-021-6 (cloth : alk. paper) — ISBN 1-59213-022-4 (pbk. : alk.
paper)
     1. Poor women—United States.   2. Poor women—Education (Higher)—
United States.   3. Poor single mothers—United States.   4. Welfare recip-
ients—United States.   5. Women college students—United States.   I. Adair,
Vivyan Campbell.   II. Dahlberg, Sandra L., 1958–   III. Series.

     HV1445 .R43 2003
     378.1'9826'942–dc21   2002035274

This book is dedicated to those whose lives speak daily to the contradictions of American meritocracy

Contents

Acknowledgments   ix

Introduction: Reclaiming Class: Women, Poverty,
and the Promise of Higher Education
in America
VIVYAN C. ADAIR AND SANDRA L. DAHLBERG   1

Speech Pathology: The Deflowering of an Accent
LAURA SULLIVAN-HACKLEY   21

I. EDUCATORS REMEMBER

1   Disciplined and Punished: Poor Women,
    Bodily Inscription, and Resistance
    through Education
    VIVYAN C. ADAIR   25

2   Academic Constructions of "White Trash," or
    How to Insult Poor People without Really Trying
    NELL SULLIVAN   53

3   Survival in a Not So Brave New World
    SANDRA L. DAHLBERG   67

4   To Be Young, Pregnant, and Black: My Life
    as a Welfare Coed
    JOYCELYN K. MOODY   85

5   If You Want Me to Pull Myself Up, Give Me
    Bootstraps
    LISA K. WALDNER   97

II. ON THE FRONT LINES

6   If I Survive, It Will Be Despite Welfare Reform:
Reflections of a Former Welfare Student
TONYA MITCHELL   113

7   Not By Myself Alone: Upward Bound with
Family and Friends
DEBORAH MEGIVERN   119

8   Choosing the Lesser Evil: The Violence of the
Welfare Stereotype
ANDREA S. HARRIS   131

9   From Welfare to Academe: Welfare Reform as
College-Educated Welfare Mothers Know It
SANDY SMITH MADSEN   139

10 Seven Years in Exile
LETICIA ALMANZA   157

III. POLICY, RESEARCH, AND POOR WOMEN

11 Families First—but Not in Higher Education:
Poor, Independent Students and the Impact of
Financial Aid
SANDRA L. DAHLBERG   169

12 The Leper Keepers: Front-Line Workers and the
Key to Education for Poor Women
JUDITH OWENS-MANLEY   196

13 "That's Why I'm on Prozac": Battered Women,
Traumatic Stress, and Education in the
Context of Welfare Reform
LISA D. BRUSH   215

14 Fulfilling the Promise of Higher Education
VIVYAN C. ADAIR   240

About the Contributors   267

Acknowledgments

WE THANK Lee Anne Bell and Temple University Press and our friends and colleagues at Hamilton College and the University of Houston–Downtown for their encouragement and support. Most important, we thank our families—especially Heather, Geryl, and Bob Adair, Ronnie Johnston, Rebekah Lockner, and Sean Lockner—who made this journey with us.

Vivyan C. Adair and Sandra L. Dahlberg

Introduction: Reclaiming Class

Women, Poverty, and the Promise of
Higher Education in America

Until the missing story of ourselves is told, nothing besides told can suffice /
We shall go on quietly craving it / In the missing story of ourselves can be
found all other missing stories.

—Laura Riding Jackson

In the fall of 1999, on a crisp, beautiful afternoon in upstate
New York, a group of educators, legislators, social-service providers,
and welfare activists met for a conference at Hamilton College.[1] Our goal
was to discuss and enrich our understanding of the plight of welfare-
recipient students in a post–welfare-reform era. One of the keynote
speakers for the event was the economist Teresa Amott, whose years of
research and publication had guided many of our own professional
careers.[2] Before she shared her thoughts on poverty and welfare reform
in the United States, Amott told the rapt audience a story that emanated
from the core of her experience. Recalling her activist roots in the 1960s,
she spoke of attending a welfare-rights demonstration as a college student after spending months organizing for legislative change. At the
rally a *Boston Globe* reporter approached Amott, the only academic in
the group, and earnestly asked: "How much do they *really* need to live
on?" In her sincerity and enthusiasm, Amott began to answer but was
abruptly silenced as one of her new welfare-recipient colleagues cautioned, "You answer that question when you have to live on the
answer!" Amott assured us that she had never forgotten that moment,
and it was clear to all in attendance that her colleague's message had
shaped the entire body of Amott's finely nuanced, respectful, and powerful work.

Many of us attended the conference as intergenerationally poor
women who were engaged in academic scholarship, as poverty-class

academics attempting to negotiate dual, and often conflicting, class identities on a daily basis. In Amott's simple anecdote we recognized a complex and powerful truth: that for far too long we had been asked to live
with shame and silence; that far too often our lives and the lives of those
we loved had been reduced to little more than the object of scholarly
investigation; and that, like Amott's colleagues, we had in that process
allowed ourselves to be spoken for and about while denied a voice in
venues of power and authority. We vowed at that moment to try to use
our burgeoning, yet still often tenuous, authority to reclaim our voices
and our stories in the classroom and in a world that both denies us and
marks us with misinterpretations of our class and value.

This collection of essays represents the fulfillment of that vow. It was
written by poor mothers and daughters who, ironically, found and then
often learned to erase their voices in the post-secondary academy. It
represents, in many cases, the first stirrings of stories that have been
heretofore repressed, denied, erased, and dismissed in society and in the
academy. We articulate and theorize what the poet Laura Riding Jackson calls "the missing stories of ourselves" to rename and reclaim our
complex relationship to the academic classroom and to prolific misrepresentations of our own class identities. These are powerful and
poignant stories that press for a hearing.

We are women who have known profound poverty—as children and
as adults—and we, like the vast majority of our sisters in poverty, bear
the material, social, psychic, and physical marks of our poverty-class origins. Our perceptions of the world and our actions have also been positively influenced by our cultures of origin. Having roots in poverty has
both hurt us and provided us with strength, community, resiliency, and
vision. Some of us are no longer experiencing the hardships of economic
poverty, but we identify our culture of origin as the poverty class and
remain grounded in that identity as surely as members of the middle
class maintain their own class identities despite economic fluctuations.

The women who have contributed to this collection are also associated with higher education and view its structure, culture, and policies
from the vantage point of poverty. Although we recognize that education is not a unilateral solution to poverty, we also know that we have
survived and positively changed our lives and those of our families
through the process and products of post-secondary education. Most of
us survived in an environment that sought to exclude, punish, and vil-

ify us because we were poor. We are living proof of both the pejorative power of public policy based on stereotypes of poor women and the liberating and revolutionary potential of higher education.

We are deeply indebted to those working-class scholars who have so brilliantly, and so bravely, come before us to articulate the anomie and sense of dislocation they experienced in concert with the power and privilege associated with higher education. Richard Sennett and Jonathan Cobb in *The Hidden Injuries of Class* (1973) and Jake Ryan and Charles Sackrey in *Strangers in Paradise: Academics from the Working-Class* (1996, 4) recognized that, for working-class men, "the conflict inherent in the hierarchy of the class system becomes internalized within the individual, upwardly mobile person." Michelle Tokarczyk and Elizabeth Fay further explore this sense of dislocation and shame in *Working Class Women in the Academy: Laborers in the Knowledge Factory* (1993). Focusing on the experiences of women marked as working class—often by virtue of their parents' economic and social positions and not their own—contributors to this collection reflected their experiences of being hired to do more work for less reward (Tokarczyk and Fay 1993, 16); of lacking material, emotional, and financial support that would otherwise enhance their careers (Tokarczyk and Fay 1993, 18); of taking on greater work loads than their middle-class peers so they could "prove to themselves and to others that they are worthy" (Tokarczyk and Fay 1993, 17); and of being silenced by the "singular [middle-class] voice of the institution" (Tokarczyk and Fay 1993, 7). The essays in Tokarczyk and Fay's ground-breaking collection also reflect that working-class female academics suffer the price of class "transformation," that they often believe themselves to be imposters (a move that can undermine their own success), and that they engage in self-hatred that makes them complicit in their own oppression (Tokarczyk and Fay 1993, 51, 55).[3]

In addition, poor women in the academy are often disenfranchised materially. Working at minimum wage, lacking health care, caring for children on our own, securing necessary social-service benefits, and attending school full time renders poor female academics silent and exhausted. Wearing the "wrong" clothes, having bad teeth, not being able to afford expensive research materials or to attend important academic conferences, coping with public censure and vilification, and stumbling with new language and methods evoke feelings of shame and guilt, again generating a sense of fear and alienation.

In C. L. Barney Dews and Carolyn Law's *This Fine Place So Far from Home: Voices of Academics from the Working Classes* (1995), contributors also evocatively described the psychic pain of embodying "the oxymoronic phrase: working-class academic." In this collection, working-class academics speak of feeling forced to "shift [their] allegiance[s]" (Law 1995, 3) and of interacting with the academy and their families of origin in ways that produce pain and dislocation. Law laments that through the process of education she "suffered a loss my present context doesn't even recognize as a loss," concluding, "my education has destroyed something even while it has been recreating me in its own image ... my success is always tempered by the guilt I feel in having chosen a life path that has made me virtually unrecognizable to my kin" (Law 1995, 2). She adds, "While one can appear to be a native in an adopted land, one is always haunted by voices from the other side of the border. These are narratives of profound conflict, of persons feeling out of place in both worlds" (Law 1995, 7). It is the unrealized dream of these scholars "not to embarrass family but to reclaim our past lives with dignity" (Law 1995, 4).

Our contributors expressed similarly profound, complex, and raw feelings about the prices they paid, and continue to pay, for accessing the fruits of education. Added to the general malaise expressed by working-class scholars is the very real poverty-bashing that poor women experience in the media, from public officials, and, crucially, at the hands of "well-meaning" professors, administrators, and peers. All too often, and increasingly in the past decade, the term "poor woman" in the United States has been yoked to images of "broodsows,"[4] "Welfare Queens,"[5] "unfit parents who view their children as nothing more than increases in welfare checks,"[6] "alligators," and "wolves who eat their young."[7] Poor women are feared, blamed, mocked, ridiculed, and punished in U.S. media and society, and hence in public policy.[8] Indeed, several contributors noted their experiences of being judged and feared for being "less than working-class," as their marital status and maternal bodies collided with racism, classism, sexism, and heterosexism in the rhetoric of poverty-bashing both in and out of the academy.[9]

In response, poor female academics have often remained silent. Indeed, poor women learn at a very early age that their stories are dangerous and obscene. As children, we are daily reminded not to share the details of our lives for fear of public sanction, and as we grow we are well tutored in shame, guilt, resentment, envy, and self-hatred—all of silence's handmaidens. These lessons are reinforced as our families are marked with debilitating tropes and punished with policy meant to control and contain our "dangerous" and "pathological" bodies.

One avenue by which some poor women transform their lives is through higher education, but even that pathway often is not benign. Our lives continue to be discounted and devalued in the post-secondary academy. In sometimes elaborate acts of confession, poor women are forced to publicly reject their cultures of origin to gain entry into academic institutions and to be viewed as worthy, "deserving" students and "legitimate" scholars. When we began our educational journeys, many of us believed (perhaps naively) that the academy was a place where we could be freed of class stigmas, a place where we would be judged on our own scholarship and hard work. Yet the process we continue to experience of moving from poverty to a professional class has been and remains full of twists and turns, carrying with it examples of rejection and loss, oppression and denial. Rather than being cleanly transformed by educational advancement and achievement, we were simultaneously erased and made painfully visible with poverty-class markers. Education does, however, provide the means for many women to secure economic solvency and intellectual fulfillment. It offers hope, even as that hope is complicated by pedagogies and policies that are ultimately detrimental to poor women.

In the United States, the standard academic lens through which poverty is examined is that of middle-class culture, which posits an adversarial stance toward the poor. When poverty is being examined, for instance, poor people are seldom called on as expert witnesses; academicians and the media rely instead on interpretations of poverty made by middle- and upper-income observers. Often in academic inquiry, more validity or status is accorded to the "disinterested" observer than to the active participant. In the case of poverty and the evaluation of higher education, this practice has too often resulted in a false inference that there is only one truth, one lens, by which the efficacy of higher education can be analyzed: the lens of the middle-class perspective. As a result, the stories of poor women are controlled or revised to conform to the middle-class lens. Too often, when poor women critique our class system and its barriers to mobility, we are further marginalized by being labeled "ungrateful," which very clearly displays that privilege is the basis for respect and access to public discourse. These moves erase the complexities of poverty and prohibit firsthand poverty-class analyses of the American condition.

When poor women do find the energy and courage to speak, they are often silenced by the fear of reprisal. This collection is a case in point. Poor women writing these essays struggled to include pivotal examples of abuse and domestic violence, unfair treatment at the hands of educational administrators, and damaging practices experienced in courtrooms, welfare offices, and social-service agencies. Ultimately, much in those sections was removed—literally excised—to avert the possibility of litigation, even though irrefutable documentation exists to validate the claims.

So, many of us learn to live a lie and to pretend that we are not poverty class. Those who are both "fortunate" enough to pass successfully and willing to bear the psychic cost of such deception throughout our undergraduate and graduate educations must continue to do so to perform our authority as professionals throughout our careers. Rita Felski points to Carolyn Steedman's *Landscape for a Good Woman* (1987) as evidence of the long-term cost that passing as middle-class can entail:

> In spite of Steedman's movement out of the working-class she remains haunted by the psychic markings from her childhood, conscious of the gulf between her background and that of her upper-middle class friends. Yet she cannot simply celebrate her origins: indeed they stand for a material and psychic impoverishment she is glad to have escaped. (Felski 2000, 12)

Forced to pass in order to survive and denied the opportunity to celebrate and take solace in our communities of origin, poor female scholars and professionals become homeless.

In this collection we begin to break this cycle, and to rupture the ubiquitous middle-class lens, by allowing poor female academics to reclaim their truths. We tell and theorize our stories, delineating the class barriers we encountered in an effort to demonstrate the effects that public policy and sentiment have on our lives. We offer analyses of the academic systems that marginalize poor women and provide counter-narratives and policy recommendations that can ameliorate the class bias of academe and allow academic institutions to fulfill the promise of providing affordable access for all classes of Americans.

As this collection illustrates, despite the enormous risk inherent in resistance, poverty-class academicians make sense of their lives, marginality, and liminality by using their experiences of class in ways that are both startling and productive. In being allowed to reclaim both our class and our experiences in the classroom, poor women reveal new insights around the ontology of class marking, resistance, and transcendence. Here, to borrow from the feminist credo, the personal becomes political, as in the process of coming to voice class is re-envisioned as psychic, economic, social, cultural, corporeal, and semiotic.

Our stories are heartfelt and impassioned, but they are not unique. We offer them as representative examples of the experiences of poor women in higher education who have been, and continue to be, denied the opportunity to speak, even while resisting and pushing against that prohibition. It is our hope that these stories will affect legislation, and educational and public policy, that for so long have operated and been justified without our perspectives; create a new politics of recognition that is immediate and resonant; and clear a space for the articulation and valuation of the stories of other poor women in and out of the academy. In this way, we hope to support them in their efforts to resist their positioning as voiceless objects of investigation, a resistance that will allow poor female scholars and educators to emerge as literate and powerful speaking subjects.

In Part I: Educators Remember, women who exited poverty via the pathway of higher education and joined the professorial ranks recall their experiences within theoretical frames, allowing readers to understand and critique the process of education as a democratic project. Vivyan C. Adair begins this section with "Disciplined and Punished: Poor Women, Bodily Inscription and Resistance through Education." Using Michel Foucault's argument about the inscription of bodies, Adair examines the closed circuit that fuses together systems of power, the material conditions of poverty, and the bodily experiences that allow for the perpetuation—and, indeed, for the justification—of discipline and punishment. She also exposes the "revolutionary" and liberatory potential of higher education to disrupt this process.

Working from a central thesis of the bodily inscription of poor women, Adair explores the processes and epistemology of resistance through which many poor women have entered into post–secondary-degree programs to "rewrite their meaning and value in the world." She warns that this process is not as simple or as positive as the myth of education and meritocracy suggests; rather, she illustrates that ultimately education can and does allow poor women "to resist and to reconsider—deconstruct and rearrange—the bodily signs of [their] own very public punishment." Adair claims that, in the end, education does not erase the indelible marks of poverty, but that it does transform the ways in which poor women are able to address class stratification, punishment, and erasure, ultimately enabling them to interrogate and critique the indelible scripts of poor women's—of our own—bodies.

Nell Sullivan's "How to Insult the Poor without Really Trying" further explores the theme of class inscription and poor women's forced silence. In this compelling essay, Sullivan uses Lacan's theory of aphanisis to describe her own fading and disappearance, her nascent erasure and silence as a white child growing up poor in the South. In rethinking her class origins, she argues that no matter how hard one works "it is not individual identity, but class identity that determines one's fitness for even a basic education and respect."

Sullivan connects childhood lessons of class to brandings and misreadings that she experienced at various junctures in academe. She remembers that experiences of "shame were also abundant in college and graduate school, but in those settings everyone always assumed that I was at least middle-class, and if not, that I would pretend to be," adding ironically that "in such settings, economic need supposedly becomes a moot (or perhaps only a mute) point." For Sullivan, poverty-class shame and invisibility force us to become complicit in our own silence and invisibility. This complicity is fueled by literary and social stereotypes that are "academically endorsed" and "in turn serve [again] to silence those who hail from the lower economic classes by inducing shame and creating the desirability of passing for middle-class." Sullivan reveals that, even in writing this essay, she "struggled with the alternating urges to remain silent . . . or to hide [herself] within an authoritative middle-class voice that passes in academe for the voice of consensus." She concludes with a plea: "We educators [of the lower economic classes] need to proclaim our heritage and refuse further complicity in our own silence and the silencing of others."

In "Survival in a Not So Brave New World," Sandra L. Dahlberg expertly continues to explore the institutionalized disfranchisement of poor women in the "academic broom closet" of higher education. As an opening metaphor, Dahlberg compares herself to the characters of Shakespeare's *The Tempest,* especially to those characters for whom "no resolution is provided." Like the play's Miranda, Dahlberg found herself longing to live in the "brave new world" of academe that promised learning, advancement, and financial security. But like Caliban, she realized that in reality, her presence in the academy was often co-opted, as she was positioned as a foil by which other "normative" and "deserving" students could "measure their own worth, their own privilege." As a result, Dahlberg tells us, she was remanded to the "periphery of higher education" unless she abandoned her "culture of origin and refashion[ed herself] in middle-class customs." For Dahlberg, access to higher education involved "a duality that required self-erasure in order to succeed . . . in a sometimes hostile environment."

Dahlberg goes on to explore the ways in which the concept of class transcendence diminishes the lives (strengths and power) of poor, single mothers in the academy; the ways in which categories of deservedness and undeservedness mirroring those of welfare reform are established and used to maintain academic class distinctions; and the pressure to pass as privileged or as middle class (or, at the very least, as working class) in institutions of higher education. In all of these ways, poor women learn to "closet themselves" to survive. The price of passing is both erasure and "a loss of family and community of origin," as Dahlberg puts it, but the price of not passing is greater still: It is failure and banishment from the brave new world of the academy.

Through the work of Adair, Sullivan, and Dahlberg, we begin to understand that misrecognition and misplaced authority are central to the co-optation and misrepresentation of poor women in the post-secondary academy. Joycelyn Moody illustrates that this misrepresentation is intensified for poor black women experiencing the "multiple jeopardies of race, class, and gender." In "To Be Young, Pregnant, and Black: My Life as a Welfare Coed," she explains that racist, classist, and sexist misrepresentation rendered her welfare experience "particularly snarled and thus deeply painful," leading ultimately to self-hatred and erasure. She convincingly argues that "the injurious censure" she received at the hands of health-care workers "compounded my sense of shame about my 'illegitimacy,' my pregnancy, and my dependency."

Moody uses these experiences of shame and humiliation to consider both inter- and intra-racial conflicts "based on (the mere appearance of) class differences," expertly exploring the confusion of class with race by both blacks and non-blacks. Further, she posits that this confusion "amplifies the pain of African American women's experiences on welfare during pregnancy and exposes the interlocking systems of oppression that stereotype and misconstrue them." In her essay she untangles the "knotted threads of the story of [her] participation in the welfare system" and confronts the injuries of racism (affected by classism, sexism, and heterosexism) that "make us all crazy." Moody ends by exposing the "exceptions" model as one that absolves the larger society of its role in her past suffering. She concludes by choosing to claim the stance of activist, proclaiming, "We are nobody's exceptions: not causalities of the latest 'war on poverty,' but sufferers of it—and proudly valiant soldiers against it."

Reflecting on public policy that responds to a rhetoric of blame and finger-pointing, Lisa Waldner's chapter, "If You Want Me to Pull Myself Up, Give Me Bootstraps," continues with an analysis of our culturally "myopic vision regarding welfare and single-parent families." Waldner begins by arguing that "for some the American Dream is not even a dream. It is a hallucination." She continues by critiquing short-sighted policy concerning poor women and education that leads to their devaluation in institutions of post-secondary education.

Waldner urges us to understand the complex intersection of public and private issues that lead to poverty and structural inequity. Some of the most salient of those issues for Waldner are "a system that refuses to promote equal pay for women and that discourages poor women from earning educational degrees or training for higher-paying skilled positions . . . and a system that does not hold men accountable for their contribution to out-of-wedlock childbearing or failure to pay adequate child support." In drawing on sociological theory and her own lived experiences, Waldner's resonant points are that we must "look beyond individuals and alleged character flaws to address systemic forces that create and re-create the welfare-class," and that we should "invest in college students, especially single-parent students, as we would any other infrastructure project."

Part II: On the Front Lines presents the stories of five poor women pursuing their educational goals. These essays present counter-narratives that offer opportunities to reframe public discourse about poor women and education. In the process of telling their stories, these women also allow us to understand better the formal and informal structures that enact and enforce their silence and erasure—and increasingly, their absence—in the post-secondary academy.

Our initial impulse was to include in this part of the collection essays that told the stories of those who had survived and overcome profoundly debilitating obstacles, but not every academic effort results in success. Too often, the system overwhelms, permanently silences, and kills hope. This is the case, as it now stands, with Tonya Mitchell. Once a thriving college student, Mitchell exemplifies the draconian policy changes brought about by welfare reform. These "reforms" disallowed higher education as a viable option for poor women and thereby eliminated hope of changing lives for the better. Mitchell's essay, "If I Survive, It Will Be Despite Welfare Reform: Reflections of a Former Welfare Student," traces her entry into college and her subsequent removal from the university less than a year short of graduation because welfare reform "forced [her] to be 'responsible' and to 'work first.'" Her displacement from the university before she had earned the degree that would allow her to earn a livable wage meant that she has less to live on than she did under welfare.

Mitchell's essay begins with a description of the humiliation she endured as a welfare mother, then describes the rage she felt when she discovered that poverty disallowed her right to autonomy and privacy. She reminds us that if you are black and poor and receive welfare benefits, then "the state pays for you and the state owns you, and there is absolutely nothing you can do about it." Her intellectual aptitude, her proven academic ability, and her hard work did nothing to ameliorate her circumstances. Of all the stories in this book, Mitchell's is perhaps the most tragically compelling, and the most important. She represents the tens of thousands of poor women whose hopes and ambitions have been destroyed by welfare reform. Furthermore, the effects of welfare reform experienced by Mitchell and others are usually excised from the public discussion on welfare policy.

The remaining essays in Part II reflect the stories of poor students who are succeeding in academe but are doing so at great cost. In "Not By Myself Alone: Upward Bound with Family and Friends," Deborah Megivern describes the alienation and dissonance she felt as an undergraduate from a very poor family entering a private college. Megivern goes on to examine more fully the tensions between familial responsibility and personal actualization, between the need for honest friendships and the imposter phenomenon she used to avoid social rejection at college. Faced with the threat of social rejection, Megivern tried to pass and, as a result, experienced episodes of depression as her successes intensified the distance between home and her academic world.

The tensions between these competing values and desires culminated in graduate school, when Megivern became a single parent to her younger siblings. At the same time, she began experiencing extreme dissonance because the ways in which poverty and the poor were being addressed in her social-work and social-science graduate courses erased or defamed the core of her being. Megivern describes how her home community—supportive through her undergraduate work—became increasingly distant when she entered graduate school and she found herself "caught in the margins between upper-class academe and my poor and working-class roots," with no clear sense of belonging in either world.

Andrea Harris examines the ways in which the stereotype of the Welfare Queen demeans, condemns, and alienates poor, black single mothers who seek fair and equal treatment under the law. In "Choosing the Lesser Evil: The Violence of the Welfare Stereotype," Harris begins with the ties between abuse and poverty, then demonstrates how poverty in turn labels poor women as "deviant," resulting in civil alienation—even when the women are acting in the best interest of their children and themselves. The Welfare Queen designation, Harris learned, evokes a visceral power that supersedes any actual individual ability or action. When she petitioned the courts for protection from her abuser, she found the judge more concerned with her status as a welfare recipient than with her determination to raise and protect her child. Legitimate complaints—for safety, legal rights, and access to higher education that allow a life without poverty (and abuse)—Harris contends, are not accorded to welfare mothers, simply because their poverty is proof that they "rejected" marriage and middle-class values.

In her essay, Harris further reveals the costs of resistance and the price she paid to secure the education that would ensure autonomy and safety for herself and her child. Yet resisting this erasure and censure and insisting on visibility and full citizenship is exhausting and dangerous. Still, Harris is determined to reinvent the image of welfare recipients, warning that, "as long as the Welfare Queen reigns in the imagery and presumptions of social narratives, my experiences are not only pushed to the periphery, but, like that of many others, they are made invisible."

Addressing the issue of invisibility and resistance, Sandy Smith Madsen declares that "educating welfare women is the stuff of revolutions." In "From Welfare to Academe: Welfare Reform as College-Educated Welfare Mothers Know It," she analyzes the circumstances and obstacles faced by welfare mothers trying to gain access to higher education, findings she obtained as a result of extensive interviews with twelve women who, like Madsen, relied on welfare while enrolled in college and university programs. Madsen notes that, "while political elites and poverty experts have gone about the business of spreading stories of immoral and idle Welfare Queens, . . . [with] the aid of a welfare check, poor mothers have transformed themselves into taxpayers with double and quadruple their former incomes." Her interviews demonstrate the resilience and determination of these women as they encounter barriers and face public humiliation.

A major concern of Madsen's work is the punitive nature of welfare policy that seeks to punish and sanction not only the welfare mother who tries to obtain higher education but her children, as well. Her interviews revealed the concerns women had about the effects of public humiliation on their children and openly address the ways in which the women avoided compliance to protect the children and themselves.

It is not always societal or programmatic constructs that thwart access to higher education. Some of the most stubborn barriers are imposed by the families of poor women who believe that, as students, they are rejecting their cultures of origin. In "Seven Years in Exile," Leticia Almanza recounts her efforts to obtain an education and the obstacles she faced both within the university structure and within the culture of her family. Almanza describes herself as a woman "born poor to migrating parents" who arrived in the United States from Mexico at age ten, unable to speak English. She was so alienated by language, class, race, and gender that teachers branded her "retarded." When she graduated from high school at the top of her class and was admitted to a selective university, it was not, however, the public school system that Almanza had to fight—it was her own family. In her quest for a university education, Almanza coped with dual senses of alienation: She would alienate her family by attending college and betray herself by not obtaining an education.

As she attempted to straddle these borders, Almanza faced other hurdles, including the unjustified loss of financial aid, the racist interrogation of her citizenship status, and a debilitating lack of allies and economic support. Eventually, these losses drove her away from college for seven years. Her success in obtaining a degree was a result of her resilience and ability to see herself as the hero of her own epic. Almanza notes, "Odysseus was not so different from us poor Mexicans: fate had dealt him a hard hand." As Almanza insinuates through her analogy to Odysseus, much of her success and failure was capricious as she battled the institutionalized "gods."

The essays in Parts I and II examine the barriers poor women encounter in higher education; those in Part III: Policy, Research, and Poor Women consider policies that affect access to higher education and advocate remedies for improved access. One function of this part is to illustrate and critique the ways in which public policies, enacted by diverse bodies and for distinct purposes, interact to produce competing mandates that harm poor female students. Only by bringing the many practices together, as they are in poor women's lives, can we begin to understand the complicated set of hidden barriers poor women encounter when they attempt to change their lives through higher education. The theoretical frame for this part is one that allows poor female academics to present analyses based on research and firsthand experience. That takes, as its first premise, the conviction that theory is at its most powerful when it allows us to understand and challenges us to work together to fight for social justice and equity.

In "Families First—but Not in Higher Education: Poor, Independent Students and the Impact of Financial Aid," Sandra L. Dahlberg examines an increasingly bifurcated financial-aid system and the impact of recent financial-aid policy on the 30 percent of college students identified as "independent." Poor, independent students are forced to cope with an aid system designed for dependent students and, increasingly, with a system that focuses on the needs of middle-class rather than poor students. Dahlberg details how aid policies are being used to create disincentives for poor students, if not implicit disbarment from higher education, when poor students are denied, through institutional and federal policy, the full benefit of the external scholarships, veterans' benefits, and child support awarded to them.

In concert with the fiscal impact of financial-aid policy on poor, independent students, Dahlberg explores the ways in which the political rhetoric of financial aid is quickly becoming aligned with welfare rhetoric when aid is allocated for poor students. At the same time, funding for merit-based aid, which supports mainly middle- and upper-class students, is increasing. As Dahlberg states, "Most certainly, notions of American higher education as a meritocracy are disrupted when 'deserving' and 'undeserving' are measured in terms of personal and familial income and not on the basis of the student's ability to succeed in college." Dahlberg's timely analysis of financial-aid policy proposes alternative practices that would revitalize the promise of equal access to higher education for all Americans.

Judith Owens-Manley's research focuses on the interplay between welfare caseworkers and welfare recipients and the effect that welfare reform has had on this already tenuous relationship. In "The Leper Keepers: Front-Line Workers and the Key to Education for Poor Women," Owens-Manley relates the results of her study of the attitudes of welfare workers and how these attitudes inform the provision of services that are crucial to poor women, particularly access to educational programs and support. One factor that underlies these attitudes is the very condition in which these social workers find themselves negatively labeled "leper keepers." It is notable that many welfare workers show some resentment toward their clients; because the social workers are so poorly paid, they find themselves "generally close to their clients in socioeconomic status" and therefore experience a sense of competition.

Owens-Manley illustrates the degree to which the administrative discretion that determines which clients will receive access to education has increased as a result of these systemic environmental problems, in conjunction with the requirements of welfare reform, and exposes the potential threat this discretion presents to poor women. Her research suggests that "until education is again regarded as a viable route out of poverty, and until welfare policy recognizes the work value of attending higher education or training, the prospects remain dismal for the long-term solvency of poor women and their families." In addition, Owens-Manley argues that as long as welfare workers are disparaged as "leper-keepers," are underpaid, and are wedged between societal mandates that posit excessive caseloads against client needs, poor women and their children will suffer needlessly and be even further restricted in their options for educational pursuits that would enable them to live life beyond welfare and poverty.

The discretion of welfare workers is of particular concern to Lisa D. Brush. In her essay " 'That's Why I'm on Prozac': Battered Women, Traumatic Stress, and Education in the Context of Welfare Reform," Brush presents findings from two studies she conducted that exposed the gaps between staff workers' perceptions of rates of battery and abuse experienced by welfare recipients and the rates of incidence actually reported by those same welfare clients. She then examines how caseworkers' misperceptions about abuse rates affect battered welfare women's attempts to obtain autonomy and solvency through education.

Brush describes and analyzes the psychic damage of battery and compares medical and social perceptions of post-traumatic stress disorder (PTSD) in veterans to the PTSD experienced by abused welfare women. Without widespread recognition of the impact of battery on welfare recipients and their children, Brush contends, abused women "face a dual trap of poverty and abuse," and she proposes education as an effective means by which battered welfare women can remove themselves permanently from this trap. Even when battery is recognized by caseworkers, she argues, the time limits for services imposed by welfare reform "undermine battered welfare recipients' [access] to education," because these women use much of their designated support time overcoming trauma, with little time remaining for educational pursuits. Thus, Brush analyzes the process through which caseworkers' discretion and misinformation collides with welfare policies to reduce poor women's already limited access to higher education.

Vivyan C. Adair concludes this part by examining the trajectory of welfare reform that has forced hundreds of thousands of poor women away from earning economic security through higher education. In "Fulfilling the Promise of Higher Education," she argues that educators committed to fostering social and economic equity through education must challenge themselves to understand how crucial post-secondary education is to low-income, single mothers; to recognize that this student population is increasingly "at risk"; and to work against legislation that at best discourages, and at worst prohibits, these students from entering into and successfully completing post–secondary-degree programs. Integrated into her discussion of recent welfare-reform legislation are findings from three studies she conducted with welfare-recipient students after welfare reform. She presents data illustrating the degree to which many poor women have been discouraged from earning college degrees, describes students' desires to further their education, and delineates the frustrating obstacles that make this endeavor difficult, and often impossible.

While acknowledging that education is not a panacea for all of society's ills, Adair's research demonstrates that access to education can aid many poor, single mothers in their efforts to embrace the lifetime challenge of becoming fully engaged and responsible thinkers, citizens, workers, parents, and community members, as it concomitantly improves their economic stability for generations to come. She concludes that we must take steps toward ensuring that education remains a truly democratic project that has the potential for enacting social change and fostering economic equity, and warns that by failing to act "we acquiesce to the production of a two-tiered educational and economic system that increasingly widens the gulf between educated and thus economically viable, and undereducated and thus economically underprivileged, citizens."

Together, these essays present a compelling and unique vision of the ideology and operations of class and of the power of education in the United States today. By engaging in remarkable acts of autobiographical theorization, contributors to this collection tell a story that has rarely been heard and is seldom given credit. The authors' frank reflections and stunning critical insights challenge us to consider a paradox that Gayatri Chakravorty Spivak analyzes in the now famous essay "Explanation and Culture: Marginalia" (1996). In the essay, Spivak reflects on the inability of the disfranchised ever to come to political voice without experiencing co-optation and transformation. Indeed, for Spivak, it is through the very practice of political articulation, crucial to authority, that the poor simultaneously gain and lose an authentic and a powerful voice. What Spivak is getting at is that poor female academics are wedged between a political rock and a hard place: We can speak through a frame of subalternity, but we are accorded no authority, validity, or power in this voice. Conversely, we can garner authority as academics but in doing so lose our authenticity—and to some degree, as Amott acknowledged, our right to speak.

A clear response to Spivak's concerns echoes throughout *Reclaiming Class: Women, Poverty, and the Promise of Higher Education in America*. With this collection, we illustrate that, as the subaltern in America, we have not forgotten (and will never forget) our voices. In reclaiming the "stories of ourselves," we produce new insights and perspectives; suggest new strategies; celebrate and critique education as a pathway out of intergenerational poverty; and resist erasure and silence. It is through education that we have begun to speak at last in clear, unified, and powerful voices.

NOTES

Epigraph: Jackson (1996, 3).

1. "From Welfare to Meaningful Work through Education" Conference, Hamilton College, Clinton, N.Y., 15–16 October 1999.

2. Amott 1999.

3. Peter Hitchcock refers to this dual marking as the "age-old but continuing predicament of the 'working-class subject' as intellectual." He adds that, when trying to make sense of working-class scholars, "the economic and social determinants that produce the former are seen to exclude the latter" (Hitchcock 2000, 21). For Hitchcock, as for the contributors to this collection, this paradox is complicated by assumptions that poor women cannot speak cogently on the subject of poverty—that they are illogical or chaotic when they attempt to speak, or that when they have learned to speak they can no longer represent their class of origin. This sentiment is coupled with the erroneous notion that poor "communities only exist as those from which one must escape" (Hitchcock 2000, 21). Rita Felski suggests that this erasure may be exacerbated by a general and "noticeable silence about class in much contemporary theory," along with poverty-class identification that is "fundamentally connected to shame and guilt" (Felski 2000, 34). On both an internal and an external level, these assumptions produce a seemingly inexorable silence in the graduate and undergraduate academy.

4. Landers 1991. Robert Rector of the American Heritage Foundation evoked the term "broodmares" to describe welfare recipients have children out of wedlock while speaking about "rising illegitimacy" as "the number one catastrophe in American today" (Rector 1996b).

5. See "Welfare Queens" 1992; Crass 1999; and Williams 1998.

6. In 1994, Governor William F. Weld of Massachusetts began using a story about child abuse in Boston to illustrate that mothers on welfare have children simply to increase their welfare allocations: See Aucoin and Lehigh 1994; see also Gillian 1995 and Rector 1996a.

7. During a congressional welfare-rights debate in 1995, Representative L. Mica (R-Fla.) held up a sign that read, DO NOT FEED THE ALLIGATORS. WE POST THIS

WARNING BECAUSE UNNATURAL FEEDING AND ARTIFICIAL CARE CREATES DEPENDENCY (*Congressional Record* 1995, H3766 16). That same year, Representative Barbara Cutin (R-Wyo.) compared welfare recipients to wolves who eat their own children (*Congressional Record* 1995, H3772 4). See Douglas 1995.

8. For a more detailed analysis of the ways in which poor women are blamed and punished for their "condition," see Adair 2000.

9. As we have argued, working-class students, like the privileged, can be read as being mobile. Indeed, our national narrative is based on the promise of upward mobility through work and sacrifice. To the degree that their presence can reinforce the myth and absolve the privileged members of the academy of guilt, working-class students are read as deserving, albeit "rough," idealized students. This is not true for the poverty class. Poor students—particularly poor, single mothers—are de-historicized and de-contextualized, and they are made to represent static "Others" who can rarely be transformed. See Adair and Dahlberg 2001.

REFERENCES

Adair, Vivyan C. 2000. *From Broodmares to Welfare Queens: A Genealogy of the Poor Woman in American Literature, Photography and Culture.* New York: Garland Publishing.

Adair, Vivyan C., and Sandra L. Dahlberg. 2001. "Welfare-Class Identities and the Rhetoric of Erasure in Academia." *Public Voices* 5, no. 3: 75–83.

Amott, Teresa. 1999. "Education and Welfare Reform." Paper presented at From Welfare to Meaningful Work through Education Conference, Hamilton College, Clinton, N.Y., 15–16 October.

Aucoin, Don, and Scot Lehigh. 1994. "Weld Using Story on Welfare Family to Aid His Case for Reform." *Boston Globe,* 25 February, 14.

Congressional Record (U.S.). 1995. H36766 and H3772 (online). Available from: <http://www.access.gpo.gov/congress/congo016.html>.

Crass, Chris. 1999. "Beyond Welfare Queens: Developing a Race, Class and Gender Analysis of Welfare and Welfare Reform." Infoshop Web site. Available from: <http://www.infoshop.org/texts/welfare.html>.

Dews, C. L. Barney, and Carolyn Leste Law. 1995. *This Fine Place So Far from Home: Voices of Academics from the Working Class.* Philadelphia: Temple University Press.

Douglas, William. 1995. "Welfare Revisions: House Passes Bill to Sweep Out 'New Deal System.'" *Newsday,* 25 March, 5.

Felski, Rita. 2000. "Nothing to Declare: Shame, Identity, and the Lower Middle Class." *Publications of the Modern Language Association (PMLA)* 115, no. 1: 33–45.

Gillian, Dorothy. 1995. "Ugly Weapons on the Hill." *Washington Post,* 25 March, B1.

Hitchcock, Peter. 2000. "They Must Be Represented? Problems in Theories of Working-Class Representation." *PMLA* 115, no. 1: 20–32.

Jackson, Laura Riding. 1996. "The Telling." In *Collected Poems of Laura Riding Jackson*. Tallahassee: University of Florida Press.

Landers, Ann. 1991. "A Loud Chorus of Outrage over Welfare." *New York Times*, 3 September, A14.

Law, Carolyn Leste. 1995. "Introduction." Pp. 1–13 in *This Fine Place So Far from Home: Voices of Academics from the Working Class*. Philadelphia: Temple University Press.

Rector, Robert. 1996a. "How Welfare Harms Kids." Heritage Foundation, 3 June. Web site. Available from: <www.heritage.org/library/keyissues/welfare. reform.html>.

———. 1996b. "Welfare Reform and the Death of Marriage." *Washington Times*, 23 February, A20.

Ryan, Jake, and Charles Sackrey. 1996. *Strangers in Paradise: Academics from the Working Class*. New York: University Press of America.

Sennett, Richard, and Jonathan Cobb. 1973. *The Hidden Injuries of Class*. New York: Vintage Books.

Spivak, Gayatri Chakravorty. 1996. "Explanation and Culture: Marginalia." Pp. 29–51 in *The Spivak Reader: Selected Works of Gayatri Chakravorty Spivak*, ed. Donna Laundry and Gerald McLean. New York: Routledge.

Steedman, Carolyn Kay. 1987. *Landscape for a Good Woman*. New Brunswick, N.J.: Rutgers University Press.

Tokarczyk, Michelle M., and Elizabeth A. Fay. 1993. *Working Class Women in the Academy: Laborers in the Knowledge Factory*. Amherst: University of Massachusetts Press.

"Welfare Queens Caught in Fraud." 1992. *Washington Post* 12 November, A1.

Williams, Lucy. 1998. "Overcoming Stereotypes." *Morning Call*, 3 July, A10.

LAURA SULLIVAN-HACKLEY

Speech Pathology

The Deflowering of an Accent

EACH SCHOOLDAY was a raveling Pavlovian chain. First a
flicker of naked bulb shocking us out of bed. Then Bus 64's engine
grinding uphill, belching sour diesel exhaust in our path like a taunt,
daring us in this chase. Once aboard, we watched the neighborhood's
grey Etch-a-Sketch landscape scroll past our windows until it disappeared into fog behind us. We dreaded the air brake sighing that
sigh of a tired old man, our cue to wade through Marlboro clouds
toward the clatter and nag of homeroom bell.

When Bus 64 screeched and coughed to a stop in front of
school one Tuesday, the driver refused to let us off. We sat, watching
all other buses unload, spilling classmates into a new schoolday.
At 8:01, a long sedan parked over our shadowed silhouettes in the
bus lane. The county school superintendent thrust himself out of
that black Lincoln, then boarded our bus two steps at a time. Grim
like somebody had just died or egged his house, he appeared to be
masturbating with his necktie, gripping and tugging and rearranging
with one fist.

"Hogtrash." He flung the word out over us all like a Frisbee
rimmed with mud for extra spin, then waited for it to settle.

"Every last one of you. Hogtrash. Never amount to nothing."

We would have searched each other's faces for clues, but
our gazes drove forward, hard swizzlestick skewers this man might
impale himself on. Bus 64 seemed to shrink, its brown vinyl closing
around us like cupped hands of beggars until we were no longer
passengers parked outside our destination; we were stepchildren
bumming a ride.

The superintendent gave his tie one more fierce yank before spinning on his heels, knocking the door open with his fist. He tripped on the last step down, but his gaffe came too late to elicit even the slightest snag of an upper lip.

The slow stream of us snaked from Bus 64 to the linoleum school foyer. Stepping down to asphalt, my jaw clamped shut. By the ring of first-period bell, I had slated my own lesson plan: to master a new language, no matter how bitter or foreign its flavor on my tongue.

My words became bullets, severe and staccato. Rappelling the cliffs where *g*s and hard *o*s had always dropped off the ends of things, I fought past the *in*s and *uh*s my lips liked to rest upon. I stiffened against the easy lean of *ain't,* the lively rhythm of twang. I bit down on all the lacy fringe of my mother's words, the slurred segues between my father's syllables, that peppery patois of the neighborhood.

The prize I knew when I heard it pronounced, years and miles from Bus 64's shuttling: "You don't sound like you come from anywhere."

NOTE

This prose poem was first published in *Kalliope* 21, no. 3: 39, and appears courtesy of the author.

I.   EDUCATORS REMEMBER

Vivyan C. Adair

1   Disciplined and Punished

Poor Women, Bodily Inscription, and Resistance through Education

Poverty is the worst form of violence.
　　—Mahatma Gandhi

In "Tired of Playing Monopoly?" (1998), Donna Langston challenges us to conceptualize class as more than a question of economic
status. For Langston, class affects "the way we talk, think, act, move,"
look, and are valued or devalued in our culture. "We experience class
at every level of our lives," Langston reminds us, so that even if our
status changes, our class marking "does not float out in the rinse
water" (Langston 1998, 128). Langston's cutting-edge work on class
mirrors my own conviction that class (de)valuation has been indelibly written on my mind and my body in ways that can be resisted but
can never be erased.

　　Traditionally, Marxist and Weberian perspectives have been employed as lenses through which to examine and understand the material and bodily "injuries of class."[1] Yet feminists have clearly critiqued
these theories for their failure to address the processes through which
class is produced on the gendered and raced bodies of its subjects in
ways that insure the perpetuation of systems of stratification and domination (Crompton and Mann 1986). Over the past decade or so, a host
of inspired welfare scholars and activists have addressed and examined the relationship between state power and the lives of poor women
and children.[2] As important and insightful as these exposés are, with
few exceptions they do not get at the closed circuit that fuses together
systems of power, the material conditions of poverty, and the bodily

Adapted from a previously published article: Vivyan C. Adair, "Branded with Infamy,"
Signs: Journal of Women in Culture and Society 27, no. 2 (Winter 2002): 451–71, courtesy of
the publisher. © 2002 by The University of Chicago. All rights reserved.

experiences that allow for the perpetuation—and, indeed, for the justification—of these systems. They fail to consider the dynamics of systems
of power that endlessly produce and patrol poverty through the reproduction of both social and bodily markers.

What is inadequate, then, even in many feminist theories of class
production is an analysis of this nexus of the textual and the corporeal.
Here Michel Foucault's argument about the inscription of bodies is a
powerful mechanism for understanding the material and physical conditions and bodily costs of poverty across racial difference and for inter-
rogating the connection between power's expression as text, as body,
and as site of resistance.[3]

In *Foucault and Feminism: Power, Gender, and the Self,* Lois McNay
reminds us that "to a greater extent than any other post-structuralist
thinker, feminists have drawn on Foucault's work" even though they
"are also acutely aware of its critical limitations" (McNay 1992, 2–3).
Particularly useful for feminists has been Foucault's theory that the
body is written on and through discourse as the product of historically
specific power relations. Feminists have used this notion of social inscription to explain a range of bodily operations, from cosmetic surgery
(Brush 1994; Morgan 1991), prostitution (Bell 1994), and anorexia ner-
vosa (Bordo 1993; Hopwood 1995) to motherhood (Chandler 1999;
Smart 1997), race (Ford-Smith 1995; Stoler 1995), and cultural imperialism (Desmond 1991). As these analyses illustrate, Foucault allows us
to consider and critique the body as it is invested with meaning and
inserted into regimes of truth via the operations of power and knowledge. However, scholars have neglected to consider the ways in which
other dimensions of social difference, such as class, are inscribed on
the body in manners as fundamental as those of sexuality, gender,
and race.

Foucault clarifies and expands on this process of bodily/social
inscription in his early work. In "Nietzsche, Genealogy, History" (Foucault 1984a, 83), he positions the physical body as virtual text, accounting for the fact that "the body is the inscribed surface of events that are
traced by language and dissolved by ideas." Foucault's powerful scholarship points toward a body that is given form through semiotic systems and written on by discourse. For Foucault, the body and text are
inseparable. In his logic, power constructs and holds bodies, which Foucault variously describes as "foundations where language leaves its

traces" (Foucault 1984b, 176) and "the writing pad[s] of the sovereign and the law" (Foucault 1984b, 177).

In *Discipline and Punish,* Foucault sets out to depict the genealogy of torture and discipline as it reflects a public display of power on the body of subjects in the seventeenth and eighteenth centuries. In graphic detail, Foucault begins his book with the description of a criminal being tortured, then drawn and quartered in a public square. The crowds of good parents and their growing children watch and learn. The public spectacle works as a patrolling image, socializing and controlling bodies within the body politic. Eighteenth-century torture "must mark the victim: it is intended, either by the scar it leaves on the body or by the spectacle that accompanies it, to brand the victim with infamy. It traces around or rather on the very body of the condemned man signs that can not be effaced" (Foucault 1984b, 179). For Foucault, public exhibitions of punishment served as a socializing process, writing culture's codes and values on the minds and bodies of its subjects. In the process, punishment discursively deconstructed and rearranged bodies.

But Foucault's point in *Discipline and Punish* is precisely that public exhibition and inscription have been replaced in contemporary society by a much more effective process of socialization and self-inscription. According to Foucault, today discipline has replaced torture as the privileged punishment, but the body continues to be written on. Discipline produces "subjected and practiced bodies, 'docile bodies'" (Foucault 1984b, 182). We become subjects not of the sovereign but of ideology, disciplining and inscribing our own bodies and minds in the process of becoming stable and singular subjects. Power's hold on bodies is in both cases maintained through language systems. The body continues to be the site and operation of ideology, as subject and representation, body and text.

Indeed, although we are all marked discursively by ideology in Foucault's paradigm, in the United States today poor women and children of all races are multiply marked with signs of both discipline and punishment that cannot be erased or effaced.[4] They are systematically produced through both twentieth-century forces of socialization and discipline and eighteenth-century exhibitions of public mutilation. In addition to coming into being as disciplined and docile bodies, poor, single welfare mothers and their children are physically inscribed, punished, and displayed as the dangerous and pathological Other. It is important to note when considering the contemporary inscription of poverty as moral pathology etched onto the bodies of profoundly poor women and children that these are more than metaphoric and self-patrolling marks of discipline. Rather, on myriad levels—sexual, social, material, and physical—poor women and their children, like the "deviants" publicly punished in Foucault's scenes of torture, are marked, mutilated, and made to bear and transmit signs in a public spectacle that brands the victim with infamy.

My own life offers evidence of this cultural phenomenon. As a child, as an adult, and even as a single-parent college student (attempting to rewrite my story and value as one of transformation and mobility), I was read and punished as a poor woman even as I disciplined my own body to patrol my physical presence in the material world. Yet it is also true that, although I was marked as deviant and pathological, I eventually learned to resist and work against debilitating class and gender markings. The ability to engage in critical thought and analysis, to counter with a new discourse of authority, and to envision the relationship among ideology, social privilege, and oppression (garnered through access to post-secondary education) provided me with the tools to begin to attempt to fully read and mitigate—although never to erase—the marks of my own punishment, discipline, and position as sign of cultural dis-ease. Ironically, it was through exposure to the *discipline* of critical analysis that I began to resist and reconsider—deconstruct and rearrange—the bodily signs of my own very public *punishment.*

TEXT OF THE BODY, BODY OF THE TEXT: THE (NOT SO) HIDDEN INJURIES OF CLASS

Recycled images of poor, welfare women permeate and shape our national consciousness.[5] Yet as is so often the case, these images and narratives tell us more about the culture that spawned and embraced them than they do about the object of the culture's obsession. Simple, stable, and often widely skewed cover stories tell us what is "wrong" with some people, what is normative and what is pathological. By telling us who "bad" poor women are, we reaffirm and re-evaluate who we, as a nation and as a people—of allegedly good, middle-class, white, able-bodied, independent, male citizens—are. At their foundations, stories of the welfare mother intersect with, draw from, reify, and reproduce mythic American narratives associated with a constellation of beliefs about capitalism, male authority, the "nature" of humans, and the sphere of individual freedom, opportunity, and responsibility. These narratives purport to write the story of poor women in an arena in which only their bodies have been positioned to "speak."[6] They promise to tell the story of who poor women are in ways that allow Americans to maintain a belief in both an economic system based on exploitation and an ideology that claims that we are all beyond exploitation.

These productions orchestrate the story of poverty as one of moral and intellectual lack and of chaos, pathology, promiscuity, illogic, and sloth juxtaposed always against the order, progress, and decency of "deserving" citizens. Trying to stabilize and make sense of unpalatably complex issues of poverty and oppression and attempting to obscure hegemonic stakes in representation, these narratives reduce and collapse the lives and experiences of poor women to deceptively simplistic dramas, which are then offered for public consumption. The terms of these dramas are palatable because they are presented as simple oppositions of good and bad, right and wrong, independent and dependent, deserving and undeserving. Yet as an intergenerationally poor woman, I know that poverty is neither this simple nor this singular. Poverty is rather the product of complex systems of power that at many levels are indelibly written on poor women and children in feedback loops that compound and complicate politically expedient readings and writings of our bodies.

I am, and will probably always be, marked as a poor woman. I was raised by a poor, single, white mother who had to struggle to keep her four children fed, sheltered, and clothed by working at what seemed like an endless stream of exhausting and demeaning minimum-wage jobs. As a child, poverty was written onto and into my being at the level of private and public thought and body. At an early age, my body bore witness to and emitted signs of the painful devaluation carved into my flesh; that same devaluation became integral to my being in the world. I came into being as a disciplined body and mind, while at the same time I was taught to read my abject body as the site of my own punishment and erasure. In this excess of meaning, the space between private body and public sign was collapsed.

For many poor children, this double exposure results in debilitating—albeit politically useful—shame and lack. As Carolyn Kay Steedman reminds us in *Landscape for a Good Woman* (1987), the mental life of poor children flows from material deprivation. Steedman speaks of the "relentless laying down of guilt" she experienced as a poor child living in a world where identity was shaped through envy and unfulfilled desire and where her own body "told me stories of the terrible unfairness of things, of the subterranean culture of longing for that which one can never have" (Steedman 1987, 8). For Steedman, public devaluation and punishment "demonstrated to us all the hierarchies of our illegality, the impropriety of our existence, our marginality within the social system" (Steedman 1987, 9). Even as an adult, she says, "the baggage will never lighten for me or my sister. We were born, and had no choice in the matter; but we were social burdens, expensive, unworthy, never grateful enough. There was nothing we could do to pay back the debt of our existence" (Steedman 1987, 19).

Indeed, poor children are often marked with bodily signs that cannot be forgotten or erased. Their bodies are physically inscribed as Other and then read as pathological, dangerous, and undeserving. What I recall most vividly about being a child in a profoundly poor family was that we were constantly hurt and ill, and because we could not afford medical care, small illnesses and accidents spiraled into more dangerous illnesses and complications that became both a part of who we were and written proof that we were of no value in the world.

In spite of my mother's heroic efforts, at an early age my brothers and sister and I were stooped, bore scars that never healed properly, and limped with feet mangled by ill-fitting used Salvation Army shoes. When my sister's forehead was split open by a door slammed in frustration, my mother "pasted" the angry wound together on her own, leaving a mark of our inability to afford medical attention, of our lack, on my sister's very forehead. When I suffered from a concussion, my mother simply put borrowed ice on my head and tried to keep me awake for a night. And when, throughout elementary school, we were sent to the office for mandatory and very public yearly checkups, the school nurse sucked air through her teeth as she donned surgical gloves to check only the hair of poor children for lice.

We were read as unworthy, laughable, and often dangerous. Poor children in our school were laughed at for their "ugly shoes," their crooked and ill-serviced teeth, and the way they "stank," as teachers excoriated them for their inability to concentrate in school, their "refusal" to come to class prepared with proper supplies, and their unethical behavior when they tried to take more than their allocated share of "free lunch."[7] One of my former classmates recently recalled:

> Whenever backpacks or library books came up missing, we were publicly interrogated and sent home to "think about" our offenses, often accompanied by notes that reminded my mother that as a poor, single parent she should be working twice as hard to make up for the discipline that allegedly walked out the door with my father. When we sat glued to our seats, afraid to stand in front of the class in ragged and ill-fitting hand-me-downs, we were held up as examples of unprepared and uncooperative children. And when our grades reflected our inferiority, they were used to justify even more elaborate punishment.[8]

Other friends who were poor as children, and respondents to a survey I conducted in 1998, tell similar stories of the branding they received at the hands of teachers, administrators, and peers.[9] An African American woman raised in Yesler Terrace, a public-housing complex in Seattle, writes:

> Poor was all over our faces. My glasses were taped and too weak. My big brother had missing teeth. My mom was dull and ashy. It was like a story of how poor we were that anyone could see. My sister Evie's lip was bit by a dog and we just had dime store stuff to put on it. Her lip was a big scar. Then she never smiled and no one smiled at her 'cause she never smiled. Kids call her "scarface." Teachers never smiled at her. The principle put her in detention all the time because she was mean and bad (they said). (Adair 1998)

And a white woman in the Utica, New York, area remembers:

> We lived in dilapidated and unsafe housing that had fleas no matter how clean my mom tried to be. We had bites all over us. Living in our car between evictions was even worse. Then we didn't have a bathroom so I got kidney problems that I never had doctor's help for. When my teachers wouldn't let me go to the bathroom every hour or so, I would wet my pants in class. You can imagine what the kids did to me about that. And the teachers would refuse to let me go to the bathroom because they said I was willful. (Adair 1999)

Material deprivation is publicly written on the bodies of poor children in the world. In the United States, poor families experience violent crime, hunger, lack of medical and dental care, utility shutoffs, the effects of living in unsafe housing or of being homeless, chronic illness and insufficient winter clothing (Edin and Lein 1997, 224–31). According to Jody

Raphael of the Taylor Institute, poor women and their children are also at five times the risk of experiencing domestic violence (Raphael 2000).

As children, our disheveled and broken bodies were produced and read as signs of our inferiority and undeservedness. As adults, our mutilated bodies are read as signs of inner chaos, immaturity, and indecency as we are punished and then read as proof of need for further discipline and punishment. When my already bad teeth started to rot and I was out of my head with pain, my choices as an adult welfare recipient were either to let my teeth fall out or to have them pulled. In either case, the culture would then read me as a toothless illiterate, as a fearful joke. To pay my rent and put shoes on my daughter's feet, I sold blood at two or three different clinics on a monthly basis until I became so anemic that they refused to buy it from me. A neighbor of mine went back to the man who continued to beat her and her scarred children after being denied welfare benefits when she realized that she could not adequately feed, clothe, and house her family on her own minimum-wage income. My good friend sold her ovum to a fertility clinic in a painful and potentially damaging process. Other friends exposed themselves to all manner of danger and disease by selling their bodies for sex to feed and clothe their babies.

Poverty becomes a vicious cycle that is written on our bodies and intimately connected with our value in the world. Our children need healthy food so that we can continue working; yet working at minimum-wage jobs we have no money for wholesome food and very little time to care for our families. So our children get sick; we lose our jobs to take care of them; we fall more and more deeply into debt before our next unbearable job; and then we really cannot afford medical care. Starting that next minimum-wage job with unpaid bills and ill children puts us farther and farther behind, so that we are even less able to afford good food, adequate child care and health care, or emotional healing. The food banks we gratefully drag our exhausted children to on the weekends hand out bags of rancid candy bars, past–pull-date hot dogs, stale and broken pasta, and occasionally a bag of wrinkled apples. We are either fat or skinny, and we seem always irreparably ill. Our emaciated or bloated bodies are then read as a sign of lack of discipline and as proof that we have failed to care as we should.[10]

Exhaustion also marks the bodies of poor women in indelible script. Rest becomes a privilege we simply cannot afford. After working full shifts each day, poor mothers who are trying to support themselves at minimum-wage jobs continue to work to a point of exhaustion that is inscribed on their faces, their bodies, their posture, and their diminishing sense of self and value in the world. My former neighbor recently recalled:

> I had to take connecting buses to bring and pick up my daughters at child care after working on my feet all day. As soon as we arrived at home, we would head out again by bus to do laundry. Pick up groceries. Try to get to the food bank. Beg the electric company to not turn off our lights and heat again. Find free winter clothing. I would be home late at night all the time. I was loaded down with one baby asleep and one crying. Carrying lots of heavy bags and ready to drop on my feet. I had bags under my eyes and no shampoo to wash my hair, so I used soap. Anyway I had to stay up to wash diapers in the sink. Otherwise they wouldn't be dry when I left the house in the dark the next morning with my girls. (Adair 1998)

This bruised and lifeless body, hauling sniffling babies and bags of dirty laundry on the bus, was then read as a sign that she was a bad mother and a threat that needed to be disciplined and made to work even harder for her own good. Those who need the respite less go away for weekends, take drives in the woods, take their kids to the beach. Poor women without education are pushed into minimum-wage jobs and have no money, no car, no time, no energy, and little support as their bodies are made to display marks of their material deprivation as a socializing and patrolling force.

Ultimately, we come to recognize that our bodies are not our own; that they are, rather, public property. State-mandated blood tests, interrogation about the most private aspects of our lives, the public humiliation of having to beg officials for food and medicine, and the loss of all right to privacy teach us that our bodies are useful only as lessons, warnings, and signs of degradation that everyone loves to hate. A poor, white single mother of three recognized her family's value as a sign at a welfare-rights rally in 1998 when she reflected:

> My kids and I been chopped up and spit out just like when I was a kid. My rotten teeth, my kids' twisted feet. My son's dull skin and blank stare. My oldest girl's stooped posture and the way she can't look no one in the eye no more. This all says we got nothing and we deserve what we got. On the street good families look at us and see right away what they'd be if they don't follow the rules. They're scared, too, real scared. (Adair 1999)

Although officially this woman has only a tenth-grade education, she expertly reads and articulates a complex theory of power, bodily inscription, and socialization that arises directly from the material conditions of her own life. She sees what many far more "educated" scholars and citizens fail to recognize: that the bodies of poor women and children are produced and positioned as texts that facilitate the mandates of a didactic, profoundly brutal, and mean-spirited political regime. The clarity of this woman's vision challenges feminists to consider and critique our commitment to both textualizing displays of heavy-handed social inscription and to de-textualizing them, working to put an end to these bodily experiences of pain, humiliation, and suffering.

Welfare-reform policy is designed to publicly expose, humiliate, punish, and display "deviant" welfare mothers. Workfare and Learnfare—two alleged successes of welfare reform—require that landlords, teachers, and employers be made explicitly aware of the second-class status of these very public bodies. In Ohio, the Department of Human Services uses tax dollars to pay for advertisements on the side of Cleveland's RTA buses that show a Welfare Queen behind bars with a logo that proclaims, "Crime does not pay. Welfare fraud is a crime" (Robinson 1999). In Michigan, a pilot program mandating drug tests for all welfare recipients began on 1 October 1999. Recipients who refuse the test lose their benefits immediately (Simon 1999). In Eugene, Oregon, recipients who cannot afford to feed their children adequately on their food-stamp allocations are advised through flyers issued by a contractor for the state's welfare agency to "check the dump and the residential and business dumpsters" (Women's Enews 2001). In April 2001, Jason Turner, New York City's welfare commissioner, told a congressional subcommittee that "workplace safety and the Fair Labor Standards Act should not apply to welfare recipients who, in fact, should face tougher sanctions in order to make them work" (Women's Enews 2001). And welfare-reform legislation enacted in 1996 as the Personal Responsibility and Work Opportunities Reconciliation Act (PRWORA) requires that poor mothers work full time in jobs that often do not provide medical, dental, or child-care benefits and that pay minimum-wage salaries that do not cover adequate food, heat, or clothing. Thus, through PRWORA, the state mandates child neglect and abuse. The crowds of good parents and their growing children watch and learn.

READING AND REWRITING THE BODY OF THE TEXT

The bodies of poor women and children, scarred and mutilated by state-mandated material deprivation and public exhibition, work as spectacles, as patrolling images socializing and controlling bodies within the body politic. That body politic is represented in Foucault's work as the other half of the discipline-and-punishment circuit of socialization. It is here that material elements and techniques "serve as weapons, relays, communication routes and supports for the power and knowledge relations that invest human bodies and subjugate them, turning them into objects of knowledge" (Foucault 1984b, 28). Again, the body and the text: text is in and of the body, body is in and of the text, in ways in which signifier and signified, metaphor and referent never replace each other but simply trace and chase each other. In this cycle of power, a template of meaning is produced through which only specific, politically viable readings of the bodies of poor welfare recipients and their children are possible.

Spectacular cover stories about the Welfare Queen play and replay in the national mind's eye, becoming a prescriptive lens through which the U.S. public as a whole reads the individual dramas of the bodies of poor women and their place and value in the world. These dramas produce "normative" citizens as independent, stable, rational, ordered, and free. In this dichotomous, hierarchical frame, the poor welfare mother is juxtaposed against a logic of "normative" subjectivity as the embodiment of dependency, disorder, disarray, and Otherness. Her broken and scarred body becomes proof of her inner pathology and chaos, suggesting the need for further punishment and discipline.

The alleged chaos of the welfare mother's inner-city "welfare culture" is illuminated in Charles Murray's "Welfare Hysteria" (1992).[11] As in other forums, in this *New York Times* article, Murray links the physical markings of poor women's bodies with a culture that is "illogical," "out of control," and "catastrophic." For Murray, poor women are "lazy due to years of government programming," and "crazed trying to meet their own selfish needs" (Murray 1992, 1).

In contemporary narratives, welfare women are imagined to be dangerous because they refuse to sacrifice their desires and fail to participate in legally sanctioned heterosexual relationships; their sexuality, as a result, is read as selfish, "unnatural," and immature. In this script, the bodies of poor women are viewed as being dangerously beyond the control of men and are, as a result, construed as the bearers of perverse desire. In this androcentric equation, fathers become the sole bearers of order and of law, defending poor women and children against their own unchecked sexuality and lawlessness. As Wahneema Lubiano points out, "As the welfare mother is constructed in this field of discourse as the synechdoche—as the shortest possible shorthand for the 'pathology' of the poor, black urban culture—so too does the absence of the figure of the father come to signify sexual instability, disorder, and immorality" (Lubiano 1992, 9).

For Republican Senator John Ashcroft, the inner city is the site of "rampant illegitimacy" and a "space devoid of discipline" where all values are askew (Ashcroft 1995). What is insidious for Ashcroft is not material poverty but an entitlement system that has allowed "out-of-control" poor women to rupture traditional patriarchal authority, valuation, and boundaries. Impoverished communities then become a site of chaos, because without fathers they allegedly lack any organizing or patrolling principle. George Gilder agreed with Ashcroft when he wrote for the conservative *American Spectator* that

> the key problem of the welfare culture is not unemployed women and poor children. It is the women's skewed and traumatic relationships with men. In a reversal of the pattern of civilized societies, the women have the income and the ties to government authority and support. This balance of power virtually prohibits marriage, which is everywhere based on the provider role of men, counterbalancing the sexual and domestic superiority of women. (Gilder 1995)

For Gilder, the imprimatur of welfare women's sordid bodies unacceptably shifts the focus of the narrative from a male presence to a feminized absence.

When welfare mothers are positioned as sexually chaotic, irrational, and unstable, their figures are temporarily immobilized and made to yield meaning as a space that must be brought under control and transformed through public displays of punishment. Poor single mothers and children who have been abandoned; have fled physical, sexual, or psychological abuse; or have refused in general to capitulate to male control within the home are mythologized as dangerous, pathological, out of control, and selfishly unable or unwilling to sacrifice their "naturally" unnatural desires. They are understood and punished as a danger to a culture that rests on a foundation of inviolate male authority and absolute privilege in both public and private spheres.

The template, or master narrative, that positions the poor, unmarried mother as sexual pariah is set against the alleged order of a universe made rational by "man's" native ability to be logical and self-reliant. The U.S. narrative combines our notions of reason and freedom with a sense of "natural" order, self-reliance, and autonomy. Where these images intersect, the narrative becomes the drama of men who are rights-bearing citizens as a consequence of their nature and their ability to order nature. The poor woman is antithetically produced in this scenario as the body that needs to be ordered sexually and socially. She is, as a result, positioned as a non–rights-bearing, non-rational, dependent, and immature antagonist. This narrative, which positions poor women as exiled by their "bodily nature," is central to the public's understanding of the workings of class in the United States. The story frames "normative" and unmarked Americans on the inside as rights-bearing, orderly, and productive citizens, while "they" are on the outside and "naturally" marginalized by their penchant—as women, as blacks, as the poor—for dependency and for their "natural" lack of order, morals, autonomy, and citizenship.

William Raspberry frames poor women as selfish and immature when he claims that "unfortunately AFDC [Aid to Families with Dependent Children] is paid to an unaccountable, accidental and unprepared parent who has chosen her head of household status as a personal form of satisfaction, while lacking the simple life skills and maturity to achieve love and job fulfillment from any other source. I submit that all of our other social ills—crime, drugs, violence, failing schools are a direct result of the degradation of parenthood by emotionally immature recipients" (Raspberry 1995). He goes on to assert that, like poor children, poor mothers must be made visible reminders to the rest of the culture of the "poor choices" they have made. He claims that, rather than "coddling" the poor woman, we have a responsibility to "shame her" and to use her failure to teach other young women that it is "morally wrong for unmarried women to bear children," as we "cast single motherhood as a selfish and immature act" (Raspberry 1995).

Continuous, multiple, and often seamless public inscription; punishing policy; and lives of unbearable material lack leave poor women and their children scarred, exhausted, and confused. As a result, their bodies are imagined as embodiments of decay and cultural disease that threaten the health and progress of our nation. Readings that position poor women's bodies and presence in the world as illegal posit an inherent connection among control, autonomy, progress, and social value. In valuing science, history, and allegedly masculine logic, progress is imagined as linear and teleological. This narrative of movement celebrates an active move from a feminized (stagnant, chaotic, abject, and dark) world to a state of masculinist autonomy, progress, discipline, and order. What the protagonist leaves behind in this foundational American myth is stasis and putrefaction.[12] As a result, the narrative sets up a series of dichotomous images that juxtapose our national obsession with movement and progress against our abhorrence for, and fear of, poor women who are constructed as static and stagnant.

In a 1995 *USA Today* article titled, "America at Risk: Can We Survive without Moral Values?" for example, the inner city is portrayed as a "*dark*" realm of "*decay* rooted in the *loss* of values, the *death* of work ethics, and the *deterioration* of families and communities." Allegedly, "all morality has *rotted* due to a *breakdown* in discipline." This space of disorder and disease is marked with tropes of race and gender. It is also associated with the imagery of "communities of women *without* male leadership, cultural values and initiative" ("America at Risk" 1995; emphasis added). In an editorial for *Newsweek*, George Will proclaims that "*illogical* feminist and racial *anger* coupled with *misplaced* American emotion may be a part or a cause of the *irresponsible* behavior *rampant* in poor neighborhoods." Will continues by saying that, here, "mothers *lack* control over their children and have *selfishly* taught them to embrace a *pathological* ethos that values *self-need* and *self-expression* over self-control" (Will 1995, 88; emphasis added).

Poor women's and children's bodies, publicly scarred and mutilated by material deprivation, are read as expressions of an essential lack of discipline and order. In response to this perception, Ronald Brownstein of the *Los Angeles Times* proposed that the Republican Contract with America will "*restore* America to its path, *enforcing* social *order* and common *standards* of behavior, and replacing *stagnation* and *decay* with *movement* and *forward* thinking *energy*" (Brownstein 1995, A1; emphasis added). In these rhetorical fields, poverty is metonymically linked to a lack of progress that allegedly would otherwise order, stabilize, and restore the culture. What emerges from these diatribes is the positioning of patriarchal, racist, capitalist, hierarchical, and heterosexist "order" and movement against the alleged stagnation and decay of the body of the Welfare Queen.

Race is clearly written on the body of the poor single mother. The welfare mother—imagined as young, never married, and black (contrary to statistical evidence)—is positioned as dangerous and in need of punishment because she "naturally" emasculates her own men; refuses to service white men; and passes on a disruptive culture of resistance, survival, and "misplaced" pride to her children rather than "appropriate" codes of subservience and submission (Collins 2000).[13] In stark contrast, widowed women who collect Social Security and divorced women with child support and alimony are imagined as white, legal, and propertied mothers whose value rests on their ability to stay in their homes, care for their children, and impart traditional cultural mores to their offspring, all for the betterment of the dominant culture. In this narrative, welfare mothers have only an "outlaw" culture to impart. Here the welfare mother is read as both the product and the producer of a culture of disease and disorder. These narratives imagine poor women as a powerful contagion capable of infecting their own children as raced, gendered, and classed agents of their "diseased" nature (Lubiano 1992). In contemporary discourses of poverty, racial tropes position poor women's bodies as dangerous sites of naturalized chaos and as potentially valuable economic commodities that refuse their "proper" roles (Collins 2000).

Gary MacDougal (1996) takes this image further by referring to the "crab effect of poverty" through which mothers and friends of people striving to break free of economic dependency allegedly "pull them back down." MacDougal affirms, again against statistical evidence to the contrary, that the mothers of welfare recipients are most often themselves "generational welfare freeloaders lacking traditional values and family ties who cannot, and will not, teach their children right from wrong." He asserts, "These women would be better off doing any kind of labor regardless of how little it pays, just to get them out of the house, to break their cycles of degeneracy" (MacDougal 1996).

It is this set of metaphors of race, class, and gender surrounding the figure of the welfare mother that inspired Raspberry to proclaim that many poor children would be "safer" in orphanages than in "fatherless ghetto homes lacking order" (Raspberry 1996). In this paradigm, the alleged "bad character" of the poor, castrating matriarch puts her children, her culture, and the country as a whole at risk. At the same time, ironically, the welfare woman is assigned no agency. In this plenitude of images of evil mothers, the poor welfare mother threatens not just her own children but all children. The Welfare Queen is made to signify moral aberration and economic drain; her figure becomes even more impacted once responsibility for the destruction of the "American Way of Life" is attributed to her. Brownstein (1994b) reads her "spider web of dependency" as a "crisis of character development that leads to a morally bankrupt American ideology."

These representations position welfare mothers' bodies as sites of destruction and as catalysts for a culture of depravity and disobedience; in the process, they produce a reading of the writing on the body of the poor woman that calls for further punishment and discipline. In New York City, Workfare programs force "lazy" poor women to take a job—"any job"—including working for the city wearing surplus orange prison uniforms picking up garbage on the highway and in parks for about $1.10 per hour (Dreier 1999). Bridefare programs in Wisconsin give added benefits to "licentious" welfare women who marry a man—"any man"—and publish a celebration of their "reform" in local newspapers (Dresang 1996). Tidyfare programs across the nation allow state workers to enter and inspect the homes of "slovenly" poor women so that they can monetarily sanction families whose homes are not deemed to be appropriately tidy.[14] Learnfare programs in many states publicly expose and fine "undisciplined" mothers who for any reason have children who do not (or cannot) attend school regularly (Muir 1993). All of these welfare-reform programs are designed to expose and publicly punish the "misfits" whose bodies are read as proof of their refusal or inability to capitulate to androcentric, capitalist, racist, and heterosexist values and mores.

Theories of class inscription allow us to read the bodily punishment of these women as a single, progressive slate on which the culture has inscribed and reinscribed continuous forces of socialization. In that the poor woman's body was, and continues to be, contextualized and given meaning in and through both discourse and public spectacles of punishment, tracing the inscriptions allows us to expose the ways in which she has been systematically marked and mapped, like a geographical terrain that produces knowledge about her human activity and value. The frantic writing of the body of the poor woman reveals the cycle that marks her body as Other and then reads that scarred body through a template that justifies the need for further punishing reform. In the process, this practice cements the allegedly "undeserving" poor woman as an emblem of chaotic and frightening meaning and as the physical and symbolic site of outlaw sexuality, excess, chaos, disorder, and disruption.

RESISTING THE TEXT: ON THE LIMITS OF DISCURSIVE CRITIQUE AND THE POWER OF RESISTANCE THROUGH EDUCATION

Despite the rhetoric and policy that mark and mutilate our bodies, poor women survive. Hundreds of thousands of us are somehow good parents, despite the systems that are designed to prohibit us from being so. We live on the unlivable and teach our children love, strength, and grace. We network, solve irresolvable dilemmas, and support one another and our families. If we somehow manage to find a decent pair of shoes or save our food stamps to buy our children birthday cakes, we are accused of being cheats or "living too high." If our children suffer, it is read as proof of our inferiority and bad mothering; if they succeed, we are suspect for being too pushy, for taking more than our share of free services, or for having too much free time to devote to them. Yet, as Janet Diamond, a former welfare recipient, says in the introduction to *For Crying Out Loud: Women and Poverty in the United States* (Dujon and Withorn 1998, 1): "In spite of public censure, welfare mothers graduate from school, get decent jobs, watch their children achieve, make good lives for themselves. Welfare mothers continue to be my inspiration, not because they survive, but because they dare to dream. Because when you are a welfare recipient, laughter is an act of rebellion."

Foucault's later work acknowledges this potential for rebellion inherent in the operation of power. In *Power/Knowledge: Selected Interviews and Other Writings* (1980), he positions discourse as an amalgam of material power and nonmaterial knowledge that fosters just such resistance. As McNay (1992) points out, for Foucault power is a productive and positive force rather than a purely negative, repressive entity. McNay notes that, for Foucault, "in relation to the body power does not simply repress its unruly forces, rather it incites, instills and produces effects in the body" (McNay 1992, 38). She adds:

> Resistance arises at the points where power relations are at their most rigid and intense. For Foucault, repression and resistance are not ontologically distinct, rather repression produces its own resistance: "there are no relations of power without resistance; the latter are all the more real and effective because they are formed right at the point where relations of power are exercised." (McNay 1992, 39)

Because power is diffuse, heterogeneous, and contradictory, poor women struggle against the marks of their degradation. Resistance swells in the gaps and interstices of productions of the self. For Foucault, "discourse transmits and produces power; it reinforces it, but also undermines and exposes it, renders it fragile and makes it possible to thwart it" (Foucault 1978, 101). Yet here we also recognize what McNay refers to as the "critical limitations" of Foucault and of poststructuralism in general. For although bodily inscriptions of poverty are clearly textual, they are also quite physical, immediate, and pressing, devastating the lives of poor women and children in the United States today. Discursive critique is at its most powerful only when it allows us to understand and challenges us to fight together to change the material conditions and bodily humiliations that scar poor women and children in order to keep us all in check.

In response to the material deprivation fostered by economic inequity and punishing public policy, many poor women work together to resist power and attempt to rewrite their value and place in the world by entering educational programs. In 1987, as a poor unwed mother, I joined almost half a million welfare recipients who had enrolled in institutions of higher education as a route out of poverty (before Temporary Aid to Need Families [TANF] restrictions implemented as part of welfare "reform" in 1996 made it nearly impossible to do so) (Adair 2001). Countless studies have exposed an overwhelming correlation between post-secondary education and the ability to exit poverty successfully and permanently (Gittell and Fareri 1990; Karier 1998; Kates 1998). But in this country, education is also touted as the "great equalizer," as a process that levels class, race, and gender difference and devaluation. According to Roslyn Mickelson and Stephen Smith (1998, 339), "Education is more than a meal ticket, it is intrinsically worthwhile and crucially important for ... social transformation ... [and] for the survival of democracy." Although it is certainly true that education facilitates economic mobility and thus freedom, my experience, and that of countless others, suggests that access to post-secondary education is a more complex experience than the myth suggests. Although education positively altered my economic value and authority in the world, the experience was also one of loss, erasure, and continued class inscription. Education allowed me to begin to resist the marks of my class position even as it continued to reinscribe class devaluation on my very body. Ultimately (and contrary to the myth), acquiring education, becoming an "educated" person, has been both an experience of profound contradiction and an act of powerful and life-altering resistance.

As a welfare mother in academe, my body was continually read and reinscribed by my professors and peers as proof of the mistakes I had made and presumably would make again. I came into academe with a scarred and mutilated body and a posture that reflected my fear of taking up space, time, or resources. Especially throughout my tenure in a graduate program, my body was read as need for further proof of my willingness to sacrifice to transcend my origin of alleged stagnation, disorder, and illogic. Sandra Dahlberg theorizes the increased pressure she experienced as a poor, single-parent student in a graduate education program:

> This rhetoric of erasure, although present at the undergraduate level, was significantly heightened in graduate school in what can easily be compared to welfare policy that is, according to Handler and Hasenfeld, "driven by the belief that the poor pose silent, insidious threats to dominant ideologies and the social order.... [and] a major threat to the economic order." ... It was one thing to obtain an undergraduate degree and move on, it was quite another to attempt to enter the professorial ranks. (Adair and Dahlberg 2001, 77)

Like Dahlberg, I was warned by my program chair as I entered graduate school that, to succeed as a student and as a graduate teaching assistant, I would have to make some of the same "tough choices" that the chair (as a woman and as a parent) had been forced to make before me. My adviser's first piece of advice was to find "superior" child care (she recommended several) and to make sure that my husband was willing to let me make graduate school and teaching my only priorities, as she had done. When I made it clear that I had no husband and could never afford her idea of child care, she simply shook her head, lamented my inability to make good choices, and refused to advise me from that point on. My adviser's sense and sentiment that I was making bad choices—

such as having the bad taste to be poor—was a portent of how my position would be framed throughout my graduate career.

My work and scholarship were similarly framed as suspect, viewed through a middle-class lens. In my graduate program, good scholarship was rewarded with coveted teaching assistantships. I was fortunate to have been offered one of these positions, even as I was reminded that the department was making the offer with trepidation, because its members suspected that I would be unreliable—as they often pointed out—because I was a poor, single mother.[15] There were a few other mothers in my teaching program, but they were never made to feel suspect, because they were able to leave their children with husbands and nannies, and evidently they had enough economic resources to attend costly conferences and take prestigious international research positions that would further entitle them to good jobs.

The teaching stipend I was so lucky to receive was about $850 a month. To teach, I had to sign a contract stating that I would not work anywhere else, even though that monthly income put my five-year-old daughter and I at less than 80 percent of the poverty level for a family of two in our area. When I applied to do extra work–study, I was reprimanded and told by one of my advisers that graduate students could live on that salary and that I would just have to "buckle down and be more budget conscious." This salary evidently could support a normative, and thus "deserving," graduate student. My position as an aberration could be used against me but was one that my teachers never really were able or willing to interrogate. My body, my child, and our material needs were simply reinscribed as pathological in a paradigm that marked me as Other, in contrast to the normative and thus allegedly deserving students.

For the entirety of my academic career, I was encouraged to perform an extraordinary amount of institutional service, so that, as one administrator pointed out, I could never be accused of being lazy or "sliding through on a pity ticket." This work further marked me materially, emotionally, and intellectually. Throughout my education, I continued to sell my blood, engage in paid medical experiments, survive on rancid and expired food-bank donations, and work and study to the point of exhaustion. My Otherness was continuously inscribed on my body at the same time that my tanned, relaxed, and collected peers were preferred and rewarded—as one of my favorite professors put it—for not being so "tightly wound," for being "natural and easy scholars who had a healthy sense of proportion and balance."

My sense of dislocation and fragmentation was particularly acute in classes where I often became both the subject and the object of investigation. Experiencing an overwhelming sense of liminality, I recall one particularly painful classroom experience in which students and teacher alike were lamenting and laughing at the inability of the poor to come to political consciousness. One student—the daughter of a doctor and a lawyer, as I recall—joked that welfare women in particular were "too busy bowling and breeding, and too numb with complacency" to fight for political equity. As the class chuckled in amused agreement, I once again felt myself ripped in two. I was laughing with my colleagues about my own existence. In the bitterness of that moment, I knew that I was homeless.

Encouraged to distance myself from class theory and working-class literature, held to uncommonly rigid time schedules and extraordinary standards, and for the most part without any mentors or colleagues to whom I could relate, I felt ostracized and confused. While my body was read as Other, I suffered from a heightened sense of alienation, yet I felt that I had to keep my anxiety over my dislocation hidden. I knew that my shabby clothes were welcomed as proof of my inferiority, but an expression of my internal pain would have irredeemably signaled my inability to transcend what were erroneously perceived as my natural bodily condition, my weakness of character, my lack of commitment, and my potential inability to survive the demands of graduate school.

I learned to pretend that I had no child at home; that I was not spending afternoons selling blood or trying to get food stamps; that I was not up all night worrying about the insurmountable debt I was accruing; that I chose to wear Salvation Army clothes; and that I did not go to costly conferences because I was doing more important things. I learned to pass, and the more I passed, the more I was rewarded. And yet, I was reminded daily that the truth of who I was was simply unspeakable.

Crucially, however, although access to education did reinscribe my body as suspect, aberrant, and untrustworthy, it also gave me the tools to critically read and negotiate those very bodily signs. In the process, it became the site of powerful communal resistance. In school I gained new and valuable work and life skills that involved the cognitive and technical abilities to communicate, organize, analyze, and think critically and creatively. I gained confidence as I acquired cultural capital and accrued a sense of worth as a "knowledgeable" and "thinking" citizen. More important, learning to think critically enabled me to envision myself in a new horizon, to reflect on life from a new vista and, as a result, to reconceptualize my place, voice, and value in the world. At one level, education made me part of the world that had for years denied me. At the same time, I was challenged to critique the very systems of power that were now offering me provisional entry.

Before I entered college, communal affiliation with other poor women had been discouraged—indeed, in many cases it had been prohibited by those with power over my life. Welfare offices, for example, are designed to prevent poor women from even talking together; uncomfortable plastic chairs are secured to the ground in arrangements that make communicating difficult. Silence is maintained in waiting rooms; caseworkers are rotated so that they do not become too "attached" to their clients; and, in fact, reinforced by "Welfare Fraud" signs covering industrial walls we are daily reminded not to trust anyone with the details of our life, for fear of further exposure and punishment. And so, like most poor women, I had remained isolated, ashamed, and convinced that I was alone in, and responsible for, my suffering. Yet as a poor, single mother–student, I began to meet, support, and resist with other poor student parents. In the throes of political activism (at first, I was dragged blindly into such actions in a protest that required, according to the organizer, just so many poor students' bodies), I became caught up in the contradiction between my body's meaning as a despised public sign and our shared sense of communal power, knowledge, authority, and beauty. Fighting for rent control; demanding fair treatment at the welfare office; sharing the costs, burdens, and joys of raising children; forming food cooperatives; running clothing banks; working with other poor women to go to college; and organizing for political change became addictive and life-affirming acts of communal resistance.

In learning to work together to overcome shared oppression, and with an urgent desire to interrupt public exhibitions of punishment, as poor, single parent-students we became increasingly aware of our bodies as sites of contestation, and we began to struggle together to fight back. By coming to understand and critique the relationships between hegemonic structures and systems and marginalized cultures, I was able to work with other poor women to contextualize, historicize, and resist the phenomenon of poverty itself. In the process, we came to understand that the shaping of our bodies is not coterminous with our beings or abilities as a whole.[16]

This process and the products of education are, of course, important to all citizens. They are crucial, however, to those who must go on to confront the continued social obstacles of racism, classism, ableism, homophobia, and sexism and to those of us who must endlessly read and negotiate the marks of both discipline and heavy-handed punishment written on our minds and on our bodies. In this sense, educating poor women is an act of subversion with the potential to liberate communities and individuals and to radically alter static and hierarchical systems of power. Becoming college-educated and earning a Ph.D. has not erased the marks of my poverty, but it has transformed the ways in which I am able to address class stratification and inequity. I now have a voice, an authority, and a community with which to interrogate, critique, and resist the indelible script of our bodies that were, and continue to be, "branded with infamy."

NOTES

Epigraph: Gandhi (1987, 11).

1. Richard Sennett and Jonathan Cobb realized that thinking of class in terms of systems obscured the human costs of being constructed within a hierarchical class system. Exploring themes found only among their "working-men," in *The Hidden Injuries of Class* they began to consider the degree to which "social legitimacy in Americans has its origins in public calculations of social value" (Sennett and Cobb 1972, 296). Yet Sennett and Cobb failed to examine directly the processes through which class is produced on the gendered and raced bodies of its subjects.

2. Mimi Abramovitz (1998, 2000), Randy Albelda (1997), Teresa Amott (1993), Linda Gordon (1995), Wahneema Lubiano (1992), Gwendolyn Mink (1996, 1998), and Frances Fox Piven and Richard Cloward (1993) have begun to unravel the historical, economic, rhetorical, and social markings of class embedded in welfare policy and poverty. Diane Dujon and Ann Withorn (1998), Bonnie Thornton Dill (1992), Kathryn Edin and Laura Lein (1997), Theresa Funiciello (1998), Donna Langston (1998), Rochelle Lefkowitz and Ann Withorn (1986), and Ruth Sidel (1998) have worked directly with poor women and their children to critique the material implications of those policies.

3. Racism, sexism, and heterosexism collide in the rhetoric of welfare-bashing. Clearly, poor women and children of color are multiply marked in this

discourse and punished in their lived lives. Their bodies are also positioned to represent the alleged pathology of an entire culture of poor women and children. Yet it is also true, as my survey results illustrate, that across racial difference the bodies of poor unmarried women and their children are marked and made to bear meaning as signs of danger and pathology, as they are both publicly punished and disciplined.

4. bell hooks (1999) said that, in the language of welfare, "poor whites have been erased, while poor blacks have been demonized." This is surely true at the level of discourse and at the systemic level, yet I would argue that at the level of the body, poor white women and children—like poor women and children of color—are both erased and demonized as the scripts of those devaluations are written on their very bodies.

5. Throughout this essay, I use the terms "welfare recipient" and "poor working women" interchangeably, because as a recent Urban Institute study made clear, these populations today are in fact one and the same (Loprest 1999).

6. In recent years, an increasingly lucrative industry has sprung up around making meaning of the presence of the poor in America. Politicians, welfare historians, social scientists, policy analysts, and all stripe of academicians produce and jealously guard their newfound turf as they vie for a larger market share of this meaning-making economy. In the shadow of this frenzied and profitable proliferation of representation exists a profound crisis in the lives of poor women and children, whose bodies continue to be the site and operation of ideology, as they are written and read as dangerous, then erased and rendered mute in venues of authority and power.

7. As recently as 1995, in the cafeteria of my daughter's public elementary school, "free-lunchers" (poor children who, without the federal free/reduced lunch program, could not afford to eat lunch, including my daughter) were reminded via a large and colorful sign to "line up last."

8. Personal correspondence with the author, 2000.

9. The goal of my survey was to measure the impact of the 1996 welfare-reform legislation on the lives of profoundly poor women and children in the United States. In early 1998, I sent fifty questionnaires and narrative surveys to four groups of poor women on the West and East coasts; thirty-nine were returned. Interviews followed with twenty of the surveyed women.

10. The adolescent psychologist Maria Root claims that a beautiful or "fit" body becomes equated with "purity, discipline—basically with goodness" (as quoted in DeClaire 1993, 36).

11. When Charles Murray first wrote about the "depravity of the welfare culture" in *Losing Ground* (1984), he was dismissed as a reactionary conservative. His theories, however, have been dusted off and are now in vogue with the political drive to reform the welfare system.

12. Catherine Kingfisher (1999, 2) notes that "the discourse of welfare reform in Aotearoa/New Zealand and the United States is pervaded by a symbolic association of the 'undeserving' poor, most notably poor single mothers, with savagery. The savage is commonly constructed as wild, uncivilized, uncontrol-

lable and living in a 'natural' state that lies outside, or historically occurred prior to, civilization."

13. In the two years that directly preceded the passage of PRWORA as part of sweeping welfare reform in the United States, the largest percentage of people on welfare were white (39 percent) and fewer than 10 percent were teenage mothers (U.S. Department of Health and Human Services 1994).

14. Tidyfare programs also require that caseworkers inventory the belongings of Aid to Families with Dependent Children (AFDC, or welfare) recipients so they can require them to "sell down" their assets. In 1994, a Section Eight inspector from the U. S. Department of Housing and Urban Development came into my home and counted my daughter's books. He then checked his list and saw that, as a nine-year-old, she was entitled to have only twelve books; calculated what he perceived to be the value of the excess books; and had my welfare check reduced by that amount the following month.

15. I contend that single mothers in academe are thought of as lacking the resources that might otherwise mitigate their "condition."

16. Many questions remain to be addressed. As feminist scholars, it is crucial to consider at what point public punishment forecloses the possibility of resistance, to appreciate and work to improve the material lives of poor women and children, to make real the connections between our understanding of poor women as subjects and our commitment to them as sisters, and to critique our own exclusionary politics that have allowed us to neglect and to silence this population of women, both in and out of the academy.

REFERENCES

Adair, Vivyan C. 1998. Unpublished survey. Seattle, Wash. June.

———. 1999. Unpublished survey. Clinton, N.Y., and Utica, N.Y. December.

Adair, Vivyan C., and Sandra L. Dahlberg. 2001. "Class Identities and the Rhetoric of Erasure in Academia," *Public Voices* 5, no. 3: 75–83.

Abramovitz, Mimi. 1989. *Regulating the Lives of Women: Social Welfare Policy from Colonial Times to the Present*. Boston: South End Press.

———. 2000. *Under Attack, Fighting Back*. New York: Monthly Review Press.

Albelda, Randy. 1997. *Glass Ceilings and Bottomless Pits: Women's Work, Women's Poverty*. Boston: South End Press.

Ashcroft, John. 1995. "Illegitimacy Rampant." *St. Louis Dispatch*, 2 July, A23.

Amott, Teresa. 1993. *Caught in the Crisis: Women and the U.S. Economy Today*. New York: Monthly Review Press.

Anderson, Dale. 1999. "County to Investigate Some Welfare Recipients." *Buffalo (N.Y.) News*, 18 August, B5.

Bell, Shannon. 1994. *Reading, Writing and Rewriting the Prostitute Body*. Bloomington: Indiana University Press.

Bennett, William. 1995. "America at Risk: Can We Survive without Moral Values?" *USA Today*, 14 October, C3.

Bordo, Susan. 1993. *Unbearable Weight: Feminism, Western Culture and the Body.* Berkeley: University of California Press.

Brownstein, Ronald. 1994. "GOP Welfare Proposals More Conservative." *Los Angeles Times*, 20 May, A20.

———. 1995. "Latest Welfare Reform Plan Reflects Liberals' Priorities." *Los Angeles Times*, 24 January, A6.

Brush, Pippa. 1998. "Metaphors of Inscription: Disclipline, Plasticity and the Rhetoric of Choice." *Feminist Review* 58 (Spring): 22–43.

Collins, Patricia Hill. 2000. *Black Feminist Thought: Knowledge, Consciousness, and the Politics of Empowerment.* New York: Routledge.

Chandler, Mielle. 1999. "Queering Maternity." *Journal of the Association for Research on Mothering* 1, no. 2: 21–32.

Crompton, Rosemary, and Michael Mann, eds. 1986. *Gender and Stratification.* New York: Polity Press.

DeClaire, Joan. 1993. "Body by Barbie." *View* (October): 36–43.

Desmond, Jane. 1991. "Dancing out the Difference: Cultural Imperialism and Ruth St. Denis's Radna of 1906." *Signs* 17, no. 1: 28–49.

Dill, Bonnie Thornton. 1992. "Race, Gender and Poverty in the Rural South: African American Single Mothers." Pp. 97–109 in *Rural Poverty in America*, ed. Cynthia M. Duncan. New York: Auburn House.

Dreier, Peter. 1999. "Treat Welfare Recipients Like Workers." *Los Angeles Times*, 29 August, M6.

Dresang, Joel. 1996. "Bridefare Designer, Reform Beneficiary Have Role in Governor's Address." *Milwaukee Journal Sentinel*, 14 August, 9.

Dujon, Diane, and Ann Withorn. 1998. *For Crying Out Loud: Women's Poverty in the United States.* Boston: South End Press.

Edin, Kathryn, and Laura Lein. 1997. *Making Ends Meet: How Single Mothers Survive Welfare and Low Wage Work.* New York: Russell Sage Foundation.

Foucault, Michel. 1978. *The History of Sexuality: An Introduction.* Trans. R. Hurley. New York: Penguin.

———. 1980. *Power/Knowledge: Selected Interviews and Other Writings, 1972–1979*, ed. Collin Gordon. New York: Pantheon.

———. 1984a. "Nietzsche, Genealogy, History." In *The Foucault Reader*, ed. P. Rabinow. New York: Pantheon Books.

———. 1984b. "Discipline and Punish." In *The Foucault Reader*, ed. P. Rabinow. New York: Pantheon Books.

Ford-Smith, Honor. 1995. "Making White Ladies: Race, Gender and the Production of Identity in Late Colonial Jamaica." *Resources for Feminist Research* 23, no. 4: 55–67.

Funiciello, Theresa. 1998. "The Brutality of Bureaucracy." Pp. 377–81 in *Race, Class and Gender: An Anthology*, ed. Margaret L. Andersen and Patricia Hill Collins. Belmont, Calif.: Wadsworth Publishing.

Gandhi, Mohandas K. 1987. *Gandhi in India, in His Own Words*, ed. Martin Green. Hanover, N.H.: University Press of New England.

Gilder, George. 1995. "Welfare Fraud Today." *American Spectator,* 5 September, B6.

Gittel, Marilyn, and Camille Fareri. 1990. "From Welfare to Independence: The College Option," report to the Ford Foundation, New York, March.

Gordon, Linda. 1995. *Pitied but Not Entitled: Single Mothers and the History of Welfare.* New York: Belknap Press.

hooks, bell. 1999. "Thinking about Race, Class, Gender and Ethics." Presentation at Hamilton College, Clinton, N.Y., 12 April.

Hopwood, Catherine. 1995. "My Discourse/Myself: Therapy as Possibility (for Women Who Eat Compulsively)." *Feminist Review* 49: 66–82.

Karier, Thomas. 1998. "Welfare Graduates: College and Financial Independence," *Policy Notes* (Bard Colldge, Jerome Levy Economics Institute, New York), no. 1.

Kates, Erica. 1998. "College Can Help Women in Poverty." Pp. 341–48 in *For Crying Out Loud: Women's Poverty in the United States,* ed. Diane Dujon and Ann Withorn. Boston: South End Press.

Kingfisher, Catherine. 2000. "Rhetoric of (Female) Savagery: Welfare Reform in the United States and Aotearoa/New Zealand." *National Women's Studies Association Journal* 11, no. 1: 1–15.

Langston, Donna. 1998. "Tired of Playing Monopoly?" Pp. 126–36 in *Race, Class and Gender: An Anthology,* ed. Margaret L. Andersen and Patricia Hill Collins. Belmont, Calif.: Wadsworth Publishing.

Lefkowitz, Rochelle, and Ann Withorn. 1986. *For Crying Out Loud: Women and Poverty in the United States.* Boston: Pilgrim Press.

Loprest, Pamela. 1999. *Families Who Left Welfare: Who Are They and How Are They Doing?* Washington, D.C.: Urban Institute.

Lubiano, Wahneema. 1992. "Black Ladies, Welfare Queens, and State Minstrels: Ideological War by Narrative Means. Pp. 323–63 in *Race-ing Justice, En-gendering Power,* ed. Toni Morrison. New York: Pantheon.

MacDougal, Gary. 1995. "The Missing Half of the Welfare Debate." *Wall Street Journal,* 6 September, A16.

McNay, Lois. 1993. *Foucault and Feminism: Power, Gender and the Self.* Boston: Northeastern University Press.

Mickelson, Roslyn, and Stephen Smith. "Can Education Eliminate Race, Class and Gender Inequality?" In *Race, Class and Gender: An Anthology,* ed. Margaret L. Anderson and Patricia Hill Collins. Belmont, Calif.: Wadsworth.

Mink, Gwendolyn. 1998. *Welfare's End.* Ithaca, N.Y.: Cornell University Press.

———. 1996. *The Wages of Motherhood: Inequality in the Welfare State 1917–1942.* Ithaca, N.Y.: Cornell University Press.

Morgan, Kathryn. 1991. "Women and the Knife: Cosmetic Surgery and the Colonization of Women's Bodies." *Hepatia* 6, no. 3: 25–53.

Muir, Kate. 1993. "Runaway Fathers at Welfare's Final Frontier." Times Newspapers Limited, 19 July, A2.

Murray, Charles. 1984. *Losing Ground: American Social Policy, 1950–1980.* New York: Basic Books.

———. 1992. "Welfare Hysteria." *New York Times,* 15 September, E1.

Piven, Frances Fox, and Richard Cloward. 1993. *Regulating the Poor: The Functions of Public Welfare.* New York: Vintage Books.

Raphael, Jody. 2000. "Saving Bernice: Women, Welfare and Domestic Violence." Presentation at Hamilton College, Clinton, N.Y., 23 May.

Raspberry, William. 1995. "Ms. Smith Goes after Washington." *Washington Post,* 1 February, A19.

———. 1996. "Uplifting the Human Spirit." *Washington Post,* 8 August, A31.

Robinson, Valerie. 1999. "State's Ad Attacks the Poor." *Plain Dealer,* 2 November, B8.

Sennett, Richard, and Jonathan Cobb. 1972. *The Hidden Injuries of Class.* New York: Vintage Books.

Sidel, Ruth. 1998. *Keeping Women and Children Last: America's War on the Poor.* New York: Penguin.

Simon, Stephanie. 1999. "Drug Tests for Welfare Applicants." *Los Angeles Times,* 18 December, A1.

Smart, Carol. 1992. "Disruptive Bodies and Unruly Sex: The Regulation of Reproduction and Sexuality in the Nineteenth Century." Pp. 7–32 in *Regulating Womanhood: Historical Essays on Marriage, Motherhood and Sexuality,* ed. Carol Smart. New York: Routledge.

Steedman, Carolyn Kay. 1987. *Landscape for a Good Woman.* New Brunswick, N.J.: Rutgers University Press.

Stoler, Ann Laura. 1995. *Race and the Education of Desire: Foucault's History of Sexuality and the Colonial Order of Things.* Durham, N.C.: Duke University Press.

U. S. Department of Heath and Human Services. 1994. *An Overview of Entitlement Programs.* Washington, D.C.: Government Printing Office.

Will, George. 1995. "The Welfare Crisis Is Better Described as a Crisis of Character Development." *Newsweek,* 12 December, 88.

Women's Enews. 2001. "Civil Rights Bad for Welfare Moms" (online), 4 May. Available from: <http://www.womensenews.org>.

Nell Sullivan

2 Academic Constructions of "White Trash," or How to Insult Poor People without Really Trying

If Jesus had said to her before he made her, "There's only two places available for you. You can be either a nigger or white-trash," what would she have
said? ... Finally she would have said, "All right, make me a nigger then—but
that don't mean a trashy one."

—Flannery O'Connor

THE MODERN LANGUAGE ASSOCIATION (MLA) is *the* professional
organization of English and foreign-language professors in the United
States and Canada, and in recent years it has been increasingly aligned
with liberal causes such as labor issues and affirmative action. At the
1995 meeting of the MLA, I attended a panel focusing on the varying
depictions of white identity in popular culture. Earlier that year, I had
completed my dissertation on representations of African American subjectivity in the American novel, and I was eager to hear papers on a topic
I felt to be intimately connected with my dissertation and, perhaps more
importantly, with my own psyche. Although many have accused the
MLA of being *too* liberal, *too* "politically correct," the panel proved that
in some respects the MLA is not nearly liberal enough. Although the
academy has made great strides in addressing and redressing racial,
religious, and gender prejudice, intra-racial class prejudice remains so
deeply entrenched, so "naturalized," that it often goes unrecognized as
such.

At the 1995 MLA panel in question, Annalee Newitz gave a presentation in which she elicited wholehearted laughter from much of her
audience with caricatures of working-class and poverty-class whites,
including a ridiculing riff on the lawn furniture and yard animals of a
poor white woman she had visited as part of her research. Later, a very
earnest Hispanic woman objected to another panelist's discussion of

white male "disaffection" because, as she said, white people could not be discriminated against. Clearly she did not include poor whites in her definition of "white *people*," because we had all just witnessed a scene of such discrimination in the ridicule that had been heaped on the "trash," who in this instance were made the butt of a nasty academic joke. There may have been other dissenters in the group, but like me, they were probably too aware of their own precarious positions as passers among the middle-class to speak up.

No doubt, Newitz had good intentions. Perhaps her presentation, "White Trash 'Class Consciousness' in American Popular Culture," was meant to illuminate the plight of poor whites and to critique middle-class privilege. Although her momentary insensitivity may have been a mere lapse of an otherwise good liberal conscience, her ironically titled paper in fact derogated poor whites and relegated them to a subordinate position by seemingly confirming and playing to middle-class perceptions of the lower economic classes. Because such critiques from without lack self-consciousness and a *lived* understanding of a white, lower–economic-class identity, they do not subvert anything—except, perhaps, the dignity and self-esteem of those who actually inhabit the lower economic strata. These critiques "from above" are often riddled with uncanny manifestations of the very prejudices they seek to eradicate in what amounts to a middle-class, liberal return of the repressed. They tend to depict poor whites as the new exotic Other, the less-than-human, the non-subject. "Trash" does not count. And what is "white trash"? Although definitions vary according to whom one asks, the term *white trash* invariably refers to a white person who has failed to reach the U.S. minimum standard of affluence but has not successfully or willingly hidden that fact. For those who invoke the term, it connotes genetically transmitted intellectual and moral deficiency. And, in a throwback to American Calvinist roots, white-trash economic status is also invoked as an outward sign of theological or biological unworthiness, a mark of cosmic judgment rather than the inevitable consequence of late industrial capitalism's requirement for concentrated wealth and cheap, expendable labor. This attitude toward poor whites also has deeply racist implications because it assumes that whites should rightfully be economically dominant.

Although my family had a home and plenty of food and love, we inhabited the economic margins because only through my mother's heroic money management could my father's blue-collar salary support a family of eleven. Things like air-conditioning, new furniture, and fashionable clothes were impossible luxuries, and many times my younger sister Laura and I wore clothes that were fifteen years out of date, handed down from sister to sister to sister. But my family narrowly avoided being considered "trash" by being conspicuously intelligent and thus confounding the stereotypes. That is, my parents understood the connection between literacy and gentility and so encouraged all nine of their children to read and excel academically. In our un–air-conditioned summers, my mother constructed a tent over the clothesline, a hideaway where Laura and I read Nancy Drew mysteries from the bookmobile. After my older sister Jane got a job at the local library, I had access to more than just the bookmobile's limited popular fare. In my nascent pretensions, I decided to read all the "classics" (there's class in "classics"), which to my young mind meant books that looked old. I read novels such as *Gone with the Wind, Pride and Prejudice,* and my favorite, *Vanity Fair.* I was fascinated by Thackeray's Becky Sharp, who inexplicably appealed to me even though I knew she was the bad girl whom I was not supposed to like. It never would have occurred to me then that Becky was a distant mirror, an economically marginal girl trying to climb out of an undesirable class designation.

I attended the elementary school considered to be the worst in Frankfort, Kentucky. Thornhill Elementary served a white, working-class neighborhood with several pockets of extreme poverty. In fifth grade, I had a very elegant teacher. I do not recall the social studies or English lessons we learned from her, but I do remember one important lesson she taught us, what I will call my socioeconomic primal scene. One day, Ann, a girl who had been "held back" a grade or two, brought a gold lamé purse to school. I am sure at that age I thought the purse absolutely beautiful. But the teacher was outraged, berating Ann before the whole class for being so "trashy" as to bring "an after-five handbag" to school. Her tirade, delivered in righteously clipped tones, implied that we should be ashamed of lacking both the essential knowledge of etiquette and the material possessions we should have had.

In retrospect, I know that Ann probably brought to school the best purse she had (it had no doubt been donated to a clothing drive by some philanthropic ex-prom queen or debutante), but even if Ann had known better, she could not have afforded better. I also know that our teacher failed us in a crucial, almost unforgivable way. She taught us social prejudices with much more conviction than she taught us reading, writing, and math. Ann, I know, never graduated from junior high, much less high school. But in 1975, I looked at this teacher as the-one-who-was-supposed-to-know, and I therefore looked to her to affirm my subjectivity, to recognize me as a worthy human being in my own right. Instead, she taught me class shame and the desirability of hiding my working-class origins.

Sometimes, however, it is impossible to hide where one comes from. In high school, I had to ride the bus to school, something that was then and still is uncool, if not downright déclassé. On one occasion, some kids in the back of the bus verbally abused the bus driver, who then refused to let any of us off at school that morning. The vice-principal, who patrolled the unloading area, boarded our bus and promptly branded us inclusively, "Hogtrash. Every last one of you. You'll never amount to nothing."[1] His double negative notwithstanding, the vice-principal made it clear that it is not individual identity, but class identity—where one came from and on which bus—that determines one's fitness for even a basic education and respect. In fact, the vice-principal served as a deacon with my father at our church, but when we were among our economic peers, my sister and I were reduced to nothing in his eyes.

Lessons of shame were also abundant in college and graduate school, but in those settings everyone always assumed that I was at least middle class or, if not, that I would pretend to be. In such settings, economic need supposedly becomes a moot (or perhaps only mute) point. In a meeting for English graduate students who were applying for coveted tenure-track teaching positions and thus facing possible job interviews at the annual MLA convention, I heard earnest advice about what to wear to these interviews. A classmate posed the "What if it snows in Chicago?" question—that is, What does one do with one's galoshes or walking shoes when one goes for an interview? The professor who once team-taught a Marxism–feminism seminar I took answered emphatically and without irony, "It's MLA, for God's sake! Buy good boots!" Translation: Middle-class identity is crucial for getting a job in academe. If one cannot afford the right clothes, one deserves to remain among the shabbily dressed, jobless preterite.

Many times, I have listened with a grim smile as colleagues and intimates have unknowingly insulted me. "Passing" among middle-class academics, I have heard all of the following beliefs articulated by otherwise intelligent, educated people:

1. "Using marshmallows in recipes is so white trash," said a colleague, discussing recipes her mother used when "entertaining" (a term rarely used by the lower economic classes). Here, economic necessity is confused with a lack of sensibility.
2. *Blue collar* means "white trash." A friend with whom I attended graduate school was lamenting her high school's lack of rigor, for which she blamed the "white trash" who made up most of the student body. When this conversation took place, we had known each other for ten years, and she had even visited my home in Kentucky, where she broke bread with my father, a former construction worker. When I asked her what she meant by "white trash," my friend said, "Oh, you know, blue-collar people."
3. Anyone who speaks with standard grammar or obtains a high-quality education must be a product of the middle class, at the very least. This belief has been articulated in multiple forms, from a colleague referring to facility with spoken language and grammar as "middle-class polish" to another exasperated colleague upbraiding me for some class-conscious comment in a meeting. "But Nell," the colleague said, "you went to Vanderbilt." My colleagues sometimes do not recognize standard dialect as the Mandarin language that it is, viewing it instead as an exclusive language "belonging" to the economically advantaged. Further, most middle-class academics have had no direct experience with financial aid outside of their graduate fellowships, which, of course, were not need-based. It seems little short of miraculous to many in the professoriate that a child of the lower-economic classes should be speaking *their* language as well as they.
4. Lower-income people have a limited capacity for learning and scholarship. As Rita Felski (2000, 34–35) notes, the lower economic classes are often depicted as "pure body" with no intellect. This stereotype of brutish carnality runs rampant in film, television (for example, *Married . . . with Children*), literature, and, as Felski notes, even the scholarship of popular culture, where members of the working class are the modern equivalent of clowns and pastorals (Felski 2000, 35). Felski notes John Fiske's influential *Understanding Popular Culture* (1989), among others.[2]

Ironically, this poor-people-are-stupid mentality plagues my own institution, an open-admission undergraduate institution whose mission is to serve the community, particularly the working classes of all ethnic origins, who make up most of our student population. In 1999, Sandra Dahlberg and I sponsored the College Bowl team and submitted a budget request for a modest $1,500, or less than one-sixth of the annual automobile allowance of the academic administrator to whom we submitted the request. Although this administrator would not commit a response to writing, she let us know through indirect channels that she did not intend to fund College Bowl, so we were forced to seek funding from a non-academic office that oversees student organizations and clubs. Meeting with an administrator in this office, I realized that the resistance we faced was symptomatic: The administration did not believe that College Bowl was a worthwhile activity for *our* students, whom they assumed could not possibly be smart enough to compete. At this meeting, the very well-heeled administrator attempted to disarm me by complimenting me on my jacket. She seemed somewhat deaf to our arguments but not blind to my clothes. At least I had worn the right thing to come a-begging: The request for College Bowl funding was finally approved.

These middle-class attitudes often go unchallenged by those who have experienced a lower–economic-class identity because of the shame engendered by that heritage (Felski 2000, 39) and the invisibility that the middle and upper classes demand of the lower economic classes (Hitchcock 2000, 21). Those of us who find ourselves among the middle class become complicit in our own silence and invisibility, disciplining ourselves to hide all traces of our origins. To be seen and heard, we must assume a middle-class identity and all its trappings. It is a *dis*grace to be poor, not to own the right boots, the right jacket, the right handbag. Moreover, in a manner analogous to the way in which the word *nigger* effaces the humanity of the African American so labeled, the term *white trash* effaces the humanity of the white subject in an effect of language that the post–Freudian French psychoanalyst Jacques Lacan calls *aphanisis*. According to Lacan, "Through the effects of speech, the subject always realizes himself more in the Other" (Lacan 1981, 188), but "when the subject appears somewhere as meaning, he is manifested elsewhere as 'fading,' as disappearance" (Lacan 1981, 218). In other words, one cannot both *mean* and *be* simultaneously. Aphanisis results when the poor white subject's meaning for the middle-class Other eclipses her being, and this happens each time someone invokes the term *white trash*.[3] The lower–economic-class invisibility noted by Peter Hitchcock (2000, 21) is in fact a prolonged instance of aphanisis, a condition I personally experienced when the vice-principal made a busload of people disappear behind his bon mot "hog trash."

Moreover, stereotypes about the poor are constantly reinforced in the various discourses that inform academic disciplines, discourses whose alleged objectivity lends them credibility. For example, Stephen Heath remarks on the class bias at the heart of Freudian psychoanalytic theory, which has been a major force in literary studies since the 1920s. Freud remarked about "servant girls" in 1907: "Fortunately for our therapy, we have previously learned so much from other cases that we can tell these persons their story without having to wait for their contribution. They are willing to confirm what we tell them, but we can learn nothing from them" (Heath 1984, 43). This dim view of the lower economic classes ensures their silence, for the academy often circumvents the question, "Who is permitted to speak?" by asking instead, "Who *can* speak?" and answering for itself that the lower economic classes, of course, are not articulate speaking subjects, much less literate ones.

Like Freud's work with "servant girls," most American literature and cultural criticism dealing with class issues represents the lower economic classes "without having to wait for their contribution." In 1997, for instance, Newitz expanded her MLA presentation and, along with Matt Wray, edited an anthology titled, *White Trash: Race and Class in America* (1997). In the acknowledgments, she reveals her economic privilege by thanking "Cynthia and Marty Newitz for the financial support which allowed me to spend time working at writing instead of working for money" (Newitz and Wray 1997, vii). Clearly, only the economic preterite have to "work for money," and the exigency of working for money insures they will remain in that state because it precludes their finding their way into print. After all, one needs "time, money and idleness" to become a published writer, as Virginia Woolf notes in *A Room of One's Own* (Woolf 1989 [1929], 94).

Yet for those who have ever actually been without money, even their mute authority apparently rests on their remaining impoverished. For example, in their introduction to *White Trash,* Newitz and Wray decry Roseanne Barr and the late Kurt Cobain as "two examples of white trash who, having escaped poverty and disempowerment through fame, nevertheless used a sense of social victimization as their own, 'white' form of hip authenticity" (Newitz and Wray 1997, 6), an accusation the authors neither explain nor substantiate. "*Faux white authenticity,*" they continue, "is not what we aim to foster" (Newitz and Wray 1997, 6; emphasis added). I am not quite sure what they were "aiming to foster" when they included the brutally insensitive piece "White Trash Girl: The Interview," a collaboration by Laura Kipnis, a professional academic who admits she only dabbles in "low taste" but "shop[s] at Saks" (Kipnis and Reeder 1997, 114), and Jennifer Reeder, a self-identified member of the middle class who "performs" the character White Trash Girl (Kipnis and Reeder 1997, 120). Kipnis explains the motives for Reeder's performance: "White Trash Girl was merely the latest expression of Reeder's theoretical conviction . . . that modes of inhabiting social classes are both embodied and performative" (Kipnis and Reeder 1997, 115).[4] Kipnis's emphasis on the performative conveniently allows her to forget that Reeder does not actually inhabit the social class she performs. Although the Kipnis-Reeder collaboration reveals itself to be an example of "faux authenticity," Newitz and Wray view its authors as being somehow more credible than Cobain and Barr, as though a parody were more valid than the real thing.

Wray and Newitz's book does contain a few thoughtful pieces—particularly "Sunset Trailer Park" (1997), co-written by Allan Bérubé and his mother, Florence—but in general it is marred by its insistence that performing "white trash" is more authentic, more authoritative, than a *lived* experience of lower economic status. In privileging this middle-class performance of "white trash," the book actually reinforces negative stereotypes. With its blithely unselfconscious title *White Trash*, Wray and Newitz's collection is indicative of the aphanisis inherent in the middle-class invocation of "white trash," the same misrepresentations of lower–economic-class whites that plague low-brow and high-brow literature alike, from Erskine Caldwell's *Tobacco Road* and *God's Little Acre* to Eudora Welty's Pulitzer Prize-winning *The Optimist's Daughter*. In the latter, Welty presents as the villain the "white trash" character Fay, a fashion miscreant who wears green stiletto heels before five in a style vaguely reminiscent of my former classmate Ann, and throttles her ailing, much older husband, Judge McKelva, whereas his proper daughter Laurel reads dutifully to him in a steady, measured voice. The literate Laurel, of course, is the novel's center of consciousness, for Welty could never imagine Fay even having consciousness. Welty writes near the end of the novel:

> But of course, Laurel saw, it was Fay who did not know how to fight. For Fay was without any powers of passion or imagination in herself and had no way to see it or reach it in the other person. Other people, inside their lives, might as well be invisible to her. To find them, she could only strike out those little fists at random, or spit from her little mouth. She could no more fight a feeling person than she could love him. (Welty 1990 [1972], 178)

Viewing the novel from another perspective, however, it becomes clear to the reader that Laurel is not, in fact, invisible to Fay. Rather, for all her conspicuousness, Fay—the *Other* person—is somehow invisible inside her life to Welty, who cannot see beyond the stereotypical notions of white trash on which she builds her novel.

After Mark Twain's *Adventures of Huckleberry Finn*, "Revelation," a story Flannery O'Connor wrote shortly before her death in 1964, offers one of the most significant literary challenges to intra-racial class assumptions. In the story, Ruby Turpin imagines being given an irrevocable choice:

> If Jesus had said to her before he made her, "There's only two places available for you. You can be either a nigger or white-trash," what would she have said? . . . Finally she would have said, "All right, make me a nigger then—but that don't mean a trashy one." (O'Connor 1983, 407–408)

Later, Ruby's class-consciousness, along with a knot on her head, is raised when the upper-middle-class college girl, Mary Grace, hurls a psychology textbook (the true emblem of the acquisition of literacy) at her, eventually leading to Ruby's vision of the masses ascending to heaven together, with the respectable class including herself, "who had a little of everything," at the rear. "Yet she could see by their shocked and altered faces that even their virtues were being burned away" (O'Connor 1983, 423). Those would be, of course, middle-class virtues, which O'Connor suggests might not be Christian virtues after all.

The desire for recognition from the Other has been mediated not only through speech but also through written language. To avoid cultural aphanisis in the United States, one must lay claim to the reading subject position and, in effect, master literacy. American cultural history is replete with representatives of marginalized groups doing just that, from the requisite account of the acquisition of literacy that James Olney notes as part of the slave narrative's "existential claim" (Olney 1985, 155) to the Cherokee apologist Elias Boudinot's argument in "An Address to Whites" (1994 [1826]) that the Cherokees' invention of an alphabet and the subsequent translation of the Bible into Cherokee proved their essential humanity. During the antebellum period, the wealthy planter class was also invested in promoting and extolling the literacy of its members. In his polemical "Southern Thought," the slavery apologist George Fitzhugh urged Southerners to improve and expand schools for boys *and* girls of the upper class (Fitzhugh 1994 [1857], 1915). "It is all important that we should write our own books," he tells his compatriots (Fitzhugh 1994 [1857], 1916). Significantly, Lewis Simpson notes that Fitzhugh's vision of the organic Southern society also included the belief that slavery should logically be extended "to the lower orders of the white race" (Simpson 1985, 171).

More recently, the "white trash reading subject," the lower–economic-class answer to Welty's Laurel McKelva Hand, has become a common feature in contemporary fiction, particularly fiction written by women who themselves come from the lower economic classes and have recognized the wisdom of "writing our own books." Dorothy Allison, Carolyn Chute, and Connie May Fowler have all challenged and problematized white class stereotypes in their novels. Particularly instructive is Katherine Dunn's *Geek Love* (1989). Capitalizing on the pervasive popular notion of the working class as virtual carnival grotesques, Dunn makes her Binewski family literal carnival folk. To outsiders, the Binewskis are visible only as grotesque bodies, the freaks of their "Carnival Fabulon," but Dunn undercuts this perspective by making the limbless Arturo a genius, albeit an evil one, and by using Oly's position both as an albino dwarf (the whitest of white, the lowest of low) and as narrator to assert the white working-class woman as the literate subject. Oly literally writes the story to save her daughter Miranda from the clutches of the wealthy heiress Mary Lick, whose father amassed a fortune from a line of frozen TV dinners marketed primarily to the working class. Miss Lick offers Miranda money to have the physical traces of her Binewski heritage surgically removed, a procedure that Oly recognizes as an erasure, an invitation to invisibility.

The manifestation of the white trash reading subject in works such as *Geek Love* is a significant trend in contemporary fiction that may represent a way to overcome the cycle of lower–economic-class stereotypes, shame, and silence. The U.S. educational system—at least, as I have experienced it—fosters negative stereotypes about the white lower economic classes that it perpetuates, even in those institutions that view themselves as bastions of liberalism, such as the MLA. These academically endorsed stereotypes in turn serve to silence those who hail from the lower economic classes by inducing shame and creating the desirability of passing for middle class, particularly in light of the academy's failure to recognize that members of the lower economic classes can be, should be, and are in fact subjects of literacy. Writers such as Allison, Chute, Dunn, and Fowler have asserted their own positions as literate subjects, and their works should be incorporated into high-school and college English and humanities curricula to insure a more accurate representation of the white lower economic classes. Critical readings of their texts, with their lower–economic-class, first-person narrators created by writers who have *been there*, would create cross-class understanding to help dispel the last acceptable prejudice in academe.

Unfortunately, these negative stereotypes are deeply entrenched, and the shame they invoke in those of us marked by them is a compelling force. Writing this essay, I have struggled with alternating urges to remain silent (as I did in 1995) and to hide myself within an authoritative middle-class voice that passes in academe for the voice of consensus. Ironically, revealing my scars makes me vulnerable to fresh wounding, especially by those who will argue that such personal experiences have little to do with public policy and institutions, and that essays such as these are tantamount to whining. Having outed myself socioeconomically, I worry that such a gesture could destroy my credibility with some in my profession, although their disapproval may not be conscious and will run the gamut from disgust to disdain to pity, all the inverted forms of shame. Yet I am willing to take this risk. It seems unlikely that the prejudice against the lower economic classes will be eradicated until more of our voices are heard in higher education, both as professors and as authors of texts, because in depending on middle-class champions or in assuming middle-class personas to legitimize our claims, we risk the perpetuation of "white trash" and other lower–economic-class stereotypes and thereby the erasure of our subjectivity.

We educators who are children of the lower economic classes therefore need to assert our heritage and refuse further complicity in our own silence and the silencing of others. Following the examples of our colleagues in fields such as African American studies, Chicano/Chicana literature, and gay and lesbian studies, we should establish ourselves as legitimate discursive subjects, both in the classroom and in print. Without an authentic audible and visible presence in academe, the lower economic classes will continue to be objects of cruel parody and distorted caricature disguised as enlightened or even benevolent critique. To build on Fitzhugh's directive to the antebellum planter class, it is essential that we who hail from lower economic classes should both write and teach "our own books," in our own voices.

Notes

Epigraph: O'Connor (1983, 407–408).

1. I am indebted here to my sister Laura Sullivan-Hackley, who sat next to me on that bus and acted as my only confidante about this incident. She recounts the incident in her recent prose poem, "Speech Pathology: The Deflowering of an Accent" (Sullivan-Hackley 1999, 39).

2. This is another manifestation of what Peter Hitchcock calls "the age-old but continuing predicament of the 'working class subject' as intellectual, in which the economic and social determinants that produce the former are seen to exclude the latter" (Hitchcock 2000, 21).

3. For more on the connection between race and aphanisis, Nell Sullivan (1996, 1998).

4. This emphasis on the performance of "white trash" reflects a recent trend in literary and cultural criticism. The notions of performance and theatricality in identity are used to undermine forms of domination justified by appeals to gender or racial essentialism. For example, in her influential study *Gender Trouble* (1990), Judith Butler argues that gender exists only in performance, and therefore gender stereotypes may be subverted through parody. In his analysis of the American minstrel tradition, Eric Lott argues, "The very form of blackface acts ... demonstrates the permeability of the color line" (Lott 1993, 6). In other words, white performances of blackness actually amounted to assaults on racial strictures. Ironically, the performances of "white trash"—particularly in such pieces as the Kipnis–Reeder collaboration—do not have the

consciously desired effect of subversion because they merely reinforce the stereotypes and because the performance of economic status works in only one direction. That is, poor people cannot fake being affluent; moreover, when they actually attain a higher economic status, they are accused of being over-reachers or of having, in Newitz and Wray's words, "faux white authenticity" (Newitz and Wray 1997, 6).

REFERENCES

Bérubé, Allan, and Florence Bérubé. 1997. "Sunset Trailer Park." Pp. 16–39 in *White Trash: Race and Class in America*, ed. Matt Wray and Annalee Newitz. New York: Routledge.

Boudinot, Elias. 1994 (1826). "An Address to Whites." Pp. 1792–1801 in *Heath Anthology of American Literature*, vol. 1, 2nd ed, ed. Paul Lauter et al. New York: Heath.

Butler, Judith. 1990. *Gender Trouble: Feminism and the Subversion of Identity.* New York: Routledge.

Dunn, Katherine. 1989. *Geek Love.* New York: Warner.

Felski, Rita. 2000. "Nothing to Declare: Shame, Identity, and the Lower Middle Class." *PMLA* 115, no. 1: 33–45.

Fiske, John. 1989. *Understanding Popular Culture.* New York: Routledge.

Fitzhugh, George. 1994 (1857). "Southern Thought." Pp. 1913–22 in *Heath Anthology of American Literature*, vol. 1, 2nd ed., ed. Paul Lauter et al. New York: Heath.

Heath, Stephen. 1984. *The Sexual Fix.* New York: Schocken.

Hitchcock, Peter. 2000. "They Must Be Represented? Problems in Theories of Working-Class Representation." *PMLA* 115, no. 1: 20–32.

Kipnis, Laura, and Jennifer Reeder. 1997. "White Trash Girl: The Interview." Pp. 113–30 in *White Trash: Race and Class in America*, ed. Matt Wray and Annalee Newitz. New York: Routledge.

Lacan, Jacques. 1981. *The Four Fundamental Concepts of Psycho-analysis.* Trans. Alan Sheridan. New York: Norton.

Lott, Eric. 1993. *Love and Theft: Blackface Minstrelsy and the American Working Class.* Oxford: Oxford University Press.

Newitz, Annalee, and Matt Wray. 1997. "Introduction." Pp. 1–12 in *White Trash: Race and Class in America*, ed. Matt Wray and Annalee Newitz. New York: Routledge.

O'Connor, Flannery. 1983. "Revelation." Pp. 405–24 in *Three by Flannery O'Connor.* New York: Signet.

Olney, James. 1985. "'I Was Born': Slave Narratives, Their Status as Autobiography and as Literature." Pp. 148–75 in *The Slave's Narrative*, ed. Charles T. Davis and Henry Louis Gates, Jr. New York: Oxford University Press.

Simpson, Lewis P. 1985. "The Mind of the Antebellum South." Pp. 164–74 in *The History of Southern Literature*, ed. Louis D. Rubin, Blyden Jackson,

Rayburn S. Moore, Lewis P. Simpson, and Thomas Daniel Young. Baton Rouge: Louisiana State University Press.

Sullivan, Nell. 1996. "Persons in Pieces: Race and Aphanisis in *Light in August.*" *Mississippi Quarterly* 49, no. 3: 497–517.

———. 1998. "Nella Larsen's *Passing* and the Fading Subject." *African American Review* 32, no. 3: 373–86.

Sullivan-Hackley, Laura. 1999. "Speech Pathology: The Deflowering of an Accent." *Kalliope* 21, no. 3: 39.

Welty, Eudora. 1990 (1972). *The Optimist's Daughter.* New York: Vintage.

Woolf, Virginia. 1989 (1929). *A Room of One's Own.* San Diego, Calif.: Harvest.

SANDRA L. DAHLBERG

3 Survival in a Not So Brave New World

AT THE END of Shakespeare's *The Tempest*, the character of Miranda, astounded by the thought of a vigorously populated world completely antithetical to her secluded island, exclaims, "Oh, brave new world that has such people in't." The cynical Prospero, her father, responds that it "is new to thee," although he readies himself for travel to his former dukedom where he will resume his position of power, wealth, and learning (Shakespeare 1974 [1611], 5.1.183–84). The remaining island inhabitants, the characters of Ariel and Caliban, do not fare so well. Ariel is "freed," but no mention is given as to the final disposition of Caliban. I, too, have felt the power of Miranda's words regarding a "brave new world." In my case, the world of academe offered the potential for learning, advancement, and financial security. Yet, often, I can identify with Caliban, the character in the play for whom no resolution is provided. Caliban, like the poor in academe, functions as a foil by which Prospero and Miranda measure their own worth, their own privilege. I have been Caliban on the periphery of higher education, allowed measured access and systematically reminded that only provisional acceptance has been granted until I abandon my culture of origin and refashion myself in middle-class customs. It was access to higher education that began my dual existence between Caliban and Miranda, a duality that required self-erasure to succeed and perseverance to survive in an unfamiliar and sometimes hostile environment.

The concept of class transcendence denotes a dual existence that positions the poverty-class academic on the periphery of a middle-class environment that is separate from her original class roots. The poverty-class person works in the middle-class arena, but her psyche remains rooted in the poverty-class culture. Middle-class opportunity is culturally represented as an unambiguously uplifting transformation by those who have not had to transcend class boundaries or to pass class lines. The process itself, however—centered as it is within the middle-class traditions of higher education—leaves unchallenged and unexplained the disruptions actually imposed on the poverty-class individuals involved. The assumption is that poor people want to "better" themselves without actually examining what is meant by "bettering" oneself or the personal costs of doing so. Much of this schism between public rhetoric regarding class mobility and the lived experiences of poverty-class people is a result of our societal inability to discuss the intricacies of poverty-class cultures without denigration and without concepts of "betterment" that ignore the positive attributes of poverty-class cultures. Through this denial we create a dichotomy and treat class distinctions similarly to racial Otherness. As Abdul R. JanMohamed says, "The function of racial difference, of the fixation on and fetishization of native savagery and evil, must be mapped in terms [of colonialist politics and culture] and ideological imperatives" (JanMohamed 1986, 82). In the case of U.S. class identities, the poverty class functions to reinforce middle-class cultural norms, mapping out cultural imperatives that equate economic advantage with moral agency. As a result, little more than a tacit awareness of the poverty class is provided to society, and that awareness is burdened with a fetishized identification. Fetishization is the pathological projection of irrational characteristics associated with an identity deemed exotic or "different" from the dominant group. When such poverty-class identities are examined at all, they function very much like the colonized racial Other, as poverty-class imagery is sexualized, fetishized, and appropriated by middle-class culture to proscribe more acceptable models of class Otherness. Further, these models pit working-class images of labor against poverty-class representations of economic failure to reinforce concepts of the "deserving" and "undeserving" poor. The poverty class remains Other as a result and unacceptable in the cultural consciousness.

Public imagery often reduces portrayals of poverty-class people to those delineated by a supposed moral deficiency. This presentation is based on a presumed lack of a work ethic that constrains the class-identity debate in terms of binary oppositions of "good and evil, superiority and inferiority, civilization and savagery, intelligence and emotion" (JanMohamed 1986, 82). Discourse surrounding class cultures—as is the case with racial discourse in postcolonialist theory—reveals that the effectiveness of this opposition "is based on a transformation of racial [or class] difference into moral and even metaphysical difference" (JanMohamed 1986, 80). What makes the "metaphysical differences" in class identity particularly problematic within academe is that individual efforts to resist complete transformation (through class transcendence or passing) further marks that poverty-class person as Other, or as morally questionable and intellectually weak. The "metaphysical differences" are accentuated if the poverty-class person—now a "middle-class" academic—professes an adherence to an alternative class-consciousness such as a working-class or poverty-class identification. At the same time, academics firmly within the middle-class culture can safely advocate a competing class consciousness because their middle-class status means that they are not Other and therefore do not pose the same cultural threats as do poverty-class individuals.

CLOSETING THE POOR IN ACADEME

Under the exercise of multiculturalism, the examination of race, class, and gender has nearly become a cliched methodology for exploring postmodern identity and subjectivity, particularly in literary and cultural studies. The intellectual exploration of subjectivity within the context of academic inquiry is, however, too often considered a self-reflexive endeavor with little connection to actuality. Examined are the ideas of race, class, and gender, whereby these Others are arbitrarily privileged within the narrow constraints of academic discourse. Postmodern radicalism moved the discussions of Otherness and marginality from the abstract practice of academic theory to the concrete arena of social and cultural reform. Doing so has offered profound insights and correctives to our cultural myopia in regard to multicultural issues and societal inclusiveness. As a result of these efforts, more access was available to non-whites and women as academe worked to diversify faculty and student populations. Identity at the intersections of race, class, gender, and sexual orientation became a topic of great interest in the academy. This interest brought about the establishment of academic programs and theoretical "schools" such as feminist theory, queer theory, and ethnic studies.

It is important to remember that there was significant resistance to ethnic studies, women's studies, and gay and lesbian studies, as challenges of "quality" often veiled an exclusivist hegemonic standard. Today these fields are thriving. But with the proliferation of theoretical constructions of identity, and the inclusion of previously marginalized

Others in the academy and in academic discourse, there is a marked exception. Within an exploration of "race, class, and gender," the advancement of U.S.-based, post–Marxist critical theories to enhance examinations of class identities is negligible. Institutions offer few class-studies courses and—under the aegis of multiculturalism—the recognition, much less the recruitment, of poverty-class academics of all ethnicities is non-existent. Institutions whose student bodies are composed of significant numbers of working-class, poverty-class, or first-generation college students would benefit by hiring poverty-class and working-class academics who could serve as positive role models for their students (Oldfield and Conant 2001). Yet even when poverty-class and working-class scholars teach at such institutions, they are often so obviously in the minority among their peers that they resort to passing, or at least engage in selective exposure.

I work at a public university with an open admission policy. The vast majority of my students are of the poverty class and the working class. Most are first-generation college students. The student body is one of the most diverse in the nation, demographically representative of the public the university is designed to serve. Even in this environment, I have to be careful when I reveal my poverty-class roots so as not to undermine my authority as a "middle-class" professor. My students, for one thing, want to see me as middle-class because they are attending college so that they can "become middle-class." The privileging of middle-class cultural norms in academe—that is, models of oral exchange, intellectual engagement, and subject matter—works to transform these students from their cultures of origin to a white, middle-class norm, a process that will always mark them as Other. While academic and economic achievement is laudable, I am concerned with the psychic contradictions that this poverty-class–middle-class duality poses for my students and for myself.

In an environment that privileges transcendence to the middle class as proof of arrival, the politics of class bias inscribe schizophrenic mandates. A colleague understands that, although the academy may value her study of ethnic women's literature and tell her that she is "one of us," the acceptance—which is often tenuous, at best, especially if she is a woman of color—is jeopardized should that same woman embrace a poverty-class background. Similarly, the set of hurdles a woman faces to come out as a lesbian in the academy is high, but attach that coming out to concurrent poverty-class identification and the dynamics inten-sify. Coming-out stories are not accorded validity when coming out means coming out of the broom closest. In the case of the white woman, white privilege is equated unconsciously to middle-class privilege, and revelations of poverty-class backgrounds are attached to an assumed rejection of middle-class norms, family shame, or grave personal fail-ure rather than acknowledged as the effects of intergenerational poverty. Poverty-class women exemplify the dualities Trinh T. Minh-ha delin-eates for women of color whose presence simultaneously affirms that "'I am like you' while persisting in her difference and that of remind-ing 'I am different'" (Minh-ha 1990, 375). It is this sameness together with difference that characterize class identities, as well. My occupation as an English professor, for instance, affirms my "likeness" to my peers and projects a middle-class status. My poverty background, however, renders me "different" from the academic norm, and I have to be cau-tious about how I act as a role model and advocate for poverty-class stu-dents, even at my open-admission institution.

It must be noted that the cultural differences and chances for oppor-tunities are as distinct between the working class and the poverty class as those that distinguish the middle class from the upper class. While recognizing the similarities, explorations of working-class and poverty-class experience and theory must be disjoined and examined separately to challenge negatively essentialized portrayals and perceptions dis-tinctly applied to each in U.S. culture. To take my field of literature as an example, lumping poverty-class representations under the rubric of the working class erases the distinctions inherent in poverty-class iden-tity and renders the poverty class invisible. At this time, alterior class identities, when examined at all in literary studies, focus on working-class identities, which, although assuredly perceived as Other in rela-tion to the middle-class norm, are not the same as poverty-class identi-ties and are not nearly as stigmatizing.

There is some indication that attitudes may be changing regarding some working-class affiliations, at least when that working-class pres-ence carries the caché of being embedded in a European culture. In "Nothing to Declare" (2000), published in a special issue of the *Publi-cations of the Modern Language Association* (*PMLA*) on class, Rita Felski contends that working-class identity can carry an aura of "radical chic" without noting that the very source of that "chic" may result from being

British working-class in America. As the special *PMLA* edition demonstrates, of the two writers who revealed working-class identities, both were British, a move that erases U.S. poverty-class subjects and critics. From a British positionality, Felski can declare with assurance the existence of a core set of working-class values that include a "tradition of respectability. . . . Frugality, decency, and self-discipline" (Felski 2000, 35). Felski elaborates this imagery by noting that "working-class women, in particular, often have a powerful interest and investment in respectability" (Felski 2000, 35). Felski must assert this "investment in respectability" because narratives of working-class respectability do not erode class biases when working-class people attempt to pass or transcend into the U.S. middle-class.

For those individuals from the poverty class, the situation is more extreme. To be poor in America is to be considered devoid of respectability and worthy values because American class stratification, unlike the presumed rigidity of the British system, is commonly considered fluid enough to facilitate upward class mobility when sufficient effort is applied. More importantly, to be a poor woman—which the vast majority of poor U.S. adults are—is to internalize what Felski refers to as the "sexualized images of lower-class women's bodies" (Felski 2000, 35). Poor American women are not represented as respectable; they are viewed as Welfare Queens and "brood mares." Both terms are sexually charged and encourage public vilification.[1] Negative perceptions of poverty enable the perpetuation of class-transcendence myths as the public discourse presumes that movement to a middle-class "norm" will eradicate the markers associated with poverty. What is missed in such presumptions of transcendence is that, although upwardly mobile, poverty-class people may welcome the reversal of economic poverty, the culture of poverty is not impoverished. I want to be Caliban *and* Miranda, equally and fully, because that is the reality of my existence. Class transcendence that denies ongoing ties to the community of origin results at best in cultural schizophrenia, or at worst in cultural suicide.

COMING OUT OF THE ACADEMIC BROOM CLOSET

The definition of Otherness is completely unsettled by the introduction of class identity in large part because the very notion of academic positionality is tied to theoretical constructs such as race theory, gender theory, and queer theory. In each case, an academic discourse exists that not only defines the field but also demarcates the boundaries of inquiry, at least to the point of deploying a set of "rules" endorsing the interrogation. In addition, academic associations and journals privilege these discourses and, in doing so, create communities that provide professional and personal validation when scholars successfully appropriate the discourses. As Maxine Baca Zinn and her co-authors note about the role of journals in feminist studies, "editors, associate editors, and consultants make important decisions about which individual pieces of scholarship will be contained in the journals' pages and what special issues will be undertaken, officially sanctioning and defining important concerns and critical scholarship in the field" (Zinn et al. 1990, 31). Discussing class is an uneasy endeavor. In confronting class, we examine our own complicity in the denigration and exploitation of others, and class criticism challenges basic precepts of American meritocracy, especially the viability of the bootstrap myth. Our uneasiness with class is best shown by the fact that, at present, there are no journals that primarily address issues of class in terms of practice or pedagogy. There is no recognized community to which poverty-class or working-class people can come out, and there is no theoretical legitimization of class positionality.

Coming out is always painful, and yet the very act of coming out, of being out—to colleagues, to students, at professional meetings—triggers unrecognized problems for the working-class academic and more so for those from the poverty-class. Gender and race complicate the matter. When coming out, gays and lesbians in academe usually are simultaneously coming out to an intact, supportive, visible academic community that fosters a sense of intellectual validity, as demonstrated by the presence of queer theory and gay and lesbian studies programs. There is a sense of belonging. There are very few communities for poverty-class scholars and students.[2] Similar to the experiences of gays and lesbians when coming out, poverty-class and working-class academics must address feelings of rejection within the family while negotiating support for educational endeavors. In addition, when coming out, poverty-class people in the academy must acknowledge and mediate the betrayal of their loved ones, because the speaker is not the only one who is outed; the family is, as well. This move exposes each family member to scrutiny for being "less than" the American norm.

I come from a family that experienced poverty in as many generations as I am aware. My father was a dropout who was disabled as a young man; he was also an alcoholic. My mother was the first high-school graduate in the family, which gave her access to fairly stable though often underpaid employment in various secretarial and clerical positions. I am the only one in my family with a university degree. My academic peers tend to come from college-educated, professional families whose members have degrees, homes, assets; some have trust funds. When I was a child, all three generations of my family lived in public housing. When my peers talk about their families and vacations in Europe, I keep silent. When I hear the term *trailer trash*, I think of my mother's twenty-year dream of owning a mobile home. The reality my family faces each and every day is so removed from the lives my peers know that it is hard to speak honestly about my family without having to make lengthy and personal explanations, to avoid having them appear as "less." I do not want to betray my family simply by talking about them. Their goals, achievements, pastimes, and joys exist in a realm different from the middle-class culture of my academic peers.

Coming out also explicitly violates working-class and poverty-class values that, Randall Collins notes, "emphasize the virtues of their own life situations. . . . [including] physical toughness, loyalty to friends, courage, and wariness toward strangers and supervisors" (O'Dair 1993, 242–43). Loyalty, then, means class loyalty, and individual actions that imply a change in class identity, real or perceived, usually distance the individual from his or her culture of origin. What this means is that my home culture and my family reward the physical and mental toughness it takes to obtain an education and to challenge the educational system that erases poverty-class identities, but they also believe that my education "changed" me because I now live and work in in an environment that is different from theirs.

When I was a child, I knew poverty, homelessness, and abuse. I also experienced love and joy. As I matured, higher education became my hope for breaking the cyclical patterns of disempowering poverty that I saw affecting my family. In that, I have succeeded in my efforts to transform my Calibanistic self into someone more resembling Miranda. But this transformation did not come until I was in my thirties. When I was in high school, I voiced a desire to attend college and to teach. My mother was adamant that I should go to secretarial school. When I rejected the idea of secretarial school, she took it as a rejection of her. When I graduated from high school in the top 10 percent of my class, I knew I had failed my mother because I could not type or take shorthand.

She saw these skills as the means to economic security. My college goals were further complicated by an extremely abusive home environment and my stepfather's mandate that I remove myself from the home immediately following graduation. I married at seventeen, just two weeks after high-school graduation. My lack of vocational training ironically provided a brief entry into community college to obtain the basic secretarial skills needed to find work. It took twelve years before I was able to re-enroll in school, followed by divorce and a return to poverty, this time with my own children in tow. When I returned to college, my family accused me of rejecting them—as spouse, parent, brother—because my embrace of education was perceived as a denial of my family and the life they wanted for me.

Assumptions of class privilege in the United States reinforce concepts not only of class shame, but also of the presumed *desire* of the poverty class to *want* to transcend class boundaries. Embedded in this concept of class transcendence is a concomitant denial that the poverty class has a valid and "distinctive social existence that creates a sense of belonging among its members" outside middle-class culture or academe (Ryan and Sackrey 1984, 107). This leaves the poverty-class person unable to "go home" and with no community to which she can truly belong. To try to discuss the ways that class shapes identity within the family is to elicit condemnation from those who believe that I am betraying secrets and shame, and denial from those who are trying to pass. At the same time, when I try to convey to academic colleagues the rich community fostered by my childhood in the poverty class, I show myself as someone different from the academic norm. To come out, therefore, is to live the psychic contradictions of competing interests and loves. And yet, to pass or transcend is to endorse the disfranchisement of our mothers, sisters, fathers, and brothers in an even more destructive act of self-denial, especially when acceptance in the new culture posits an "exceptional" status. Being exceptional implies a severance from the culture of origin, implies a need to remove myself from poverty-class culture, implies that I "never really belonged" to poverty-class culture in the first place. Exceptionalism obscures the reality that others like me exist but were not given the opportunity of higher education. Such realities disrupt the widely held myth of American meritocracy.

Middle-class America assumes the validity of a meritocratic academic system because it presumes a set of available resources that makes success primarily a matter of skill level. For middle-income people, academic skills can be capitalized on in large part because the resources are in place to support opportunities (tutoring in high school and college, SAT preparation programs, awareness of college-application procedures, and money to pay for private college counseling services). For those of the poverty class, skills and intellect alone cannot compensate for the lack of these resources. Without resources, skill levels and intellect are often irrelevant. Regardless of academic potential or demonstrated ability, the windows of opportunity given to the poor are, as a result, much more limited in scope than for middle-class or upper-class people whose financial stability ensures many choices and options at various stages in life. Quite literally, poor people may have but one chance to implement changes in their lives through education. I succeeded in my educational goals because I had two chances at higher education. Many universities, including the private university at which I earned my bachelor's degree, do an admirable job of recruiting and supporting poor students, and I was supported even though I did not have a profile that reinforced the school's stated mission to serve talented, traditional students. I naively thought that graduate school would be more accepting of class diversity. I was wrong. My openly class-stratified, traditional-age–based undergraduate university was far more gracious in terms of class, and I was not prepared for the hostility and deliberately imposed obstacles I faced in graduate school because of my class.

I probably should have tried harder to closet myself when I began graduate school. As it was, programmatic policies negated such efforts, because my graduate department was notified about which students were receiving financial aid. In this way, the department could claim in its promotional materials for prospective students, and in its report to the university community, that the department was "supporting" greater diversity among its ranks and "offering financial support" to a larger percentage of graduate students. Of course, these reports did not indicate the number of students on need-based financial aid, even when that aid was primarily in the form of student loans. Yet receiving such aid immediately marked me as both Other in a department that privileged wealth and allowed the program to assert that my support needs were already being met so that departmental awards and funds could be diverted to students not receiving support who were, by definition, not needy. I realized quickly how my poverty-class background negatively marked me in the program. I tried to pass as a "poor" but middle-class graduate student by hiding my poverty-class roots and allowing the department to believe that my poverty was chosen, situational, and avoidable.

In graduate school, my poverty was situational only in the sense that I could have abandoned my goal of a Ph.D. to secure temporary economic gain. Not having any financial support from my family, and lacking any assets, placed me in a high-need category for financial aid, and my children and I lived well below the poverty level during those years. I was intent on entering the profession; however, I had to prove my commitment to graduate studies in ways that threatened my viability as a student and as a mother. My level of "commitment" was evaluated very differently from the methods used to evaluate my middle-class, single, non-parent peers.

To demonstrate my "academic worthiness" and "commitment," I was asked to perform hours of unpaid service for the department—on top of my paid work obligations and parental duties (and my graduate course load). It was precisely because I had children that I was told to perform the added ten to twenty hours per week of service—to prove that I could "keep up" with my childless peers. No one seemed concerned that I was being asked to do far more than my peers, and judged as being less while doing more, to prove that I could "compete." Simply producing high-quality work was not a sufficient indicator of commitment or academic success. I had to prove that the negative (and erroneous) poverty stereotypes of being intellectually deficient and lazy did not apply to me. My success was held hostage to a combined expectation of extreme exceptionalism and super-mom effort in what I perceived as an attempt to see whether I possessed a moral work ethic that would allow me passage into the middle-class while imposing barriers to discourage my progress.

My difference was clearly based on my class background and the ways in which my poverty affected my mothering. There were many mothers in the program, but they demonstrated the proper "commitment" by hiring nannies for their children. I could barely keep a roof over our heads and food on the table; I could in no way consider hiring a nanny and made the mistake of saying as much. It was then that my commitment was questioned and I was marked as Other. I missed a class session when my children had chicken pox, and that single absence went into my permanent record, with a question about my "viability" in the program. My affluent peers, however, were applauded for trips to Europe and elsewhere, and viability was often reinforced as a result of such absences for "worthy" endeavors. I write about these incidents not out of bitterness or because of failure or regret. I simply want to see the playing field made more even for students, to have class diversity encouraged in academe in terms of pedagogy and representation. I know, from firsthand experience, that the price the poor pay for success is greater than that required of their more affluent peers. We have to recognize these inequities within our profession and within higher education—and how our silence and denial encourages the perpetuation of these practices—before we can challenge ourselves to alleviate the inequities that are too often used to justify the "failure" of poverty-class students in higher education.

My entry into the academic profession came later in life, as is the case for many poor people, not because of a lack of academic ability or a lack of desire to attend college after high school. In high school, I lacked a middle-class awareness of higher education that included understanding application procedures, even though I was in the college-prep track. I lacked the financial support to attend college and was unaware of opportunities for financial aid (and not advised of them by school personnel). I did not have the familial support that facilitates success because my family was more unaware of college procedures than I was. My family is still unfamiliar with higher education and unable to comprehend fully what I do for a living as a university professor. In obtaining an education and an academic position, I learned to negotiate the dual identities posited by Trinh T. Minh-ha as "like you, not like you" in both of my two worlds.

THE CLASSROOM

The underlying societal conviction is that class is a chosen identity and the inability to obtain middle-class success is a matter of individual failure, not the result of institutionalized marginalization in areas such as employment and education—particularly, higher education. Such assumptions are classist, and the regularity with which they are pronounced renders classism the only form of discrimination and prejudice that is socially acceptable today. Further, conflating class identity with race in the cultural imagination creates a sanctioned form of racism "justified" by the presumed behaviors of the so-called underclass. The sociologist Herbert P. Gans cautions that the "danger of the term [underclass] is to use it as a racial code-word that subtly hides anti-black and anti-Hispanic feelings, since race need never be mentioned" (Gans 1991, 33). Martin Gilens (1999) explores the development of the race–welfare conflation that instigates a public critique of welfare and welfare recipients. Gilens's research suggests that much public criticism has its roots in erroneous and racist assumptions regarding work ethics and individualism. Gilens reminds us that "the American public thinks that most people who receive welfare are black, and second, the public thinks that blacks are less committed to the work ethic than are other Americans" (Gilens 1999, 3). The fact that class has a history tied to race reinforces the binary qualities expressed by JanMohamed in which the dominant culture maintains power by regularly redefining the terrain in terms of class and race. This allows the culture of the racial Other and the poverty-class Other to be perceived as "uncontrollable, chaotic, unattainable, and ultimately evil" (Jan Mohamed 1986, 83). The portrayed inter-relationship between race and class further inscribes both race and class as sustainable markers of Otherness, while the dominant middle-class culture fluctuates between vilifying one and both in tandem, cementing the divide between themselves and these Others in U.S. society.

Gender further complicates perceptions of poverty. Linda Gordon notes that "most Americans think of women—single mothers—when they think of 'welfare'" (Gordon 1990, 9). The popular rhetoric of the single mother insinuates that poor women have a preference for motherhood outside more economically stable two-parent families. But this implication obscures the fact that many single mothers were once married, and that many of these women are experiencing poverty because they left dysfunctional or abusive marriages to protect themselves and their children. Wholesale vilification of these single mothers endorses domestic abuse and makes women and children the scapegoats of a destructive patriarchy that punishes the victims for the ills of society. It also obscures issues regarding paternal responsibility. In addition, to conflate race with poverty, and gender with poverty, is to participate in the re-entrenchment of racist and sexist public policies. As Gilens points out, the intense contemporary "racialization of the public images of the poor occurred fairly suddenly and dramatically between 1965 and 1967"

(Gilens 1999, 105). Although not a focus of Gilens's research, the emergence of race-based class imagery during the height of the civil-rights and women's rights movements cannot be viewed as coincidental. The resultant rhetoric of welfare and poverty-class circumstances, then, work to erode civil rights by fostering coded racist and sexist inscriptions on the cultural imagination.

Even with the widespread recognition of what Diana Pearce (1978) terms the "feminization of poverty," little regard is given within the framework of feminist discourse to ameliorating the effects of class bias and erasure within the realm that we, as educators, can control: our classrooms. University curricular innovations regarding ethnic studies and women's studies changed public discourse, political policies, and, increasingly, societal behavior and attitudes. A similar transformation is under way with gay and lesbian studies in addressing homophobia. Ignoring class in the classroom reinscribes negative public policies and attitudes that permit or encourage the systematic discrimination of the poor; it also legitimates a venue for racism and sexism. There are, however, indications of change.

In our classrooms, pedagogies that effectively examine class identities and U.S. classism challenge the ways in which the "natural lottery of birth" shapes access to higher education (Appiah and Gutmann 1996, 147). Methods to include poverty-class discourses in the academic arena are emphasized in recent textbooks that focus specifically on class (Lauter and Fitzgerald 2001; Solomon 1999; Zandy 2001). These texts examine the rhetoric inherent in class-transcendence myths that negate the Caliban–Miranda duality of poverty-class students and scholars. As teachers, we need to interrogate the politics of passing and class transcendence by examining how higher education reinforces the concepts of class transcendence as the model of achievement for poverty-class students and scholars. To do so, we must explore what it means to pass and to transcend class borders and examine how higher education, and our classroom pedagogies, facilitate or inhibit such work.

A distinction needs to be made between the terms *class transcendence* and *passing*, as well, because the severity of liminality produced by each differs. *Passing* is transitory and usually viewed in terms of impersonation, which allows one to pass in the realm of a different cultural context but return to the home culture. *Class transcendence*, however, designates a more permanent removal from the culture of origin, the ideology of which is the dominant motif of U.S. class politics. Transcendence, or the bootstrap myth, as Felski notes, presumes that

> the example of sexual passing suggests a strong disjuncture between a felt identity and an act of impersonation, yet this does not seem to be true of class, at least not in the same way. For example, if one has become upper-middle class as a result of social mobility, then one really is upper-middle class—class being, in one sense, nothing more than the sum of its material manifestations. (Felski 2000, 38)

Felski correlates passing to the gay and lesbian experience because of the ability to "hide" identity markers. She recognizes that the "cultural and psychological dimensions" of class complicate definitions, and she grapples with the seeming contradictions, but she still notes that class identity is "escapable" because "as a signifier, class seems to differ from race and gender. . . . One can change one's class in a way that one cannot, for the most part, change one's sex or race" (Felski 2000, 38). I do not believe that we can truly escape our class backgrounds, and becoming educated and working in academe does not transform me into a wholly middle-class person. Transcendence assumes that I want to deny or abandon my Calibanistic qualities. I do not. I have now, and always will have, aspects of Caliban and Miranda as integral parts of me. We need to replace dual existences predicated on oppositional identities with concepts that promote plural identities. Otherwise, the transcending body is relegated to an imposter role, while the appropriated text of her upward mobility is used as an endorsement for middle-class norms.

Perhaps the class-cultural gap is best delineated by Peter Hitchcock in his discussion of working-class representation, in which he rightly charges that

> critics of class culture come to terms with the logic of visualization as a historical, epistemological, and cognitive imperative. Otherwise, working-class representation is reduced to a laundry list of perceptions—the clothes, the hair, the voice, the hands—as if the nature of class were manifest purely in physical attributes. (Hitchcock 2000, 24)

Hitchcock also points out that "the difficulty for most readers of working-class culture is to maintain the aesthetic as a viable category" of analysis (Hitchcock 2000, 25). If it is difficult to address working-class identities in the abstract venue of literary and cultural analysis, how do we tend to poverty-class identities when they appear in the persons of our students and our peers? How do we tend to these identities when, as Felski states, working-class "respectability" is juxtaposed against the "sexualized images of lower-class women's bodies" (Felski 2000, 35)? The result is a double-distancing of the poor from significant cultural critique and representation. This double-distancing denies academic endorsement of the poverty class as a legitimate field of inquiry, and in doing so, it erases the lived experiences of poverty-class people and complex analyses of the interactions between the poverty class and dominant American culture.

American society wants to assume that obtaining a college education is always a positive occurrence that triggers a desirable class transcendence as the college graduate realizes increased lifetime wages and cultural opportunities as a result of the degree. We want to believe the myth of meritocracy based on fair access and support for promising scholars. In reality, for the neediest of financial-aid recipients, these advances come with long-term financial commitments that will inhibit their economic viability, as well as that of their children, for years to come.[3] These are financial burdens that effectively inhibit access for many poor people. Our universities, especially at the graduate level, reinforce class bias and prejudice by creating additional obstacles so that the poor student must prove her worth. Yet these same obligations are not levied against middle-class and affluent students whose worth is evident in their economic status and in their undergraduate degrees from expensive, elite schools. We need to understand that when a poor woman succeeds in academe, she has not only succeeded in her studies; she has also triumphed over systemic classism by overcoming personal and financial burdens that are added to the inherent stresses of education because she is poor. When this student cannot handle the added stress—on top of the rigors faced by all students—she is a "failure." I wonder how successful middle-class and affluent students would be if they had to mediate obstacles and stresses on par with their poorer peers. I had to fight to obtain an education. I had to fight the state courts and an ex-spouse, the financial-aid system, poverty itself, and often the needs of my own children. Poverty-class students have to battle cultural ignorance within the family, as well, while they learn how to live a dual existence and stay sane. We have learned to split our innermost selves to live simultaneously in two very different worlds. It is time that we challenge ourselves to alleviate inequities that are too often used to justify the "failures" of poverty-class students in higher education.

The doors of higher education are closing quickly, and they are shutting out too many of our poorest citizens. Without examining the role higher education plays in the perpetuation of poverty and civic disfranchisement—through the reification and endorsement of economic policies that limit educational access for the poor, and in the ways that the poverty class is taught and conceived of in our classrooms—we will be unable, as a culture and as teachers committed to multicultural inclusion, to prevent poor students from being further disfranchised from academic pursuits. When, and only when, we address these issues and remedy these inequities will we be able to proclaim that academe is the "brave new world" that allows both Caliban and Miranda to exist with equal dignity.

NOTES

1. In her study of literary and cultural representations of poor women *From Good Ma to Welfare Queen* (2000), Vivyan C. Adair traces the development of class and gender-based representations such as the Welfare Queen who is erroneously vilified as lazy and reproductively irresponsible. Susan Thomas discusses the stereotypes of poor women as they are inflicted on poor black women whom society often represents as "brood sows" who "maximiz[e] their take from the public trough" (Thomas 1998, 429).

2. The Center for Working-Class Studies at Youngstown State University in Youngstown, Ohio, is one of the few sustained programs designed to promote the study of the working class and the poverty class. In addition to sponsoring courses in working-class studies at the university, the center, under the leadership of Sherry Linkon and John B. Russo, hosts a biennial conference on working-class studies and is promoting the adoption of similar programs of study at institutions nationwide. Working-Class Academics is an organization that provides both professional and emotional support to working-class and poverty-class faculty and graduate students. Started by Barbara Peters and Jim Vander Putten, the organization holds an annual conference.

3. See chapter 11 of this volume for a comprehensive discussion of financial-aid policies and practices.

REFERENCES

Adair, Vivyan C. 2000. *From Good Ma to Welfare Queen: A Genealogy of the Poor Woman in American Literature, Photography, and Culture.* New York: Garland.

Appiah, K. Anthony, and Amy Gutmann. 1996. *Color Conscious: The Political Morality of Race.* Princeton, N.J.: Princeton University Press.

Felski, Rita. 2000. "Nothing to Declare: Identity, Shame, and the Lower Middle Class." *PMLA* 115, no. 1: 33–45.

Gans, Herbert J. 1991. *People, Plans, and Policies: Essays on Poverty, Racism, and Other National Urban Problems.* New York: Columbia University Press.

Gilens, Martin. 1999. *Why Americans Hate Welfare: Race, Media, and the Politics of Antipoverty Policy.* Chicago: University of Chicago Press.

Gordon, Linda. 1990. "The New Feminist Scholarship on the Welfare State." Pp. 9–35 in *Women, the State and Welfare,* ed. Linda Gordon. Madison: University of Wisconsin Press.

Hitchcock, Peter. 2000. "They Must Be Represented? Problems in Theories of Working-Class Representation." *PMLA* 115, no. 1: 20–32.

JanMohamed, Abdul R. 1986. "The Economy of Manichean Allegory: The Function of Racial Difference in Colonialist Literature." Pp. 78–106 in *"Race," Writing, and Difference,* ed. Henry Louis Gates, Jr. Chicago: University of Chicago Press.

Lauter, Paul, and Ann Fitzgerald, eds. 2001. *Literature, Class, and Culture: An Anthology.* New York: Longman.

Minh-ha, Trinh T. 1990. "Not Tou/Like Tou: Post-colonial Women and the Interlocking Questions of Identity and Difference." Pp. 371–75 in *Making Face, Making Soul, Haciendo Caras: Creative and Critical Perspectives by Feminists of Color,* ed. Gloria Anzaldúa. San Francisco: Aunt Lute Books.

O'Dair, Sandra. 1993. "Vestments and Vested Interests: Academia, the Working Class, and Affirmative Action." Pp. 239–50 in *Working-Class Women in the Academy: Laborers in the Knowledge Factory,* ed. Michelle M. Tokarczyk and Elizabeth A. Fay. Amherst: University of Massachusetts Press.

Oldfield, Kenneth, and Richard F. Conant. 2001. "Exploring the Use of Socioeconomic Status as Part of an Affirmative Action Plan to Recruit and Hire University Professors: A Pilot Study." *Journal of Public Affairs Education* 7, no. 3: 171–85.

Pearce, Diana. 1978. "The Feminization of Poverty: Women, Work, and Welfare." *Urban and Social Change Review* (Winter–Spring): 28–36.

Ryan, Jake, and Charles Sackrey. 1984. *Strangers in Paradise: Academics from the Working Class.* Boston: South End Press.

Shakespeare, William. 1974 (1611). *The Tempest.* Pp. 1611–38 in *The Riverside Shakespeare,* ed. G. Blakemore Evans et al. Boston: Houghton Mifflin.

Solomon, Barbara, ed. 1999. *The Haves and the Have-Nots: Thirty Stories about Money and Class in America.* New York: Signet.

Thomas, Susan L. 1998. "Race, Gender, and Welfare Reform: The Antinatalist Response." *Journal of Black Studies* 28, no. 4: 419–46.

Zandy, Janet, ed. 2001. *What We Hold in Common: An Introduction to Working-Class Studies.* New York: Feminist Press.

Zinn, Maxine Baca, et al. 1990. "The Costs of Exclusionary Practices in Women's Studies." Pp. 29–41 in *Making Face, Making Soul, Haciendo Caras: Creative and Critical Perspectives by Feminists of Color,* ed. Gloria Anzaldúa. San Francisco: Aunt Lute Books.

JOYCELYN K. MOODY

4   To Be Young, Pregnant, and Black
My Life as a Welfare Coed

For black women, the personal is bound up in the problems peculiar to multi-ple jeopardies of race and class, not the singular one of sexual inequality.
　　—Deborah K. King

I WAS ON WELFARE during the winter that Alex Haley's miniseries *Roots* first aired on television. I watched *Roots* every night of its dura-tion in the subterranean TV room of my college dorm. For eight con-secutive nights, two or three other women who also did not have tele-vision sets in their rooms watched the show in the basement with me. They were not the same few women each night, but all of them were white and, as I recall, strangers to me. Like them, I was a student at our small, private, Southern, Roman Catholic college that was exclusive in every sense of the term. Unlike them, I was black and pregnant. Although I do not remember discussing the groundbreaking show with these college women, I am confident that we were affected differently by *Roots*'s revolutionary camera images.

Nieman Reports recently published an article by Franklin D. Gilliam, Jr., a political scientist at the University of California, Los Angeles, titled "The 'Welfare Queen' Experiment" (1999). Gilliam's article analyzes media coverage of changing welfare regulations to argue that our media consistently demonstrate irresponsibility in shaping American attitudes toward the welfare system and the groups who depend on it. Gilliam asserts that social-science research has found that certain kinds of cov-erage definitely

> have an impact on public opinion about race and welfare.... Given the lack of meaningful inter-group interaction, most white Americans learn about blacks (and other minorities) through the lens of a distant camera. What this camera focuses on, who it gives voice to, and what it excludes all influence how people think about race-related issues. (Gilliam 1999, 50)

Reading Gilliam's study of the media manufacture of the Welfare Queen rivets me back to January 1977 and the complex, shameful feelings I vented and retained as I mourned the plight of Kunte Kinte's racial progeny, myself included. While Gilliam's research analyzes images of blackness, femaleness, poverty, and welfare in television and other media, and ultimately holds media accountable for perpetuating negative and dangerous stereotypes of black women and the poor, this chapter examines my own internalization of deleterious media images.

To put it bluntly, their misrepresentation of me led to my self-hatred. My whole adult life has been a struggle for self-love and personal fulfillment. Barbara Smith has lamented that "there is not a black woman in this country who has not, at some time, internalized and been deeply scarred by the hateful propaganda about us. There is not a black woman in America who has not felt, at least once, like 'the mule of the world'" (Smith 1995, 262). Smith, now an acclaimed writer and scholar, asserts: "As with most black women, others' hatred of me became self-hatred, which has diminished over the years, but has by no means disappeared." Smith praises black feminism for enabling black women "to understand that we are not hated and abused because there is something wrong with us, but because our status and treatment is absolutely prescribed by the racist, misogynist system under which we live" (Smith 1995, 262).

In my case, besides my personal self-hatred, others' unquestioned acceptance of negative media images has hurt me deeply and enduringly. In this chapter I explore how the confusion of class with race, by both blacks and non-blacks, amplifies the pain of African American women's experiences on welfare during pregnancy and exposes the interlocking systems of oppression that stereotype and misconstrue them. I try to untangle the knotted threads of the story of my participation in the welfare system and my pregnancy at age nineteen, which led to my welfare experience. To do this, I use a methodology developed by Maxine Baca Zinn and Bonnie Thornton Dill (1996) called "multiracial feminism." Zinn and Dill, two scholars of color, theorize feminism from a more inclusive model than the models of feminism developed by the white, middle-class women who preceded them. Rather than generalize about women's experience from a hegemonic base, multiracial feminism examines women's lives across lines that seemingly divide women, such as those of race and class. Zinn and Dill cogently explain that this approach to interpreting women's experience succeeds because it considers women of color "not merely as gendered subjects but as women whose lives are affected by our location in multiple hierarchies" (Zinn and Dill 1996, 321). Indeed, my location in multiple hierarchies as a young Southern woman reared in a working-class but upwardly mobile, Presbyterian black family and attending an exclusive Roman Catholic college rendered my welfare experience particularly snarled and thus deeply painful.

I matriculated in the welfare system through the resourcefulness of a compassionate priest who knew my predicament. In all likelihood completely unfamiliar with the steps needed to secure such succor, he nevertheless arranged a series of services to preserve my physical and mental health. Within days of sharing my embarrassing news with him, he had effected my access to welfare for prenatal care and my sessions with a female Catholic Charities psychotherapist. I suspect that before assisting me, Father Ernest had no experience (or interest, for that matter) in such crucial life necessities. It is a mark of his devotion to duty as both priest and professor that he cared for me as he did. Once he and other Jesuits had set me up with prenatal and mental-health care, however, I felt on my own. A weird blend of shame, humility, and gratitude prohibited me from reporting on my developments at the Board of Health and Catholic Charities. There are probably diverse reasons the priests did not question me about my experiences: their own shame at my dishonor; their regard for my privacy; perhaps an awareness of the limitations—or conversely, the extent—of their power, their duty. In any case, looking back now as a mature lesbian, I am fascinated that this transitional period in my life was so filled with faithful men.

After the priests, the person on whom I depended most was a woman. It still stings me to remember that each time I went for a checkup, my anguish began as embarrassment at having to ask a ride from the only one of my classmates I could trust not to divulge my shameful secret *and* who had a car. Needless to say, my friend was white. She was also unusual in our crowd in that she was Southern and Presbyterian. Although these attributes generally established a bond between us, I sensed that years of whiteness training in Bull Connor's Birmingham and her own moral code could not keep her from judging me as immoral because I had proved unchaste. I remember the stony tension of those six-mile drives from the suburban college to downtown

Mobile. She would drop me off at the front of the hospital, to return for me an hour or so later. Meanwhile, I was subjected to what I can only describe as the brutal mishandling of my o'erteeming body. Indeed, one of the most debilitating aspects of my welfare experience was the treatment I received at the hands of my prenatal–health-care providers, and that came after the monthly, then biweekly, then weekly interrogation at the front desk.

"Name?"

"Joycelyn Moody McDaniel," I would respond, invoking the surname of the man I had married to spare myself the added humiliation of being unwed in my identifications as black, poor, and pregnant.

"Address?"

Here it comes. I swallow. I give the name of the private college I attend.

"What?"

I repeat the reply.

"What are you doing here? You don't belong here." Sometimes the words ended there, but more often they were followed with others, to the effect of, "If you can afford to go to that college, then you don't need to be on welfare." In any case, they humiliated me.

My humiliating prenatal-care experiences reveal a fascinating and perhaps surprising phenomenon about blacks and class. They ironically subvert the findings of a recent study of the impact of class on African Americans' attitudes toward social-service programs conducted by Leslie Inniss and Jeralynn Sittig (1996). Specifically, these social scientists inquire: "[Is] the experience of being black in U.S. society so encompassing and so similar for all blacks that, regardless of their subjective or objective social class, they tend to support social welfare programs?" (Inniss and Sittig 1996, 176). My routine check-ups suggest that the answer to this query is a resounding no. The county-hospital staff, many of them black women, regularly rejected me. They insisted that I did not merit welfare because I was a student at a private college. They suggested that I was defrauding them individually and robbing the state blind in the process by stealing funds not allotted to me—apparently oblivious to the fact that less than 6 percent of the national budget is allocated for *anybody's* welfare (Jackson 1997, 44). Although the black hospital staff might generally have tended "to support social welfare programs," thereby validating Inniss and Sittig's findings, they disapproved of my particular need and access, and they did not hesitate to tell me so. Under their critical gaze, I embodied "the specter of Black women who procreate irresponsibly and have no aspirations beyond maximizing [our] take from the public trough" (Thomas 1998, 429). No wonder that their injurious censure effectively compounded my sense of shame about my "illegitimacy," my pregnancy, and my dependency.

Inniss and Sittig's study further finds that class status for blacks is determined by "status within the community, having stable family relationships, and other such attitudinal criteria" (Inniss and Sittig 1996, 178). In other words, regardless of the class to which a black person might "objectively," statistically, be assessed as belonging, African Americans themselves use diverse, albeit specific, cultural formulations to assess class status. The criteria in these formulations include the stability of the (patriarchal, heterosocial) family unit and certain political or ideological alliances or shared belief systems rather than economic figures and the amount of money one has or the resources to which one has access. From this line of thinking, perhaps the hospital workers' negative attitudes toward me had to do with their judgment of me, based on my college enrollment as well as on my aesthetic appearance and exteriority as "black middle-class." They did not know, perhaps would not have cared, that I was at the college on maximum financial aid, which meant loans so extensive that I paid them in full only recently—my last check was exuberantly written out on 1 April 1999, although I graduated in May 1979.

When I set out to analyze the persistent and pernicious confusion of class with race, using my young black pregnant self as case study, I had expected to confront ways that whites in particular tend to associate blacks with the working and lower classes and with the poor and rarely think of themselves in these terms. A precise example appears in "Learning in the Dark," a remarkable essay by Frances A. Maher and Mary Kay T. Tetreault, the white feminist authors of *The Feminist Classroom* (1996). In that article, Maher and Tetreault describe their visit to a classroom at Maryland's Towson State University, where they found that a majority of white and working-class students vehemently opposed affirmative action because they equated it with quotas for the unqualified and therefore undeserving. The students thus concluded that affirmative action functions to their economic detriment, their own class location and their potential gains from affirmative action notwithstanding (Maher and

Tetreault 1996). Although I realize (as the white students in the article probably did not) that racism and white supremacy in U.S. society also result in African Americans' similar assumption that all the wealthy are white and all the poor are colored, I nevertheless had not expected to address in this essay ways that *blacks* conflate race with class. Virtually no American is exempt from this blurring of reality, though. The temptation to judge others' racial authenticity or social conformity is too great, too much an American way of life. When African Americans judge one another as inauthentic, this often translates as something like, if Papa was *not* a "rolling stone," then "you must be tryin' to be white." Regrettably, such rigidly diametrical thinking validates the novelist Barbara Neely's grievous assertion, "Racism makes everybody crazy."

The madness of racism pervaded my youth, during which my father was a postal letter carrier, and my mother what is today called a stay-at-home mom who worked intermittently outside the home. In many ways, I had an auspicious childhood, for which I am immeasurably thankful. Compared with most of my classmates in Mobile's segregated schools, I certainly grew up with a sense of my family as upwardly mobile, although this is a term that I do not recall hearing before attending graduate school. With these autobiographical details, I am trying to convey a very complicated situation to illustrate how class and race are often confused in the United States. Inniss and Sittig speak indirectly to this irrationality. Analyzing the intersection of race and class phenomena, they conclude that where African Americans place themselves in the U.S. class structure "is particularly important in a study of the values and attitudes held by blacks" because that placement attests to blacks' awareness of the existence of an internal class hierarchy, an intra-racial stratification of disparate economic levels. Such consciousness of stratified economic levels is contrary to non-blacks' general lack of consciousness that we are *not* an economic monolith (Inniss and Sittig 1996, 180). We know that class is more a sociological concept than an indicator of personal affluence. In addition, when African Americans claim one class designation over another, they also imply "a willingness to be associated with the behaviors and values commonly attributed to members" of the particular class they claim (Inniss and Sittig 1996, 180).

A recent conversation I had with my mother illustrates the point. Pondering my salary, which always seems insufficient, I was marveling to my mother at her and my father's ability to raise four children so efficiently in the 1960s Deep South on a postal employee's salary. She told me, as she always does when we have this conversation, that she and my father struggled, that it was hard, that they managed to hide the extent of our family's poverty from us children. For once, I pressed her: "But how, Mama? Why didn't I know we were poor?"

My mother said, "Because I combed your hair everyday and put a ribbon in it." Astonishing, but that is the answer my mother gave me.

So I pressed harder, silently remembering the many times those ribbons had roused other girls' envy. "What else?" I asked.

"We never ate dinner without our table mats on the table."

"Hunh?"

My mother didn't skip a cheerful beat. "Well, it's like this. Sometimes there was nothing more than pork-'n'-beans and bologna for dinner. But if you serve it on a clean table with a nice table mat underneath, it doesn't taste so bland, does it? That kind of thing kept you and your brothers from seeing how scared your daddy and I was."

In this way, my mother articulated both of my parents' middle-class aspirations and the illusions they conjured to teach my brothers and me that we merited a slice of the American pie. Our poverty was not so dire that we could not afford "nice table mats," but I know that they scrimped and saved to devise such extensive illusions of our just desserts. Perhaps higher aspirations are no less written on the body than poverty is. For some early-womanhood manifestation of my childhood ribbons apparently marked me as my parents' daughter; the hospital's black personnel shrewdly read in a glance my emergence from an intact, upwardly mobile family. Their efforts to undermine my sense of right to access felt like betrayal, for it must have been clear to them that I was very afraid. They did not say, "Go find your family, who could apparently support you if you'd ask them; go find them and get away from this place that demoralizes young, black women and induces shame and guilt." And conversely, they did not say, "You are welcome here; we have made this clinic safe for women who are poor, alone, and pregnant." Instead, they effectively demonstrated that the madness at the intersection of race and class—and women and rights and welfare—infects even women whose paid labor entails healing, help, and nurturing. Thus, I learned that black women on welfare are not protected by the racial and ideological similarities and "loyalties" of black women who are not on welfare. Surely, those social-service workers would have

argued in favor of my right to safe, legal, abundant, and nurturing prenatal care, yet they felt licensed to condemn me because of my concurrent enrollment at a private college. The discourse of welfare and the
myths that black women are sucking the welfare system dry and "getting more than they deserve" are so profound they they infect even relationships among African Americans, ties that are otherwise exempt from
media distortions. As important as education traditionally has been and
remains to black people, skepticism among blacks about who merits
welfare aid invariably trumps race loyalty when the welfare recipient
is a college student who seems to be transgressing the system and getting over.

But quiet as it is kept, African Americans usually support one
another's getting over, especially our gettin' some get-back from the
government. What the black social workers seem to have challenged
was not my right as a black woman to receive assistance but, rather, my
right to assistance as a black woman who apparently already enjoyed
certain privileges ostensibly and usually reserved for whites. When
Inniss and Sittig (1996, 186) assert, "Neither education nor occupational
prestige, two of the traditional indicators of class, was a significant predictor of spending support," they imply that welfare traditionally has
been supported by blacks with and without education, and with and
without prestigious jobs. Such a conclusion confirms my empirical
knowledge. However, the prickly verbal harangue—or, alternatively,
silent vicious contempt—to which I was subjected could not have been
based on what I actually had. Indeed, I had qualified for welfare support because I had no money and no prospect of getting any. I was privileged with resources that made my college life possible, though: financial aid and endless loans and a familial background that cultivated my
confidence to overcome the obstacles that might have made the private
college (seem) off-limits to local, black, college-age women. Intra-racial
conflicts based on (the mere appearance of) class differences can negate
blacks' assumed support of all black women on welfare. Inasmuch as
they apparently determined that I "did not belong on welfare," the black
staff did not seem to realize that "subjective class identification and/ or
objective class indicators are [actually deceptive and thus] poor measures of class among African Americans" (Inniss and Sittig 1996, 193).
Moreover, my experience at the Board of Health revealed to me that I
could be racially encoded by other African Americans. As Gilliam has

shown, "while poor women of all races get blamed for their impoverished condition, African-American women commit the most egregious
violations of American values" and moral mandates for virtuous
women—according to the invidious gender script of the Welfare Queen
(Gilliam 1999, 50). The hospital's prenatal staff treated me as if I were
both errant thief and sexual deviant, even though I had married primarily to avoid precisely this type of recrimination.

Gilliam's research further demonstrates that, swayed by reckless
media, "the public dramatically overestimates the number of African-
Americans in poverty and similarly . . . people underestimate the number of poor whites" (Gilliam 1999, 50). In addition, Gilliam's subjects
expressed the belief "that individual failings [are] the cause of welfare. . . . [The participants in his study] indicated that they believe welfare recipients cheat and defraud the system, that they abuse the system by staying on too long, that welfare undermines the work ethic, and
that welfare encourages teenagers to have kids out of wedlock" (Gilliam
1999, 51). Intellectually, these findings do not surprise me, yet I still feel
astonished at how grossly they diverge from my own unhappy experience. To be sure, much of the agony I suffered while on welfare derived
precisely from my own internalized, invalid belief that "individual failings" had led to my personal predicament as a pregnant teen. These feelings were compounded by the religious conversion that I was also then
undergoing. Whether I judged other welfare recipients as "failures" I
cannot recall and may not be relevant. My own judgment of myself as
having failed, though, was situated in the cultural context of my rising-
middle-class family and in the political climate of my Southern hometown in the post–civil-rights era. After all, certainly one reason I had
been admitted to an all-white college in 1975 (twenty years after *Brown
v Board of Education of Topeka*) was that it had expanded its admissions
policy in accordance with positive political progress. The times they
were a-changin'—but my own changes as a black girl struck me not as
advancement but as backsliding.

My reputation for chastity ruptured, I seemed to prove what
Gilliam's participants believed: that the welfare system promotes illicit
teenage sex—sex that is illicit because it occurs among teens and, as the
pregnancy betrays, because it is unprotected. As Susan Thomas bitterly
notes, another argument for controlling poor women's bodies is the
myth that poor women "indulge in intercourse and become pregnant

solely for the purpose of obtaining or supplementing an existing welfare check" (Thomas 1998, 421). Thomas's "antinatalist response" to contemporary welfare reform, published in a 1998 volume of the *Journal of Black Studies,* quotes a Georgia welfare director who sagely declared that "anyone who thinks that a woman goes through nine months of pregnancy, the pain of childbirth and 18 years of rearing a child for $45 more a month . . . has got to be a man" (Thomas 1998, 433).

For me, as for many contemporary women, welfare *saved* me as a teenage mother rather than made me into one. Indeed, according to Thomas, "most babies born to welfare mothers in one recent study [conducted *twenty years* after my days at the college] were conceived prior to welfare receipt" (Thomas 1998, 433). When I became pregnant, I had already begun the process of freeing myself from my parents as an adult college woman. To have to return to them at that point, especially with the shame of my pregnancy and amid the tension my religious conversion to Catholicism had wrought, would have been more than I could bear—*if* my parents had been financially able to support me. The father of my child was himself a floundering college student and had no resources to speak of, so I knew that I could not depend on him—*if* I had wanted to. When I think of the "choices" that led to my welfare access, I am stunned that there are those who surmise that my participation was in any way voluntary. And when I remember the sadness of the women around me in the hospital in those months, I know that I was the rule rather than any exception to it. Most of those women were not also college students; none of the others attended the private college with me in that year.

Then, as now, I recognize my good fortune in having professors who graciously heard my "confessions" of pregnancy with the same charity and benevolence as the Jesuits who saved my life, and my son's, by locating prenatal and mental-health–care resources for a lonely, disgraced, precocious black teen. When I begged permission to run, hands holding back morning sickness, from my 8 A.M. Spanish class, Dr. Charles Kargleder simply indulged the request and honored my privacy. The next year, my prose poem about my tortured connection to my infant son—I dare say, the only submission on the subject he received—drew no moral criticism from Dr. Charles Boyle, only praise and advice. Although I turned to few folks in those days, each at the college honored my strained performance of normativity, for which I remain deeply grateful. Their indulgences assuaged my difficult pregnancy, but again I regard myself more rule than exception among black mothers on welfare.

In conclusion, in spite of the taboo of the term *victim*, especially among feminists, I want to underscore my unexceptionality by proclaiming the victimhood of my pregnant, coed self. I was only one of thousands of women suffering the degradation and demoralization that ensues from the kind of irresponsible media coverage that Gilliam's research denounces, and even more from the multiethnic U.S. public that so heartily embraces the stereotypes that media perpetuate and makes victims of so many, too many. The feminist comedian Lily Tomlin has quipped that America must indeed love the underdog—it creates so many of us. I am one more.

In "Designing an Inclusive Curriculum" (1995), her excellent essay on transforming college curricula to examine more women more fully, the black feminist scholar Elizabeth Higginbotham cautions against a pedagogy of exceptionality. She argues against introducing women of color into the curriculum by declaring them "exceptional." Denouncing this method as "very common" in contemporary classrooms, she writes:

> In contrast to marginal treatments of women of color . . . where the population of women of color is seen as an undifferentiated mass, this approach holds up a few models—nonvictims—for admiration. In the case of black women, this is often done under the guise that racism has not been terribly difficult for them. The subtle message to students is that if successful black women could achieve in the face of obstacles, other black women failed to attain the same heights because of faulty culture, lack of motivation, and other individual deficits. (Higginbotham 1995, 483)

As both black feminist educator and former welfare recipient, I am moved and affirmed by Higginbotham's cogent claims. The "exceptions" model she castigates functions to absolve the larger society of its role in my past suffering. That model lays the blame for my misery as an expectant mother on welfare not where it belongs—at the feet of those who harmed me body, mind, and soul, then held me up as transcendent exemplum. I would not have my oppressors so easily pardoned. Further, those who would admiringly label me exceptional or unique actually maintain my suffering with the suggestion that I continue to be isolated from other women, "classed" off from them. Enduring myths about welfare are rooted in racist ignorance and sustained by elitist ignorance of every sort; those myths injure and wound and scar. When feminists invoke cliches to hail the recognition of former welfare recipients as heroic "survivors," they not only perpetuate racist and classist assumptions about poor women, they also finger the wound of victimization, oblivious to its raw-edged pain—or awestruck by it. We are nobody's exceptions, not casualties of the latest "war on poverty" but sufferers of it—and proudly valiant soldiers against it.

NOTE

Epigraph: King (1995).

REFERENCES

Gilliam, Franklin D., Jr. 1999. "The 'Welfare Queen' Experiment." *Nieman Reports* 53, no. 2: 49–52.

Higginbotham, Elizabeth. 1995. "Designing an Inclusive Curriculum: Bringing All Women into the Core." Pp. 474–78 in *Words of Fire: An Anthology of African-American Feminist Thought,* ed. Beverly Guy-Sheftall. New York: New Press.

Inniss, Leslie Baham, and Jeralynn Sittig. 1996. "Race, Class, and Support for the Welfare State." *Sociological Inquiry* 66, no. 2: 175–96.

Jackson, Derrick. 1997. "Why Do Stereotypes and Lies Persist? *Nieman Reports* 51: 44–45.

King, Deborah K. 1995. "Multiple Jeopardy, Multiple Consciousness: The Context of a Black Feminist Ideology." Pp. 294–317 in *Words of Fire: An Anthology of African-American Feminist Thought,* ed. Beverly Guy-Sheftall. New York: New Press.

Maher, Frances A., and Mary Kay T. Tetreault. 1996. "Learning in the Dark: How Assumptions of Whiteness Shape Classroom Learning." Pp. 411–38 in *Knowledge, Difference, and Power: Essays Inspired by Women's Ways of Knowing,* ed. Nancy R. Goldberger et al. New York: Basic Books.

Smith, Barbara. 1995. "Some Home Truths on the Contemporary Black Feminist Movement." Pp. 254–67 in *Words of Fire: An Anthology of African-American Feminist Thought,* ed. Beverly Guy-Sheftall. New York: New Press.

Thomas, Susan L. 1998. "Race, Gender, and Welfare Reform: The Antinatalist Response." *Journal of Black Studies* 28, no. 4: 419–46.

Zinn, Maxine Baca, and Bonnie Thornton Dill. 1996. "Theorizing Difference from Multiple Feminism." *Feminist Studies* 22, no. 2: 321–32.

Lisa K. Waldner

5   If You Want Me to Pull Myself Up, Give Me Bootstraps

At a 1999 state capital demonstration in favor of higher spending on university financial aid, a group of students called on Minnesota's Governor Jesse Ventura to do more for more single-parent college students. Governor Ventura was less than enthusiastic, retorting, "Is that the government's job—to make up for your mistakes?" (Healy 1999). As I read these words in the *Chronicle of Higher Education,* I was metaphorically slapped back fifteen years to my days as a single-parent student and welfare recipient. Although it has been a long time since I have cashed an assistance check, I feel the welfare-stigma sting whenever a public official uses the struggling underclass as a punching bag.

As a sociologist and former welfare mother, I argue that it is poor public policy to underpin government programs with a "you made your own bed, you can lie in it" mentality. Instead of finger-pointing responses that continue to pass judgment but fail to provide solutions, society should focus on creating *real* opportunities for resource-challenged single parents to become self-sufficient. Give each welfare recipient a pair of bootstraps to climb the ladder out of poverty and on to self-sufficiency. For some, the bootstraps that fit best are a university education. Although this seems like a simple truth, U.S. society is often loath to engage in this type of long-term social planning. Our myopic vision regarding welfare, single-parent families, and social policy is a product of American cultural values, the hierarchical nature of the U.S. stratification system, and a refusal to discuss honestly the consequences of class, race, and gender. Poor public policy or not, the current welfare system reflects deeply rooted, shared cultural beliefs in rugged individualism and the equality of opportunity. Both are considered core American values (Williams 1965). Welfare mothers seemingly violate these beliefs and have the additional burden of causing the "breakdown" of the American family. David Blankenhorn, a conservative policy pundit and author, writes, "Almost the entire current welfare system ... constitutes a direct economic subsidy for out-of-wedlock childbearing. Taken together, far too many government activities end up taxing marriage to fund family fragmentation" (Blankenhorn 1995, 231). "Fragmented," "dysfunctional," "morally suspect"—these words are used to describe the families maintained by welfare mothers, the "undeserving" poor. In this environment, I doubt my own story would provoke much sympathy.

I had my first child when I was a junior in college at age twenty. I became pregnant when I was nineteen, the night of my graduation from community college. As a product of a working-class family, I was the first in my family to attend college. When I found out I was pregnant, I was devastated. Initially, going to college was important because I wanted more than what my father had, working dangerous jobs for low pay. I wanted to avoid the humiliation my father faced every time he used food stamps to pay for groceries, and the hurt my mother felt when social workers asked her whether she needed nutritional information because her children were growing up overweight, nourished on a diet of macaroni and other foods that fit my parents' budget but not our waistlines. College was a necessity if I was to have any chance of social mobility. I wanted to climb the class ladder out of the ranks of the working poor for my child's sake, as well. I faced incredible odds not only because I was female, single, and pregnant, but also because (regardless of gender or ethnic categories) social mobility is the exception, not the rule.

That social mobility is the exception flies in the face of cultural values of rugged individualism and the equality of opportunity. We collectively assume that social-class mobility is achieved through individual effort, and we believe everyone has the same opportunity for success. The Sam Waltons and Bill Clintons of the world have seemingly updated the Horatio Alger myth. The humble beginnings of Walton and Clinton, and their subsequent achievements, are used as proof that opportunity does exist and that it is accessible to all who exert the effort to be successful. This view assigns blame to all individuals who fail to escape poverty. Yet the successes of Clinton and Walton are extraordinary exceptions rather than a general rule.

Societies that provide opportunities tend to have a greater level of upward mobility. When one compares the United States with less industrialized nations, one finds more social mobility in the United States

(Beeghley 1996). However, the majority of this mobility is short-distance mobility, such as moving from the poverty class to the working class or from the position of an unskilled worker to semi-skilled work (Beeghley 1996; Gilbert 1998). A son of a farmer is more likely to become a farmer or a blue-collar worker than the CEO of a large corporation or the president, as did Walton and Clinton, respectively. Short-distance mobility is more prevalent than the more popularized rags-to-riches tales because there is a great deal of occupational inheritance in U.S. society (Beeghley 1996). In other words, sons of doctors tend to grow up to become doctors or assume occupations of a similar status, such as lawyer or accountant. Although long-distance mobility does occur, it is far less common. Robert Hauser analyzed data from the General Social Survey for the years 1982–90 and found that only 8 percent of upper-class white-collar male workers (professionals, managers, officials, non-retail sales work) had farmers for fathers. The mobility of women has not been studied as extensively, yet we do know that "women's occupational achievement, like men's, is powerfully influenced by class origins" (Gilbert 1998, 146). Currently, U.S. society burdens welfare women with stigmatization while denying the harsh realities of potential mobility. We blame poor women for intergenerational poverty without recognizing that they are following the same occupational inheritance norms as the rest of society.

A college education can create a pathway for upward mobility by circumventing the effects of a less-privileged family background. But, notes Dennis Gilbert, "if college graduates are equalized in this sense, access to college remains very unequal. There is, for example, an enormous gap in the college participation rates of young adults from high- and low-income families" (Gilbert 1998, 175). If equality of opportunity truly existed, the college-participation rates of lower-income students would be higher. Although the empirical evidence strongly demonstrates that the playing field is not level, the perception of equality of opportunity continues to be part of our cultural ethos. I was able to leave the ranks of the working poor because I finished my undergraduate education despite the stares and gossip of my dormitory mates and financial-aid policies that favored incoming freshmen over community-college transfer students. The class bias in the treatment of community-college transfer students who often have working-class origins is readily apparent in my case. Although I had a proven collegiate academic record, it was not until after a full year with a nearly perfect academic record that I was offered college work-study and several grants that made my senior year financially easier. I managed because my parents took in their grandchild, enabling me to finish my junior and senior years. Although the pre–welfare-reform system was not perfect, it did provide some resources that allowed me to stay in school. Almost two years later, I had my second child outside marriage.

I was a single parent with two children to care for, yet I had dreams of earning a Ph.D. and becoming a college professor. I was able to fulfill my higher-education and career goals through a combination of factors, including personal tenacity, moral compromises, a welfare bureaucracy that was not yet fully reformed, and occasionally interactions with a caseworker who defined his job more in terms of a captain navigating people through the rough waters of government welfare policy than as a taskmaster employed to punish errant women. An example of this was my experience with the work incentive program (WIN). WIN began in 1968 and required that all adult recipients with children older than six sign up for job training (Jensen 1998). As a second-year graduate student, I was trying to hold off the bureaucracy long enough to finish my masters' thesis. By spring, I could stall no longer. I made an appointment with my assigned Job Corps worker, who informed me that having two children under age six did not exempt me from registering for job training. It seems that by attending graduate school, I voluntarily took myself "out of the home," thus negating the under-six exemption. The irony of the situation was that under pre–welfare-reform rules, if I had chosen to be a full-time homemaker with no job outside the home, I was allowed to do so until my youngest child was six. Because I was already actively engaged in training for my chosen profession, I could not claim the child-under-six exemption. Further, most states do not consider college education (undergraduate or graduate) job training (Adair 2001; Jensen 1998; Wolfe and Gittell 1997).

By defying the stereotype of lazy Welfare Queen, I found myself residing between the bureaucratic equivalent of a rock and a hard place. Perhaps because of welfare stereotypes, my situation had not been anticipated by program rules. With my dream evaporating in front of me, the Job Corps program officer began asking me several questions about my class schedule. He determined that, because I was taking classes at night, I was not a full-time day student and did not need to register for the program. Clearly, the rules were not designed for such narrow interpretation, but I will always be grateful that he chose to use the system to help me.

Although I dodged the job-training bullet, by the summer of 1987 I was running out of time. Retroactive budgeting, or determining the amount of a welfare check by using income earned two months previously, made it difficult to pay bills. My graduate-assistant salary of $450 per month was not paid over the summer. Money I had earned in May was already spent paying May bills. Like most welfare mothers (and a good many Americans of all classes), I lived from check to check. Having no money to pay my July rent, I spent everything in my checkbook buying food, paying the outstanding bills I could afford, and doing my laundry. I wrote my landlord an apology note, enclosed a check covering the late-rent fee, swallowed my pride, and called my caseworker. I requested an emergency grant to cover my unpaid rent. My request was granted, with the caveat that any future budget problems would require a caseworker to take over my finances. In other words, some government bureaucrat was going to control my checkbook and require me to submit all my bills for payment approval. What is important to remember is that I was perfectly capable of managing a budget and balancing a checkbook. What I could not overcome was the system's inability to take into account any periods of temporary unemployment or underemployment. With three more years of a Ph.D. program, I knew I was not going to get through on a combination of welfare assistance and part-time work as a graduate student teaching assistant.

All of this financial instability took a toll on my children, who were toddlers at the time. After my oldest child came to live with me, both my son and my daughter were left in questionable but "affordable" day-care situations that I would never use today. Currently, women who must work to maintain their eligibility for welfare benefits often leave their children in substandard day care (Mink 1999). I had adequate clothing and supplies only through the assistance of my family, but my family's resources were limited. I might add that the welfare system required that I report any gifts of money, so I always asked my parents to give in-kind gifts such as food or clothing. The time I could not pay my rent, the groceries I bought consisted of ten packages of five-for-a-dollar dry noodles and two large cans of tomato soup. This was to last me two weeks. My young children subsisted on the few food stamps

I managed to save out of my May allotment. I just could not bring myself to go to the local food pantry. Self-loathing brought about by internalizing negative societal messages concerning welfare mothers meant that I would go hungry. My kids also had to deal with a parent who was chronically overworked and somewhat depressed, as there never seemed to be enough resources to pay rent and put food on the table. Out of sheer desperation, I agreed to do a variety of things that to this day are difficult for me to admit or accept. Providing for my family and getting through school were my top priorities, and I was willing to do just about anything to get through, including marrying my children's father, who until this time had refused to pay child support.

Marrying the father of my children was just another in a long string of moral compromises I made in those two years on welfare. I agreed to get married provided that he would *let* me earn a Ph.D. I knew the day that we married that I was not in love. I convinced myself that I could learn to love him if I tried hard enough. We stayed married for well over ten years, through my Ph.D. program and my first tenure-track job after graduate school. It was neither the worst situation in the world nor the best. He tried to be a decent father to our children, but I was never able to dismiss the anger that I felt because of his refusal to support our children unless we married. I am not sure today that he even understands or remembers his reluctance to pay child support before our marriage. He loves his children and has probably repressed some of the unpleasant memories of that time in our relationship. What I clearly remember is his anger over my initial ending of our relationship and his response of hiring a lawyer to defend himself in a paternity suit. His lawyer was able to stall for quite some time, and the suit was not dropped until we were engaged. By marrying a man I had determined at one time was not right for me, I was participating in a state-sanctioned form of prostitution. He took me off the welfare rolls while I exchanged wifely duties for a level of financial security that would make graduate school possible.

This decision to marry only delayed the inevitable family "fragmentation" that Blankenhorn abhors. Unfortunately, policy forums continue to float the idea of encouraging welfare mothers to marry the fathers of their children. At a recent forum, Robert Rector, senior fellow at the Heritage Foundation, a conservative Washington think tank, suggests that these parents "be encouraged to marry, perhaps by giving them a brochure on the advantages of marriage and connecting them to programs that work on relationship skills" (Hopfensperger 2001, A4). A piece of paper listing the advantages of marriage and a few phone numbers is not valid assistance. There are myriad reasons that men and women who conceive out-of-wedlock children decline to get married. These reasons have little to do with ignorance of marital advantages or a lack of interpersonal skills. Biological fathers may lack the financial means to support their children; mothers may fear domestic violence or child abuse. I made a poor marriage decision because it seemed like the only way out of poverty for my children. Admittedly, marriage did provide some economic relief, and it not only made me "respectable," it enabled me to join the ranks of the middle class.

CLASS MATTERS

American cultural values color our perception of the class system and prevent an honest discussion of the realities of class. Because we believe in the American dream, we dismiss the importance of class. The phrase "pulling yourself up by your own bootstraps" expresses this belief in individualism, or the ability of citizens to rise to the top through their own efforts (Henslin 1997). We celebrate the American dream and emphasize individual responsibility in its pursuit. For some, however, the American dream "is not even a dream. It is an hallucination" (MacLeod 1987, 2). As part of ideal culture, individualism is a motivator encouraging the working class to achieve.[1] There is nothing wrong with equating hard work with rewards, as long as opportunities for success are created and rewards are not limited to a specific group of people. The cruel irony of rugged individualism is that it fails to acknowledge existing systemic barriers such as poverty, racism, or sexism or deficiencies in the educational system that frustrate the ascendance of the working class and poverty class. Promoting individualism renders invisible class, race, and gender roadblocks (Henslin 1997). In U.S. society, individual responsibility is promoted while social responsibility for creating the means or opportunities for achievement is deemphasized (Kerbo 1991). We must reject the promotion of individual responsibility while continuing to ignore systemic forces that make it difficult, and often impossible, to self-direct and ultimately determine social location as defined by income, education, and occupation.

Working-class, welfare, and poverty are unimportant concepts if we imagine that anyone can leave a status behind through hard work. However, in the United States, social class is both an ascribed and achieved status. Social class is ascribed because we do not choose the class we are born into; it is achieved because some movement between class levels is possible through higher education and work. Let us not pretend that only achievement matters, because the best predictor of adult class position is the class into which one is born (Kerbo 1991). The fact is that class matters, because we do not all start out in the same place. Some of us begin our lives with a few more rungs to climb. When we are pushed off the ladder—as I almost was in graduate school—or are prevented from grabbing hold in the first place, the American dream is little more than a fantasy. It is a tool of oppression used by every self-righteous advocate of personal responsibility. We need to remember that welfare mothers must climb the rungs while holding on to their children.

Americans both deny and create social class. We deny class divisions by subscribing to a classless ideology of individualism and equality of opportunity (Kerbo 1991), yet at the same time we construct a class hierarchy with the welfare class at the bottom. The lower strata functions to make the rest of us feel better about our current position in the pecking order. Herbert Gans (2001) suggests that poverty continues to serve the non-poor because having someone beneath you takes the sting out of not being middle or upper class and allows for the creation of divisions both between and within classes. Gans argues that this is similar to the tendency of the upper class to distinguish between old money and the nouveau riche. We also create distinctions within the middle class between those who were born middle class, those who achieved it by moving from the non-welfare working class, and those with a welfare history. As I am regularly reminded, those previously "on the dole" are not bona fide middle class when compared to those who were born middle class or moved up from the non-welfare working class.

Despite my current middle-class status, some will always define me as less than middle class, a type of sub-class, because of my welfare history. My former welfare status overshadows all my other achievements, including graduating magna cum laude, attending graduate school, and earning a Ph.D. My experiences with this are analogous to how society treats ex-cons. By continuing to stigmatize ex-cons, we never let them pay off their debt to society. I first realized that I would never be able to pay my debt while attending a baby shower for one of my colleagues. One of the guests was ranting about lazy welfare mothers. (How a generic discussion about babies ended up on "welfare babies" is another essay.) This group of intelligent, college-educated women, many with Ph.Ds, was discussing motherhood and child-care experiences when someone told the proverbial friend-of-a-friend story. The principal subject allegedly ran a day-care center and had one welfare client who had trouble paying for day care. In addition, the story presented the poor woman's child as *always* "dirty" and sick (they left out covered with rat bites). This poster mom for welfare reform was held up as representing all welfare mothers. Although I could have passed as a middle-class professional, I decided to "come out" as a former welfare recipient to challenge the Welfare Queen stereotype that was being proffered. The Ventura-like responses from these women reaffirmed my belief that, as a society, we neither forgive nor ever let a welfare mother forget where she comes from. One woman actually told me I had no business going to school because my bad choices should not be rewarded with *her* tax dollars.

In our society, we treat welfare mothers like criminals, but we rarely punish their male co-conspirators whose failure to pay child support precipitates the need for welfare. According to some, we should not stigmatize or punish the complicit men, because "they do not think of themselves as deadbeats because they do not think of themselves as dads. These guys never signed on to anything. They never agreed to play by any fatherhood code. They do not have—they have never had—any explicit obligations to either their children or to the mothers of their children. By what reasonable principle do they owe anybody anything?" (Blankenhorn 1995, 135). This type of reasoning blames women while letting men off the hook for their role in creating this so-called welfare family crisis.

THE REALITY OF GENDER

Gender is a necessary prism through which we must view single parenthood, because it is usually women who are left with the responsibility of raising children and absorbing the blame for single parenthood, poverty, and welfare participation. Although poor single parents, both male and female, need support to increase their chances of success, let us not pretend that both men and women equally face the problems of raising children and finishing their educations. No social scientist discusses the "masculinization" of poverty. However, half of all single-parent families headed by women live in poverty (Henslin 2000). The feminization of poverty is due to divorce, births to unmarried women, lower wages paid to women, a lack of job opportunities in the labor market, and inadequate child-care resources (Anderson 2000; Henslin 2000). Welfare-reform advocates need to look at *all* of the reasons that female–single-parent families are more likely to live in poverty. Rather than emphasizing divorce and out-of-wedlock childbearing in general, reform advocates need to address the complex reasons that contribute to divorce and out-of-wedlock childbearing, including domestic violence, child abuse, and substance abuse by fathers. We need to recognize that many of these mothers are single parents because they put the safety and well-being of their children first (Brush 2003).

Believing that all or even most welfare mothers are in their positions because of behavior committed or omitted is to blame the victim. According to D. Stanley Eitzen and Maxine Baca Zinn (1999), the values of rugged individualism and equality of opportunity are what provide an ideological basis for a victim-blaming society in which homeless men are defined as lazy; drug addicts as weak; and welfare mothers as morally deficient. Because welfare mothers derived their status through divorce or out-of-wedlock childbearing, they are viewed as morally tainted by society at large. Labeling welfare mothers less virtuous serves to deflect attention from the actual lack of opportunity in U.S. society, thereby maintaining the status quo.

Gans suggests, "The poor can be identified and punished as alleged or real deviants to uphold the legitimacy of conventional norms. The defenders of these norms must be able to find people who can be accused of being lazy, spendthrift, dishonest and promiscuous" (Gans 2001, 324). In other words, our stereotyping of welfare mothers as lazy and sexually loose promotes expectations that citizens should be hardworking and chaste. Again, there is nothing wrong with promoting hard work and sexual virtue. Gans's argument is that the poor—and, I would argue, especially welfare mothers—pay the price for all moral transgressions and the societal need to promote certain behaviors while discouraging others. Laziness and sexual promiscuity are found in all social classes, genders, and ethnic groups. By focusing attention on welfare mothers, the behavior of the middle and upper class is under-scruti-nized. Welfare mothers cannot reject or challenge the labels, because "they lack political and cultural power to correct the stereotypes that other people hold of them" (Gans 2001, 324). Welfare mothers, then, are used as scapegoats in the promotion of the larger social order.

This ingrained tendency to engage in victim-blaming can be cir-cumvented by practicing what C. W. Mills (1959) called the "sociologi-cal imagination." Mills's concepts "personal troubles of the milieu" and "public issues of social structure" offer another way to view welfare mothers. Mills defined personal troubles as occurring "within the char-acter of the individual and within the range of his immediate relations with others" (Mills 1959, 8). In contrast, public issues "have to do with matters that transcend these local environments of the individual and the range of his inner life" (Mills 1959, 8). For Mills, identifying and cor-recting the deficiencies of individuals solve problems due to individual characteristics. Identifying and correcting deficiencies within the system solve problems that are social in origin. The problem is that we collec-tively assume that problems with social origins are primarily personal in nature. This is articulated by a belief that, if welfare women stopped being lazy and sexually active, they could pull themselves out of poverty. In reality, the solution is not so simple, as most issues usually are a combination of individual and social causes. Although it is true that some individuals engage in self-destructive behavior, that behav-ior is often a response to oppressive conditions and the absence of any realistic means to change their situation (Kozol 1995). Welfare mothers do not exist because some women are lazy and promiscuous. Welfare moms are created by a system that refuses to promote equal pay for women and that discourages poor women from earning educational degrees or training for higher-paying skilled positions, such as plumber or welder.[2] Welfare moms are created by a system infused with gender discrimination by guiding women into lower-paying positions, such as secretary.[3] Finally, welfare moms are created by a system that does not hold men accountable for their contribution to out-of-wedlock child-bearing or for their failure to pay adequate child support.

As a constant supply of low-paid laborers with little power and no voice, welfare women make up a reserve army of workers that can be exploited on demand for low-paying jobs, with little if any benefits, and fired when their usefulness has ended (Gans 2001). Welfare recipients participating in the Work Experience Program (WEP), for instance, were working as New York City subway-car cleaners for less than minimum wages but with hopes of becoming permanent transit workers. The hopeful cleaners were informed of a hiring freeze as the five-year wel-fare-limit deadline neared (Bernstein 2001). Who benefits from the coercion of the welfare class? Everyone from the social worker who has a job doling out benefits, to corporate managers who need cheap workers who can be laid off at the hint of economic downturn (Gans 2001). The WEP participants cost New York City $1.80 per hour. Permanent transit workers doing the same job make between $11 and $19 an hour, with union benefits (Bernstein 2001). With an economic recession and city revenue dwindling, in part because of September 11, what is the incentive to hire permanent workers when welfare recipients can be had so cheaply? The implication of Mills's insight is that we cannot solve the socioeconomic crisis of welfare mothers and their children by telling women to "cross their legs." We must look beyond individuals and alleged character flaws to systemic forces that create and re-create the welfare class.

Failing to differentiate between private troubles and public issues occurs because welfare mothers are not considered among the "deserving" poor. Thus, they are easy targets for politicians and conservative policy pundits who want to deflect attention from systemic deficiencies by framing the issue as a "personal trouble." In 1994, U.S. Representative Jim Talent of Missouri, then in his first term, filed a bill intended to reduce out-of-wedlock births by capping welfare payments and requiring welfare recipients to work. This bill was based on the assumption that welfare mothers deliberately have more children to avoid working or getting married. Talent's welfare solution is framed as a response to "personal trouble," because individual characteristics of promiscuity and greed are perceived as the cause of alleged escalating welfare costs. Talent justified his bill by remarking, "We must remove the *enormous* economic subsidy for people to form families that are dysfunctional" (Associated Press 1994, A9; emphasis added). Not only are welfare mothers considered sexually loose and greedy, but their families—their children—are represented as dysfunctional because they are poor.

The difference among Representative Talent, Governor Ventura, and me is that I want my government to invest in college students, especially single-parent students, as it would any other infrastructure project. We already know that spending money on the education of welfare mothers is a good investment, as the essays in this volume show. By constructing opportunities such as subsidized child care for college students with children, and making welfare programs more compatible with higher-education goals, we can transform welfare recipients into taxpayers and societal stakeholders who continue to invest in the system. People with college degrees or advanced training make more money. Those women who earn more can provide better for both themselves and their children. As a full-fledged taxpayer, I have paid back the system many times over the cost of my financial assistance and will continue to do so for the rest of my working life. For every woman like me, there are many more who did not make it. Yet if we want poor women to pull themselves up by their bootstraps, we must give them bootstraps. To not provide opportunities, but still to expect women to attempt the class-ladder climb, is like asking them to scale Mount Everest without equipment. It is not impossible to make the climb, but very few will succeed, and countless casualties will result from attempting to reach the summit.

NOTES

1. *Ideal culture* is defined as group goals. It can be contrasted with reality or *real culture*, the values and behaviors actually followed (Henslin 1997).

2. In 1995, the median income for year-round, full-time female workers was 71.4 percent of what men earned (National Committee on Pay Equity 1998).

3. Sex segregation in the workplace is demonstrated by figures that show that in 1995, women made up 8.4 percent of all engineers but 98.5 percent of all secretaries (National Committee on Pay Equity 1998).

REFERENCES

Adair, Vivyan C. 2001. "Poverty and the (Broken) Promise of Higher Education." *Harvard Educational Review* (Summer): 217–39.

Anderson, Margaret L. 2000. *Thinking about Women: Sociological Perspectives on Sex and Gender,* 5th ed. Boston: Allyn and Bacon.

Associated Press. 1994. "Republican Welfare Reform Plan Cuts Benefits for Unwed Mothers." *Houston Post,* 29 April, A4.

Beeghley, Leonard. 1996. *The Structure of Social Stratification in the United States,* 2nd ed. Boston: Allyn and Bacon.

Bernstein, Nina. 2001. "As Welfare Comes to an End, So Do the Jobs." *New York Times,* 17 December. Available from: <http://nytimes.com/2001/12/17/nyregion/17welf.html>

Blankenhorn, David. 1995. *Fatherless America: Confronting Our Most Urgent Social Problem*. New York: Basic Books.

Brush, Lisa D. 2003. "'That's Why I'm on Prozac': Battered Women, Traumatic Stress, and Education in the Context of Welfare Reform." In *Reclaiming Class: Women, Poverty, and the Promise of Higher Education in America*, ed. Vivyan C. Adair and Sandra L. Dahlberg. Philadelphia: Temple University Press.

Eitzen, D. Stanley, and Maxine Baca Zinn. 1999. *Social Problems*, 8th ed. Boston: Allyn and Bacon.

Gans, Herbert J. 2001. "The Uses of Poverty: The Poor Pay All." Pp. 322–28 in *Down to Earth Sociology: Introductory Readings*, 11th ed., ed. James M. Henslin. New York: Free Press.

Gilbert, Dennis. 1998. *American Class Structure in an Age of Growing Inequality*, 5th ed. Belmont, Calif.: Wadsworth.

Healy, Patrick. 1999. "The Continuing Education of Jesse Ventura." *Chronicle of Higher Education*, 4 June, A12.

Henslin, James M. 1997. *Sociology: A Down-to-Earth Approach*, 3rd ed. Boston: Allyn and Bacon.

———. 2002. *Essentials of Sociology: A Down-to-Earth Approach*, 4th ed. Boston: Allyn and Bacon.

Hopfensperger, J. 2001. "Welfare Experts Say Challenge Ahead Is to Keep Up Momentum." *Minneapolis Star Tribune*, 27 October, A4.

Jensen, R. H. 1998. "Welfare: Exploding the Stereotypes." Pp. 242–48 in *Race, Class, and Gender in the United States: An Integrated Study*, 4th ed., ed. Paula S. Rothenberg. New York: St. Martin's Press.

Kerbo, Harold R. 1991. *Social Stratification and Inequality*, 2d ed. New York: McGraw-Hill.

Kozol, Jonathan. 1995. *Amazing Grace: The Lives of Children and the Conscience of a Nation*. New York: Crown Publishers.

MacLeod, J. 1987. *Ain't No Making It: Leveled Aspirations in a Low-Income Neighborhood*. Boulder, Colo.: Westview Press.

Mills, C. W. 1959. *The Sociological Imagination*. New York: Oxford University Press.

Mink, Gwendolyn. 1999. "Aren't Poor Single Mothers Women? Feminists, Welfare Reform, and Welfare Justice." Pp. 171–88 in *Whose Welfare?*, ed. Gwendolyn Mink. Ithaca, N.Y.: Cornell University Press.

National Committee on Pay Equity. 1998. "The Wage Gap: Myths and Facts." Pp. 234–41 in *Race, Class, and Gender in the United States: An Integrated Study*, 4th ed, ed. Paula S. Rothenberg. New York: St. Martin's Press.

Williams, R. M., Jr. 1965. *American Society: A Sociological Interpretation*, 2nd ed. New York: Knopf.

Wolfe, L., and M. Gittell. 1997. *College Education Is a Route out of Poverty for Women on Welfare*. Washington, D.C.: Center for Women Policy Studies.

II. ON THE FRONT LINES

Tonya Mitchell

6   If I Survive, It Will Be
     Despite Welfare Reform
     Reflections of a Former Welfare Student

In 1993, I found myself to be everything that America loves to hate and blame for its ills: I was young, black, pregnant and unwed, and poor. Yet for some strange reason, I had not felt—and, as a result, did not at the time recognize—the vehemence with which I would be judged as a social pariah, as an outcast, as a Welfare Queen. My mother had raised my brothers and sisters and I with very little money, yet we had come from a loving, clean, and stable home. My father drank away any money we ever had and had left us by the time I was seven. Yet my mother worked diligently to provide us with love, intellectual stimulation, dignity, a sense of direction, and an appreciation for education. So when I found myself pregnant at age seventeen, my only thought was that, like my mother before me, I would work hard, continue my education, and raise a happy and healthy child. Little did I suspect that things could in any way be harder for me than they had been for my mother. Little did I know that racism, classism, and sexism intersect in the ever popular rhetoric and practice of welfare-bashing, and that my toughest battle of all would be to save my sense of self and worth in a contest that costs many their souls and their self-respect.

My first recognition of the stigma that poor single mothers face came with my initial visit to the welfare office in my third month of pregnancy when I applied to receive medical benefits. Racism was rampant in the county office: As I approached the reception desk, a clerk looked at my small, brown, and still not showing body and bitterly remarked, "Pregnant, I suppose!" From there, it went downhill. During my screening, the caseworker sarcastically stated, "I suppose you don't know who the daddy is"; stifled a laugh when I said I planned to finish my GED and go on to college; and glared at me when I told him that I refused to have my teachers—who did not yet know I was pregnant—sign notes for the welfare office stating that I was still in school and in good standing. To be frank, I was shocked. I had always known and hated racism when I saw and experienced it, but this was something more. It was racism mixed with the sense that someone had the right to hate me, to laugh at me, to disrespect me openly and blatantly because I was black and poor, because I was pregnant, and because I was alone.

I have never backed down in my life, and I was certainly not going to when my unborn child's health depended on my perseverance. So I sat and silently suffered the caseworker's sarcasm and disrespect, but I left with medical coupons in my hand. This, however, did not guarantee that life would be any easier, because I found that many doctors, and most private physicians, can and do refuse to take new patients with medical coupons. The stigma of being a welfare mom was already being read on my body as I went from practitioner to practitioner, begging them to see me and to check on the health of my baby. Finally, I was allowed to see a nurse practitioner at a public medical clinic that operated on a sliding-scale basis. It is at least officially against the law to discriminate against a person on the basis of their race or gender, but it is evidently just fine to refuse to serve them on the basis of their poverty read through receipt of state-issued medical coupons. The final shock of the day came when I found that I was pregnant with twins.

I did go on to finish my GED, and three weeks after the birth of my babies I entered a community college with every intention of finishing at the top of my class, then going on to earn a four-year college degree. I know many feel that welfare is a trap from which one cannot escape. But for me, welfare meant the ability to be a good mother to my baby girls, the freedom to earn an associate of arts degree, the choice not to depend on the man who had gotten me pregnant and who was a manipulative and dangerous person with a temper to be feared and avoided at all costs. I found a very small apartment near the college, which I received for reduced rent in exchange for managing the five other units. Every day, I took my babies to a clean and wonderful child-care center, where I also worked in the afternoons. Between dropping the girls off and spending the afternoons with them, I found a paradise in my studies. I had the opportunity to listen to brilliant professors and excited students. There were great music and drama programs to attend for free. I was nurtured and encouraged by teachers and new friends, many of whom were also single parents trying to earn degrees. My world completely opened up as I learned to think in new ways and about subjects to which I had never been exposed.

It was also hard to be in school. It was particularly difficult being in those classes where welfare-bashing was delivered as academic gospel. In one sociology class, the professor opened the discussion by telling the class ridiculous anecdotes about lazy poor women sitting at home collecting welfare checks so they could buy color television sets with which to watch the *Oprah Show.* He had no proof for these allegations, no foundation on which to generalize in his obscene little stories. But he did encourage others to join in with their own ideas of the outrageous misdeeds that the poor inflict on our country—all of which seemed to be pulled out of thin air. I remember sitting and listening and feeling ill, given how exhausting my routine and that of my single-mom–student friends were. But, of course, I was too hurt, too shamed, and too afraid to be "outed" to protest.

As hard as it was in school, being a welfare mom was far more oppressive on the outside. Oftentimes on buses, between school and the grocery store or the laundry, I would try to read my homework while my babies slept in their stroller. One day, a well-dressed Latina businesswoman put her cell phone down to look at me with disgust and say, "I wish I had time to read. Some of us have to work for a living." When I went to grocery stores and used food stamps, it was O.K. as long as I was buying only beans and rice. But as soon as I tried to buy a treat for my family—say, a decent cut of meat or some good baby food for my girls—customers and clerks invariably commented, "Well, how nice that you can afford brand names on taxpayers' money when I can only afford generics."

As a poor single mother, you soon learn to give up your ideas about privacy. When the grocery-store check-out clerk announces over the intercom, "I need food-stamp change on three," and everyone stares at you; when you have to change your babies' diapers in the welfare office's public waiting room because there are no changing tables in the bathrooms; and when you must recount again and again to some paternity official the details of the sexual act that led to your pregnancy, you know you have given up your sense of autonomy and privacy. The state pays for you and the state owns you, and there is absolutely nothing you can do about it.

It was also often difficult to go home exhausted at the end of the day and then cook dinner, clean my house, clean the apartment building, play with the babies, and start my homework, which I sometimes did throughout the night. Money was so tight that my five-foot, two-inch frame went down to about ninety-eight pounds and we often had our electricity shut off because I could not pay enough on my bill to keep it on. But we had our own tidy and safe place; the girls were healthy and happy, and I was in school and falling in love with the idea of becoming a medical professional.

In my two years as a community-college student, I had three Bs; the rest of my grades were As. In my second year, I started studying chemistry, biology, and physiology, and I loved it. I will never forget the day I mastered the Krebb's cycle or the oral exam on the physiology of a pig embryo, for which I received the highest grade in my class. Every other weekend, I started trading off with another single-mother nursing student, and we took turns going to a medical clinic to do volunteer work helping nurses care for poor folk. I felt alive and needed and valuable. I was really excited about working in a health-care field someday, where I would have the opportunity to work with and really help populations who were so under-served because of racism and poverty. I had dreams of opening a clinic where poor women of color could come for free health care and where they would be treated with the respect and dignity that they deserved. These dreams fueled my studies. When the choice came between getting an LPN degree or an associate's degree so that I could transfer to the university to earn a degree in nursing—at times, I even fantasized about becoming a doctor—the choice was clear. I earned an associate of science degree, then applied to the university, confident that I would be accepted. In the spring of 1995 came the second-happiest day of my life (the first was the day I gave birth to my twin daughters) when I received my letter of acceptance.

On that same day, however, the world came crashing down on my head when I was assaulted in my own home while preparing my daughters to go with me to the grocery store. During the attack, I feared for my life and that of my babies. That night, we slept in a safe house set up by the YWCA, and I spent the next three months in that safe haven, preparing to start school. Despite my pain and fear, I honestly thought that I could leave behind my past to become a productive and respected parent, taxpaying citizen, and worker.

I loved being at the university, and my girls were thriving and happy. University professors pushed me harder and harder, and sometimes I thought my head would explode with all the new information and ways of thinking. We were poor, and I was always tired, but we were moving forward. Yet I was in school for only a few months when President Clinton signed the Personal Responsibility and Work Opportunity Reconciliation Act of 1996 into law, and my life and my ability to be a responsible parent and medical practitioner was forever altered.

I was called into the welfare office in the next term and told that, because I had been deemed "work ready," I would have to start a job or I would be dropped from TANF (Temporary Aid to Needy Families, or welfare) immediately. This meant that I would lose not only the money I needed to pay the bills but also that I would lose medical benefits and food stamps for my girls. I had to comply. I was not even allowed to finish that term at the university, because higher education had not been written in to my Personal Plan prior to 1996. Even I had to admit that there was no way I could work that many hours and go to school and care for my daughters. Although one of my professors went with me to petition the state, to show transcripts and testify about my promise as a student, my case was denied, and I was forced to be "responsible" and to "work first."

The state helped me to find a job at a nursing home, where I have now been working for almost three years. Because the nursing home is located about an hour by bus away from my apartment, I have to leave home at 5:15 in the morning, and I do not get home from the girls' child-care center until after 7:30 in the evening. I make $6.35 per hour at my job, and I have to pay a good portion of my monthly check for health care for my children and myself. I do have help from the state with child care, but I have lost medical benefits and food stamps, so life is much harder for me now than it was before. It also contains very little hope.

Clearly, welfare reform and the Personal Responsibility Act changed my life. Now it is even worse. I do not have the money I need to pay my rent and bills, and I have to put my twins in awful day care for about ten hours a day while I work in this dead-end job. My girls are generally asleep when I drop them off in the early morning and sound asleep by the time I get home in the evening. But even if they had been able to stay awake, I am usually too tired to read to or play with them. This is what breaks my heart the most.

All I wanted was to be a nurse and help care for people. I had a very high grade point average, and I know I would have earned a nursing degree if I had been allowed to stay at the university. Nurses earn about $25 an hour. But I am stuck here. I guess it is where the state thought I belonged all along. I should have known better than to think that I could help myself and my kids to a better life.

There are just two more comments I want to make about being hated as a poor black woman who tried to exit poverty through education. My family, my friends who are poor, and my children and I are families of love and support. It is hunger and exhaustion and pain that I want to leave behind, not the people I treasure so much. Second, I think it is important to think clearly about the ways in which racism intersects with classism and sexism to make us so hated and punished as welfare mothers. A professor at the university once told me that bell hooks had said in a lecture that "poor black women are demonized and poor white women are erased" in the rhetoric of welfare-bashing. In practical terms, what this means is that everywhere I go, people know and assume that I am "one of those women." There is absolutely no place for me to hide. Poverty is apparent on me because of the fact that I do not have money to buy good clothes, do fashionable things with my hair, or get my teeth fixed. But that obvious poverty is deeply connected to the other obvious thing about me, which is my race. The two are inextricably seen on my body. If I were well-to-do, I believe, my material condition might to some degree neutralize the way my body is read and hated. If I were white, I might be able to hide my position, at least temporarily. But as a poor, black, young, and unmarried mother, there is nowhere to hide. And so they think they have put me where I belong and will keep me stuck here. But they will fail, because I will never give up. Some day, God willing, I will return to school and pull my children out of poverty, not because of but *despite* welfare reform.

7 Not By Myself Alone

Upward Bound with Family and Friends

ONE WEEK before Christmas when I was ten years old, my younger brother and I stepped off the school bus to find two police cars parked at the base of our family's long driveway. Our family lived on a farm outside a small Iowa town, where everyone knew the police officers by name. One of the officers I knew from school stepped from behind his car and greeted me. He introduced me to the unfamiliar policeman, told me not to worry, and explained that my brother and I were to go away to a neighboring city. This would be the extent of the explanation either man offered to us.

Without question, my brother and I stepped into the back of the police car and began the half-hour ride to Waterloo, one of the larger cities in Iowa. During the ride, a thousand thoughts entered my mind. Quickly, I decided that my parents must have died. I grabbed my brother's hand and squeezed it for support. As the oldest of five siblings, I was immediately aware of my new responsibilities as head of the household.

The police officer drove us to a hospital where my fears were allayed. My parents were alive, and sitting with a cadre of solemn adults, each member dressed in a suit. Alone, I was taken right away into a room with more people in suits. They began asking me what I ate for breakfast, how often I ate, and how many clothes I had. Instincts told me to lie, and I constructed a story of regular meals, warm clothes, and an average home life. In another room, my brother was apparently not as savvy. That night the local news reported that five children had been found in an unheated farmhouse with no fresh food in the home.

My parents agreed temporarily to sign over custody of my siblings and me to the state. Child Protective Services divided us between two foster homes. Throughout the separation of our family, the public debated the parenting skills of my mother and father. My parents were alternately accused of doing drugs, being physically abusive, and being generally lazy. During a series of court battles, my parents went to the media to tell their story, emphasizing the lack of social services for underemployed two-parent families. Public pressure may have assisted in the reunification of my family, but it took several months to bring closure to this event. Our family left our small rural home to live in the moderately urban city of Waterloo.

There had been poverty in my family from the time I was able to talk until the day the police officers met me at the bus stop. From that time until the present day, there would continue to be poverty in my family. Nevertheless, the experience with Child Protective Services would be pivotal in my life and in the lives of my family members. That situation held a power—a power that made poverty something I thought about during the course of each day. The strain of the experience with social-services intervention eventually led to my parents' divorce. Although both of my parents had a history of mental illness, the helplessness they experienced at the hands of the state increased their symptoms to levels that affected their ability to function. For example, my mother frequently woke my siblings and me in the middle of night. Wild-eyed, she would demand that we thoroughly scrub the house as she insisted that the police or Child Protective Services could arrive at any moment to deem our house filthy. She was sure they would find reason to take her children from her again.

During my young adolescent years, my mother struggled to keep the family alive on welfare. Our clothes were ill-fitting; our meals were supplied by a combination of the Salvation Army, food stamps, and the county food bank; and we occasionally spent time in the local homeless shelter. At one point, mice lived in my mattress, and lice invaded each family member's hair. My mother's paranoia about Child Protective Services led her to handpick each nit from our hair until the infestation was eliminated. Lice shampoos were available only by doctor's prescription at that time. She was afraid that a doctor would report the lice to the state. My father dutifully sent meager child-support payments, because it was all he could afford on a janitor's salary.

My role in the family became increasingly important as I assumed responsibility for the checkbook, under-the-table income supplementation, and co-parenting. Following a suicide attempt by my mother, I was able to conceal from Child Protective Services her extended absence that left we children alone during her psychiatric in-patient hospitalization. Meanwhile, I studied furiously in high school to maintain good grades. I had a few close friends who supported me emotionally; however, the majority of the students at the high school I attended rejected me. I had neither the "right" clothes nor the disposable income to attend after-school activities. In addition, I lived on the wrong side of the river, in the predominantly African American community. Much of this time in my life was spent in isolation, occasionally interrupted by physical, emotional, or sexual violence that were commonplace in my neighborhood.

The staff and students of the federally funded educational program Upward Bound became my lifeline during my adolescence in the mid-1980s. The program was situated on a college campus nearly two hours away from Waterloo. Upward Bound staff members brought low-income adolescents to the campus each summer for six weeks, and occasionally for weekends during other seasons of the year. Their goal was to familiarize students with college life while bolstering self-confidence and study skills. I rarely needed assistance with homework, but feelings of alienation left me vulnerable to bouts of self-doubt and hopelessness. I engaged in self-destructive behavior that ranged from substance use to running away. Beginning at age thirteen, I engaged in sexual relations with older boys to gain social approval. Typically, I ended up feeling used and unloved. The Upward Bound staff was there to counter each negative experience with support and reassurance.

My summers spent at Upward Bound were often interrupted so that I could work on farms as a fieldhand in an activity called corn detasseling. My family needed the extra money. When I was old enough to work in general labor, I often missed Upward Bound activities to work as a prep cook at a restaurant. However, the influence of Upward Bound was so great that, even without the full benefit of the program, I gained the courage to join extracurricular activities at high school. I became part of after-school plays and the speech team, and I even spent one season as a member of the color guard.

With the support and persuasion of Upward Bound staff, I completed a single college application. The staff seemed instinctively to know that I would need ongoing support during my time in college, so the application they supplied to me was for the college at which my Upward Bound program was located. A college education sounded like a dream; my family was real. Apprehension about leaving my family to attend college led to ambivalence, which in turn led to procrastination. Completing the college application required the direct oversight of Upward Bound staff. Even after I was accepted to the college, I experienced a great deal of indecision. I was responsible for managing finances in my family, and my younger siblings were more like my own children than my brothers and sisters. However, I desperately wanted to escape poverty through higher education.

I felt that I deserted my family when I was seventeen so that I could attend college. I told myself that going to college would serve my siblings well, because I would be providing a positive role model for them. Despite helpful scholarships and hefty educational loans, I had to work more than thirty hours a week as a waitress at an off-campus restaurant and as a cook at the on-campus cafe. Whenever I could spare the money, I mailed a check to my family.

The college I attended is a private institution, and the majority of the students come from middle-class to upper-middle-class families. With my class load and work schedule, I did not have a lot of time to get to know other students. My main companion was my roommate, who was a fellow graduate of the Upward Bound program. Our similar backgrounds allowed me to feel comfortable, and my roommate was not shy about broadening our social circle. Through her influence, I was able slowly to meet other students who differed significantly from me in their understanding of the world. I decided to make a fresh start at college, and I became excited about the prospect of finally "fitting in." I bought clothes that I could not really afford, and I had my hair styled. I did not mention my history to my new friends, and I mimicked their style of speaking and interacting. Unfortunately, I began to develop the sense that I was an imposter. I felt as though everyone was superior to me—more confident, more attractive, and more socially at ease.

My fear of social rejection intensified when my roommate decided to move out of the state. Suddenly, I was left with acquaintances that knew only a phony version of me. Without being honest about my background, it was difficult to develop intimacy with new friends. I rarely felt I could relate to their conversations about topics as mundane as watching *Star Wars* (my family had never been able to afford to see movies) and complaints about allowances that were *cut down* to $200 a month. In addition, many would-be friends were frustrated with my seeming unwillingness to spend more time in social activities and less time at work. I returned to old dating patterns wherein I used my sexuality to attract mates, only to be left feeling used and dirty. Most of my thoughts were of home, where my friends knew me well and continued to support me across the distance. It was less than a complete school year before I seriously contemplated dropping out of college.

Shortly thereafter, I began to feel suicidal, so I sought out the Upward Bound staff. I had vowed to avoid relying on Upward Bound staff, but the situation seemed desperate. Staff members spent hours talking to me about my family concerns and my internal turmoil regarding my social relationships. My family had begun falling apart as two of my brothers dropped out of high school, and my mother required further psychiatric hospitalizations. While the assistance of the Upward Bound staff was invaluable, I also sought the help of a counselor. By a stroke of fortune, the counselor I was assigned at the college's psychological services was a working-class man who had attended a private college.

While I was able to verbalize some of the alienation I felt on campus, my counselor's own class background allowed us to have a silent understanding. When I was not capable of describing my feelings, he seemed to be able to fill in the blanks. He listened as I told him about my anger and resentment, feelings that arose even in the classroom. For example, in a political-science class, the professor discussed cutting aid to families on welfare. Fellow students expressed extremely negative and stereotypical views of poor people, and I was too afraid to challenge their thinking. An economics professor assigned the works of writers such as Charles Murray, co-author with Richard Herrnstein of *The Bell Curve: Intelligence and Class Structure in American Life* (1994). We were assigned an essay by Charles Murray titled, "What's So Bad about Being Poor?" (1998), which romanticizes poverty. Years of hardship had left me numb and virtually unable to cry, but reading this essay caused weeks of internal wrenching and waterless tears.

What I needed more than anything was a personal identity that would allow me to develop social closeness on campus like the closeness I shared with friends at home who did not attend college. Although counseling was not able to provide me with an identity, I became less afraid of telling some friends about my background. Following my carefully timed disclosures, some people became distant, but other friends accepted me more fully than I had ever been accepted in my life. These friendships would not be without challenges. For example, a serious argument developed with a good friend when her father bought her a new wardrobe worth more than a thousand dollars. Because I was having trouble paying for food despite a full work schedule, I resented her fortune, especially because she did not have to work. I remember becoming moody and argumentative to the point that a loud and painful dispute ensued. I never told her the source of my hostility, and later we were able to move beyond the incident.

As I neared graduation from college, the encouragement of Upward Bound staff and my college advisers led me to consider graduate school in social work or psychology, my two majors. I had both a love of teaching and a desire to conduct research. Although a doctorate degree seemed attainable, it also felt as though I was overstepping the bounds of reasonable upward mobility. In addition, my family was deteriorating as poverty further threatened their survival. By this time, two of my brothers were heavy drug users, and most of my other siblings had dropped out of high school or even junior high. These were children who had maintained solidly high grade point averages and who scored in the top 3 percent on standardized tests. Yet their futures were in serious jeopardy. Going to graduate school meant that I would have to postpone having a livable income; hence, I could not provide better circumstances for my siblings.

Following an old pattern, I completed only one application to a doctoral program in social work and social science. I decided to let the admissions committee determine my future. Whenever I considered graduate school, I felt selfish for abandoning my siblings. Although I had never promised to return and take them from poverty, I had silently promised myself to do just that. Here I was considering studying social work, and to the best of my knowledge the people in the most need were directly related to me. When I was accepted to graduate school, I reasoned that two of my younger brothers who were closest to me in age were beyond help. Their substance abuse and skirmishes with the law made them seem unreachable by any effort I might be able to make. I believed that I could still finish graduate school and have a good job in time to support my youngest siblings through their teen years.

My life until graduate school had been an alternating series of misfortunes and dumb luck. Through a blind roommate match I again experienced dumb luck when I was paired with an African American roommate from the East Coast. We had compatible personalities that allowed us to become fast friends, but we also shared some overlap in our backgrounds. She was the daughter of a doctor and a chemical engineer, but her earliest childhood years had been spent in financial strain. Although she attended private prep schools, her family's finances were compromised when her parents divorced; her mother was a poor medical student, and her father was not providing financial support. She described times of going hungry at school, because her mother could not afford to buy food. She was familiar with being left out by peers in school because of both her financial standing and her race. Her presence in my life was vital to my success at graduate school. Our friendship gave me a sense of grounding, and at least I could comfortably relate to someone who understood my poverty.

During the day, my new best friend went to her graduate program in engineering, and I went to my classes in social work and psychology. I was immediately uncomfortable in my new surroundings. As in many graduate programs, the faculty wanted the incoming cohort to bond. In one of our introductory meetings, each student was asked to provide an introduction to the group. The descriptions of lives spent in exotic lands, degrees earned at the best colleges, and interactions with important people left me frightened about my ability to stand next to my fellow students. Over time, we participated in a seminar designed to introduce us to the program. There were many opportunities to get to know one another academically and personally. There was a formality and stiffness to social interactions that created intense anxiety for me. I was afraid of failing to follow social protocol. I was afraid to eat, and I was certain that I would say the wrong thing at any moment. As the members of my cohort described their research interests, they mentioned the names of great scientists and theorists that were completely new to me. I could not understand how everyone could be nodding in familiarity or interrupting to disagree with a particular theoretical stance, and yet they did so comfortably.

It did not take long to discover that one's identity was politically and socially important. When their social identity was apparent, students would describe their personal experiences with becoming aware of racial or gender discrimination. When an identity might be easily hidden, students regularly mentioned their sexual orientation or their religious background followed by accounts of systematic alienation. There was a great deal of prestige attached to pointing out some way in which the program was failing to meet the needs of one group or another. The heterosexual, financially stable, white men were schooled in places that taught them to speak about the pains of recognizing their privilege, so their enlightened views warranted some attention in classes. My ever lingering shame and vulnerability about my background prevented me from discussing my economic history, so my edited personal description sounded hollow. It became obvious that the assumptions about me went something like this: naive and sheltered middle-class woman from a conservative, private college in the heart of the Midwest—consequently, an area barren of diversity and progressive thinking. It was pointless for me to express my thoughts on multiculturalism; they were easy to dismiss.

We read Peggy McIntosh's essay "White Privilege" (1990). I had been exposed to the essay in my undergraduate classes, and I felt I could acknowledge my privileges. Back in those college days, if I even felt the tempting pull of denial, I had only to think about my friends in my hometown neighborhood. I had witnessed firsthand the oppression they faced. For example, during my eighth-grade year, my best friend, who was black, and I hopped off the city bus at a McDonald's on the west side of the city. One of the customers asked her in a threatening tone what she thought she was doing "on this side of the river." There were plenty of other subtle examples of racial prejudice, hatred, and disadvantage for me to call on from my memory.

Yet something about the atmosphere in my graduate classes made reading the essay on white privilege challenging. I could easily recognize and accept most of the examples of white privilege that were listed, but several of the items seemed particularly untrue for me. For example, McIntosh mentioned, "I can go home from most meetings of organizations I belong to feeling somewhat tied in, rather than isolated, out-of-place, outnumbered, unheard, held at a distance, or feared" (McIntosh 1990, 32). I tried to imagine a time since I had begun college that I could have agreed with the statement and found there was no use in trying to do so.

My classes on poverty were especially challenging. It felt as though people who had never gone hungry were essentially discussing my family, my friends, even me, as though we were all objects. Theories about social structure that tended to focus on only urban isolation or racial discrimination were intertwined with theories of poor peoples' marriage patterns, procreation, work habits, and inability to delay gratification. Sometimes my frustration overcame my feelings of inadequacy and vulnerability, and I expressed my disagreement in class. I did not challenge the theories we discussed; rather, I challenged the ways in which we even bothered to pose the research questions. For example, expert researchers had apparently found that women in low-income neighborhoods were reluctant to get married, and these same researchers determined that these women were responsible for marriage patterns in poor neighborhoods. I nearly choked as I thought back to the vicious fights that girls had over boys in our neighborhood. I personally had had a knife to my neck following the circulation of an incorrect rumor. Each of the girls in my neighborhood prayed that her man would ask for marriage, but these men were "players," and being tied down was not in their plans. (There are many sociological reasons for this behavior on the part of the men, but the middle-class participants in this class on poverty issues were pointing all of the blame toward the "marriage-rejecting" women.) When I shared my firsthand knowledge by presenting a hypothetical scenario, I did not have the credibility to be heard in class. At any rate, personal experience often is not a legitimate basis for disagreement in graduate school, whereas it is a form of truth for poor people.

As I progressed through the first few years of graduate school, I became bolder about discussing my background with select students. When I could be honest, it was easier to talk about the financial concerns I held regarding my family. Although I had some experience interacting with economically advantaged friends in college, I found that I was still learning how to develop friendships with people who seemed so foreign to me. For example, rather than enjoying spontaneous social activities, my new colleagues scheduled "fun" in a day planner. We did not have a lot in common, because they did not eat meat or listen to either of my favorite forms of music. It also felt impossible to become close to some types of graduate students or faculty members. Specifically, there were those who seemed hypocritical, as they were unaware of the irony when they lightly swirled a glass of fine red wine and bemoaned social ills from poverty to infant mortality. After all, they were sitting at a social gathering held in a home that could have graced the cover of *House Beautiful.*

The friendships I formed in graduate school were never quite as comfortable as those I made at home, but I found that I needed to cultivate these graduate-school friendships quickly or I would literally be alone. What was the source of this urgency? The last remnants of long-distance friendships with people from my hometown neighborhood were dying. In ways I could not understand, these old friends who had been so supportive for years found that I had changed too much. I still felt like the street kid standing in line at the Salvation Army for lunch, but they insisted that I had become a different person. They told me that they did not like the way I saw subtle messages about race or gender in children's cartoons. They told me that education had caused me to drift away from God. Caught in the margins between upper-class academe and my poor and working-class roots, I was becoming miserable in a way that compromised my mental health significantly. I was beginning to despise academe, and yet I felt compelled to continue on the career path to which I had committed. I also knew that I could not go home. My friends had become distant beyond the miles between us. My family was in a constant state of crisis that overwhelmed my ability to cope. In fact, my brother David took own life during my time in graduate school.

Three things carried me through the remainder of graduate school. First, my thirteen-year-old sister was arrested for shoplifting. I could not bear to watch her follow a negative life path, so arrangements were made for her to come to live with me. Some of the nagging feelings I had about abandoning my family were alleviated as I took legal custody of one of the children I had previously been responsible for raising. Taking care of my sister was not easy, but it was easier than carrying unbearable guilt. Two years later, my youngest brother also came to live with me. With a graduate assistant's meager income, their presence would mean the accumulation of astronomical student-loan debt. Although I reached the federal maximum in loan debt, I am also grateful that my university allowed expanded budgets for students with dependent expenses. Other institutions of higher education do not necessarily provide student loans that allow for dependents, and it was important for my siblings to live with me in an environment where they gained so much from wealthy school districts, safe neighborhoods, and exposure to edifying experiences. My sister entered college during my seventh year of graduate school.

The second experience to help me through graduate school came when the Upward Bound staff again provided me with invaluable information. They sent me an e-mail message about a conference of working-class academics. The conference description included a focus on topics such as the "imposter phenomenon," alienation from home and family, and resentment and anger over financial disadvantage. Attending the conference allowed me to feel at home with strangers; we had a "silent understanding" that I had come to value in my days with the college counselor. Through the conference and participation in the online discussion group, I gained the strength I needed to feel more comfortable in academe.

The third factor that assisted my completion of the Ph.D. was the support and guidance of my academic adviser and mentor. She is an established, exceptional researcher who managed to stay down-to-earth and accessible. I have little doubt that my attraction to working with her came when I observed her subtle working-class habits and mannerisms. Although we never specifically discussed our individual interpretations of being working class in academe, it seems that we had a "silent understanding." When I began to undercut my own abilities and skills, she pushed me to reach farther than I otherwise would have. For example, the National Institute of Mental Health (NIMH) has a competitive dissertation grant award for people doing research in my field. I really did not believe that I was capable of winning this award, but my adviser provided a great deal of encouragement, so I applied and received the NIMH grant.

There were many nights during graduate school when I walked out to the family-housing parking lot, leaned up against my car, and asked the stars for guidance. Doubt about my ability to complete graduate school was my constant companion. I have completed numerous applications for occupations away from academe; yet these applications were never submitted. I know that I have a great deal of turmoil ahead of me as I encounter the enormous strains of being a new faculty member. Nevertheless, I have been fortunate in that I have many of the supports I need to conquer that hurdle, as well.

Reflecting on my academic and personal chronicle from a child on welfare to self-sufficient faculty member, I realize that my good fortune has been crafted by caring people, innovative yet difficult-to-access social programs, and anti-poverty policies. Of course, I worked hard, but there are so many others with my background and circumstances who were unable to access the supports that would have allowed them to enjoy the same successes. My story of upward mobility is exceptional, not because I am a unique individual, but because so many others do not have the social scaffolding necessary to move up academically or economically.

REFERENCES

Herrnstein, Richard, and Charles Murray. 1994. *The Bell Curve: Intelligence and Class Structure in American Life.* New York: Free Press.
McIntosh, Peggy. 1990. "White Privilege: Unpacking the Invisible Knapsack." *Independent School* 49: 31–33.
Murray, Charles. 1988. "What's So Bad about Being Poor?" *National Review,* vol. 40, 36–39.

ANDREA S. HARRIS

8   Choosing the Lesser Evil
The Violence of the Welfare Stereotype

I WAS NOT born into poverty. In some sense, it might be accurate to say that I was born into a middle-class black family. My father worked at a naval base, and my mother was an accountant. I am the middle child, with a sister before and a brother after me. We had a nice family home, a huge backyard with pear trees, a patio with a built-in grill, Sunday dinners, and family vacations. On the surface, we were a happy, middle-class black family, until I was eleven and my parents finally separated. My father was extremely abusive. I vividly recall one morning when my mother fled the house barefoot and dressed in pajamas in an attempt to get away from my enraged father. She left with the intention of taking refuge at my aunt's house a few blocks away. My dad put me in the car and sped out of the driveway. He turned the corner, and we spotted my mother in tears, running. I watched the scene unfold as if in slow motion: my mother being almost hit by the car, then dragged to the car by my father as she screamed and clawed like a frightened creature. Once in the car, my father repeatedly slapped away her meek pleas for freedom until we arrived at the school parking lot. I watched as she attempted to get the attention of a white woman who was getting out of a nearby car. The woman turned her head without even acknowledging my mother and kept going. Somehow my mother managed to get out the window. My parents ran all through the school, my mom screaming for help, my dad compelled by rage, and me, helpless and frozen with terror and shame. No, I was not born into poverty but into something else that breeds not only poverty but also self-destruction—violence.

Like the presumptions politicians make about poverty, violence is often seen as the result of the victim's own bad decisions. Yet my mother was a victim of violence—victimized within her home by my father and victimized by the social narrative that persuaded her that welfare was only for those women who made bad choices, for those women who were bad people. She so embraced this narrative that, rather than carry the stigma associated with welfare, she stayed in an abusive relationship.

I will never forget the story that she told so many times. Swearing that she would never ask a handout of a white person again, she always spoke with unrelenting conviction when she told the story of how she, at sixteen and pregnant with her oldest child, my sister, went to apply for welfare. After being continuously placed after the white people who came into the office, despite the fact that she was there before them, she finally met with a social worker. My mother described her as a "wrinkled old white woman." After the worker reviewed my mother's forms, she explained that my mother would be eligible for $11 a month in food stamps. Even in Georgia in the 1970s, that amount was not sufficient to provide adequately for a mother and infant. When my mother asked how she was to make it on so small an amount, the woman cruelly lectured my mother on the irresponsibility of "niggas" like her who "gap their legs open" and then fail to take responsibility for their own actions. With no other options, my mother humbly accepted the vouchers and the woman's harsh words.

Although my mother did find a job the same day and later returned the check with a few words of her own, she did not throw away the woman's conceptualization of welfare. She did not challenge the notion that what the woman said was in fact true. I think that it is this experience that crystallized her resistance to seeking aid, even in a situation in which we were all abused first by my father, then by my mother's significant other. She maintained that it was better to be victimized in the privacy of the home than to be demonized publicly and by the entire society.

It is still ironic to me that this same woman is now an adamant opponent of welfare in any form, characterizing the typical welfare recipient in the same way that she was by that "old wrinkled white woman" years ago. Once I was at her home while she visited with one of her friends, an older black woman. As they broached the subject of welfare, I felt myself cringe. I was immediately on edge, anxious to eavesdrop and hear how this woman—who had been abused and without resources, who then abused and allowed her own children to be abused, and who eventually left me at sixteen, permanently displaced—would stand on the issue of welfare. I stood in shock, in complete disbelief, as I listened to my mother declare that "ain't nothing wrong with them women on welfare except they need to get off they ass and go to work."

FIGHTING THE MYTH

I entered the university less than one month after the birth of my daughter. I came to college as a homeless single parent. In the conventional political view, I am another tragic image of the ghetto, poverty, and the dysfunctional single-headed household. Whether such descriptions are applicable to my situation is almost irrelevant, as I am swallowed into the categorical abyss of "unwed black teenage mother." The responsibilities that come with each of the respective titles I bear—mother, student, worker—always seem to conflict with one another. Yet in the context of my status as a welfare recipient, these roles are eclipsed by the pervasive image of the Welfare Queen. It is this myth of the chronic welfare dependent that pervades most political discourse on the subject of welfare reform. It is this myth that circumscribes my reality and pushes to determine my value in the world.

These images have been a source of psychological pain and frustration for me. From welfare offices and family law courts to the university, I am seen and devalued as only an unwed black mother. These simplistic devaluations belie the material conditions of my struggle. For my child and I, I receive a monthly Temporary Aid to Needy Families (TANF) grant in the amount of $440 and $210 in food stamps. The average cost of a one-bedroom apartment in the area, according to current market analysis, is $600 a month. With an eviction notice every month that qualifies me for the rent assistance needed to cover the remaining balance of rent, rotating between paying the heat and the phone bills, using local clothing and food banks, clipping coupons for basic necessities, and often going without, somehow we survive.

Even these minimal supports cost me dearly. I can recall very vividly an early experience I had at the welfare office. The woman behind the counter stood firmly with a look of disdain on her face as she addressed the recipient in line in front of me. When the intake worker spoke, it was as if the young mother before her, instead of being an adult capable of receiving and following instructions, were a child. The intake worker did not volunteer any additional information to assist the woman; instead, she made the process so difficult that it seemed she was guarding the key to the national treasury, as opposed to providing an application for state assistance. Given what I know now of public opinions concerning welfare, it is indeed plausible that the worker understood her duty to be such a guard. After all, welfare recipients are routinely depicted as draining the national treasury.

While I was considering whether to question the worker's obvious rudeness, the young mother (described as "unruly and vulgar") was escorted out of the building by a security guard. I decided to hold my tongue, a strategy that would serve me well in the future. When my turn came, I politely and humbly requested information about applying for assistance. After a staccato series of questions, I was handed three forms. I remember the look on the intake worker's face when I responded to her question about whether I was in a high school or GED program. When I stated that I was attending the university, she looked stunned and incredulous. Obviously doubting the veracity of my claim, the worker quipped, "Well, we'll need proof of that." When I assured her that I could obtain an acceptance letter or a current schedule, she stated sarcastically that my financial worker would have to review my program and determine whether it was acceptable.

One form was to be completed by my daughter's child-care center to confirm what I listed as my activities during my daughter's school hours. (As if I would not be the most reliable person to report my own activities.) Another form was to be completed by my landlord—in this case, University Family Housing. I stood before that financial worker obviously distressed that she wanted me to parade my welfare status to each public space I used: the university, the child-care office, my job, my landlord. I was well aware of the shame I would experience through such a process. Overwhelmed, I asked whether all of this paperwork was really necessary, and the intake worker angrily responded, "We have to confirm anything you tell us. Either you want the child care for working or not." Once again, I bit my tongue. I needed her help to seek safety from a sexually abusive situation, to prevent my infant daughter and I from becoming homeless again, and to change our lives by completing a college degree.

I continued to seek assistance from the welfare office, on and off, for the four years I attended school. After welfare reform went into effect, I was informed that the state's Department of Social and Health Services would not support me if I stayed in school. As if I had committed a crime, the worker who cautioned me that I would be terminated from the welfare program if I chose to attend school (as opposed to working) questioned my "ignorance" in thinking that I was "entitled" to assistance while earning a bachelor's degree. She reminded me that I should have taken up a vocational skill and been satisfied with that.

What is at stake here is the lack of those very choices that bring a woman to the welfare office in the first place. It is assumed that a woman's presence in a welfare office, seeking assistance, is proof of her incompetence and the error of her ways. Thus, welfare caseworkers maintain and limit the options available for each woman who needs aid. In a sense they become judges, assessing not only applicants' financial need, but also their moral states, their intellectual capacities, their ability to think for themselves, and their desire to care for their children. With each visit, they remind us that, had we made the "right" decisions, we would not be there, at their mercy and prey to their judgment.

My position and value as a young, unmarried black mother, was similarly framed in my experiences with the court system. My encounter with family law court first came in 1995. I was eighteen, and my daughter was a newborn. Like many poor and abused women, I went back several times to my daughter's father, finally resolving—as his hands were around my neck and my days-old infant was in my arms—that I had to escape. I had never called the police before, but that time I went so far as to file a petition for protection in county court.

When I stood before the judge, pleading my case, I felt both empowered and powerless. Although I was proud that I had taken an independent step toward freedom and safety, I learned that in the judge's eyes I was reduced to stereotypes about my race, gender, and financial condition. I had wanted so much to have the right kind of family, to be a model of black love, and the thought that I had failed weighed heavily on my mind. The judge made it clear, however, that my commitment to my daughter's and my own safety were irrelevant because I had marked both of us with the stigma of welfare. Rather than focusing on my immediate and urgent need for protection, he lectured me on my need to "get off of welfare."

My concerns and pleas fell on deaf ears on many more occasions. When my daughter's father and I were before the court on the issue of a parenting-plan proposal that gave him weekend visits, I expressed my concern for his lifestyle and its negative impact on our child. Rather than addressing my well-founded fears, the judge proceeded to question what he assumed to have been my affiliation with gangs while I was with my daughter's father. Of course, I never had any such affiliation. What the judge was really questioning was my ability to have a legitimate complaint about the safety of my child, given that I had allegedly put her in harm's way by being on welfare. In his eyes, I was responsible for exposing my daughter both to her father's bad choices and to my own.

In another instance, I addressed my concern that a child in a home frequented by my daughter during paternal visitation shot himself in the stomach with a gun found under a pillow. The judge cynically asked, "Oh, *you* have a problem with guns?" and rolled his eyes upward. Evidently, he felt that as a single, black welfare mother I was cunning and manipulative and could not possibly have a legitimate concern for my child's well-being. My "welfare baby" and I were both marked as disposable, and in his view I was incapable of logical, reasoned, or rational thought. Had I been of a different class, a different race, a different gender, I imagine, the judge would have been concerned about everything from the physical to the emotional well-being of my child and myself. Instead, his framing of my case as that of a welfare mother precluded that possibility even in a place that I had presumed to be a site of "truth" and equity.

On many occasions, judges ridiculed me and lectured me about my status (or lack thereof) as a welfare mother, and, as a result, paid little attention to the accusations of violence from which I sought protection. In fact, in one instance, when I sought a protection order after I had been assaulted, the judge declared that he would not change the visitation schedule because the violence directed toward me had nothing to do with the safety of my child. Charles Murray (1992) argues that welfare irrevocably condemns children. The judge seemed to buy into this notion while dismissing my concerns. He expressed his opinion that I could have no legitimate concerns about my daughter's father and his parenting abilities, because I, as a single black welfare mother, had doomed us both in the first place. When I was before the court one time, I took the opportunity to ask the judge about the appropriate time frame for notification if I was accepted to an out-of-state law school. The judge responded, "*You* are applying to law school?" He proceeded to chuckle with an air of "as if," and then dismissed me by stating, "Worry about that *if* you get there."

Despite the way I have been treated by family, in welfare offices, and even in the courts, I have continued to pursue the education that altered my life. I entered higher education and fought to stay in school because I needed an education. I needed an education to learn, to grow, and to strengthen and hone my thinking, reading, and writing skills. I needed an education to regain self-esteem, purpose, and focus. I needed an education to fight against the debilitating stereotypes that confronted and confounded me at every turn. And finally, I needed an education for the credentials and authority required to change my life and the life of my daughter economically and socially.

Going to school is hard. I am currently a first-year law student, and the work is often staggering, but it is the other battles that erode my stamina. At times I feel as though I have to fight against the world. In any given week I simultaneously do battle with the court system, the welfare department, biased teachers and ignorant students, and damaging public images. Many times, I retreat to the arms of my beautiful and innocent daughter as a much needed refuge against the battering I experience in the world because of my race, my class, and my gender. At times I am overwhelmed and break down in exhaustion and tears. At other times, when everyone rejects, hurts, and denies me, it simply increases my resolve to continue my battle.

Staying alive becomes a challenge unfamiliar to most of my fellow classmates. Often I go to school hungry, overcome with fear for my personal safety and that of my daughter, and exhausted by what feels like a never-ending and unwarranted battle that leaves me scarred and hurt. There are days that we have no electricity in our house and we wear coats that are not quite warm enough for our chilly climate. Yet I persevere, and learn, and became stronger and stronger. While I grow and change, I watch my daughter become a child with a clear and unshakable vision of herself as a good, worthy, and valuable human being.

I live and go to school with dozens of poor women who are similarly fighting to change their lives through education. In sharing resources and child care, my friends and I lean on one another, offering strength for support and shoulders to cry on in times of frustration. "Gotta do what you gotta do," said one of my friends, speaking of our situations as students on welfare. Laughing one minute and angry the next, not a day goes by that we do not remark on how we struggle with the stigma associated with our status as single black welfare mothers and students.

Most often we share our efforts to subvert our status as welfare women, particularly in the grocery store. We laugh at our need to demonstrate that, when using food stamps, we should use our student rather than our county identifications to demonstrate that, although we are on welfare, we are also "doing something" to better ourselves. Yet even this exchange reveals the extent to which we internalize the narrative of the Welfare Queen, desiring to distinguish ourselves from the Other.

It is clear that my body has become the political battleground on which America has waged its war against the poor. Even as I began to identify myself as a single mother, I am conscious of the ways in which my mind is processing how I should preface or qualify the title with redeeming characteristics: I am a poor single mother, but I am a single mother because . . . ; I am a poor single mother, but I am also a student . . . ; I am a single mother, but I am a good parent. On a daily basis I am reminded that I need an explanation. If I can say that I am a single welfare mother because I refused to stay in an abusive and oppressive relationship, or if I can say that I am a single welfare mother but I am also a student, then maybe I can write myself back into social acceptance. Maybe I can surface from the abyss of the category "welfare woman."

In struggling to claim the complexity, the struggle, and the value of my life, I become engaged in an ideological and material battle to resist being submerged or subsumed under my status as a welfare recipient, under the violent stereotype of the Welfare Queen. For as long as the stereotype of the Welfare Queen is alive, I am written out. It does not matter that I am attempting to support a child; it does not matter that I am working and in school. It does not matter that I am escaping abuse and homelessness. It does not matter that others are disabled, in the process of seeking skills, or seeking mental stability. As long as the Welfare Queen reigns in the imagery and presumptions of social narratives, my experiences are not only pushed to the periphery, but like that of many others, they are made invisible. Through education I hope to battle this oppressive stereotype and its oppressive material implications. As an attorney I will fight for poor women and for the equal treatment of people of color. My hope is that I will be able to change the conditions of my family's life while never forgetting who I am or what we have been through.

REFERENCE

Murray, Charles. 1992. "Welfare Hysteria." *New York Times,* 15 September, E1.

SANDY SMITH MADSEN

9   From Welfare to Academe
Welfare Reform as College-Educated
Welfare Mothers Know It

I WAS ON the National Dean's List. I was listed in *Who's Who among Students in American Universities and Colleges.* I was investigated. I was spied on. A welfare investigator came into my home and, after thoughtful deliberation, granted me permission to keep my belongings. Afterward, I began receiving hate mail from the neighbors she had queried. They thought the hours I kept were odd; perhaps I was selling drugs. One anonymous letter writer suggested in explicitly porno-graphic terms that there was one occupation for which I was qualified. Like the witch hunts of old, if a neighbor reports you as a Welfare Queen, the guardians of the state's compelling interest come into your home and interrogate you. While they do not have the right to set your body ablaze on the public square, they can forever devastate heart and soul by snatching away children. Just like police officers, they may use whatever they happen to see, or think they see, against you. Full-fledged citizens have the right to deny an officer entry into their homes unless they possess a search warrant; mothers on welfare fork over citizenship rights for the price of a welfare check. In Tennessee, constitutional rights go for a cash value of $185 per month for a family of three (Urban Institute 1999). The investigation occurred within the first few months of my stint on welfare. It served to put me on notice that I did not possess the price of constitutional rights.

Being a welfare mother and a college student is a schizoid experience. Within academe you gain an enhanced self-esteem; you walk among an elite class. Off campus, you are the underclass. It is common for poor women to dress up in an effort to pass or gain respect by transcending class, but try pulling out food stamps when you are dressed in anything but rags. Welfare mothers are clearly the site of a variation on the same old theme of women who are damned if they do and damned if they don't stay in their place. In the years immediately preceding welfare reform, almost half a million welfare claimants were "out of place," or enrolled in higher education (*Congressional Record* 1994).

Those who accept the dominant construction of welfare mothers as an inherently inferior class of women will hold the view that it is only the very exceptional welfare mom for whom higher education is an option. I submit that the salient difference between welfare mothers who pursue higher education and those who do not is that some have been strong enough to resist the definitions imposed by an overclass that measures the worth and potential of human beings on the basis of rank in class, race, and gender hierarchies. Feminism was a life-saving liberatory theory for me in that it enabled me to reject the battery of psychologically abusive verbal assaults that politicians and poverty "experts" repeatedly fire at women such as myself. Women who internalize the propaganda spawned by the "overclass"—which purports that by virtue of race, class, gender, or status as mother-but-not-wife, one is beyond hope, uneducable, forever excluded from membership in the so-called cognitive elite (Herrnstein and Murray 1994), and thus inherently inferior—will be hard pressed to summon the confidence required to pursue higher education, even if the opportunity should present itself. Yet in the words of the former welfare mom and women's studies scholar C. Ditmar Coffield:

> So much of this welfare reform policy seems to be oblivious to the fact that many welfare recipients would be much better suited as Ph.D. candidates (based on their intellectual potential) than as burger flippers, street sweepers, or housekeepers. The fact that someone doesn't have literacy skills or hasn't taken a high school diploma has a lot more to do with the structure of our educational system; with systematic, institutionalized gender, race, and class oppression and with our propensity toward the reproduction of social, political and economic inequality than it does with their intellectual abilities. (Coffield 1999, 18)

Given the enormity of the obstacles faced by single mothers in the United States, it is remarkable that so many have found their way to higher education. Certainly, the numbers would be even greater if public policy actually encouraged and supported education as the route out of poverty. Instead, U.S. welfare policy assaults such women with a politics of deliberate discouragement. Despite studies that consistently find that higher education leads to higher wages (Spalter-Roth and Hartmann 1991; U.S. Bureau of the Census 1998) and substantial research indicating that post-secondary education is the most certain of paths for welfare moms to lift their families out of poverty (Gittell, Gross, and Holdaway 1993; Gittell, Schehl, and Fareri 1990; Karier 1998; Kates 1991), with few exceptions welfare reform consists of policy that pushes high-school–educated women into jobs with poverty-level wages and provides minimal training for everyone else. The new welfare law's active discouragement of ambitious women has effectively forced tens of thousands, perhaps hundreds of thousands, of poor women to drop out of school and relinquish the dream of a college education (Kahn 1998; Schmidt 1998). Instead, single moms sign up for the low-wage jobs more befitting the all-pervasive image of "welfare mother," as childlike, dependent, ignorant, immoral, and idle woman. These are the very same stereotypes that have been applied to women throughout history. We are still struggling to prove them wrong.

Like roughly half of all mothers on welfare, I went to the welfare office after the dissolution of a nuclear family (McFate 1997, 133), and I went because I simply could not figure out how to provide the attentive care that all children require while working for wages for most of their waking hours. When President Clinton signed the Personal Responsibility and Work Opportunity Reconciliation Act of 1996 (PRWORA), I was entering my senior year at a public university in Tennessee. My daughters and I had been living a rather remarkable life as a household of impoverished, but happy, honor-roll students. My flexible college schedule, financial aid, and the meager welfare subsidy enabled me to drive my children across town to some of the city's best schools. The city did not provide transportation for the students of magnet schools; the city's best schools were, in effect, reserved for families who could afford to have a mother in the home. With the aid of a welfare check, I was just such a mother. I scheduled classes and sporadic paid employment around the lives of my children, drove them across town to three different magnet schools, helped them with homework, and attended school functions. When they were home, I was home. College was family-friendly. Then, on 22 August 1996, Clinton signed the welfare-reform bill and thus joined with conservative forces in the mandate that I end my lazy, immoral ways and get to work.

Adding the mandated work requirement to my weekly schedule as full-time student, sporadic part-time wage earner, and solo caregiver to four daughters was a prescription for failure. I was already functioning in a chronic state of sleep deprivation. Even so, I might have tried it but for the requirements of Learnfare. Like many responsible mothers who find themselves at the mercy of an abusive welfare state, I had gone to considerable trouble to protect my children from the harmful effects of the government-promoted welfare stigma. But Learnfare requires moms to notify schools, at three-month intervals, that their children are members of the inferior welfare class, a class designated by a corps of elite white men and their representatives as beneath them in every way, and thus termed the underclass. The lowered expectations of teachers and the biased treatment accorded such children has been extensively documented. Moreover, the long years of the welfare debate had taken its toll. I was worn down by the verbal abuse hurled down at women such as myself by political elites whom I had once thought of as my elected representatives. An increase in poverty and heartbreak seemed preferable to the increase in intimidation, control, and intrusiveness promised by welfare reform. Convinced that welfare reform would both harm my children and force me out of school, I refused to sign the so-called Personal Responsibility Plan. Instead, I stayed in school and dropped out of welfare. Although this is just what welfare reformers have in mind, and just what they term successful welfare reform, it was a decision that would cost my children dearly.

My conviction that the law would force me into a dead-end job that would neither allow me to support my family, nor permit me to provide the care and supervision that children require, persuaded me that my options were akin to those I face every election year: this evil or that evil. I sent my daughters to live with their father, who was a superior breadwinner but a decidedly inferior caregiver. For the first time in their lives, my girls were forced to spend a great deal of their lives fending for themselves. I worked longer at waged work and devoted far less time to the important work of parenting. In effect, I gave up the costly habit of investing time in the work of caring for children. If it did not pay money or grades that would lead to money, I had no time for it. Alleged experts on women's poverty routinely present mothers who rely on welfare as unfit, or rotten, mothers (Herrnstein and Murray 1994; Murray 1984, 1988)—and welfare policy does its very best to make it so. By the end of that grim year, my daughters had lost their places on the honor roll, and one had come close to death. In a perpetual state of hunger, I went from dress size 12 to size 6 that year; but thin was in, and I was welfare-free. Eventually, I earned a bachelor's degree and a graduate fellowship at a university in another state. The harsh truth is that, although my family was utterly devastated by a law that pretends to be concerned with the welfare of families, my children and I are among the fortunate. For unlike other single-mother families in the grip of an abusive welfare state, my daughters and I evaded homelessness. Unlike some families, we are all still living.

AGAINST ALL THE ODDS: WELFARE MOTHERS IN ACADEME

In self-defense, I began to look around for other women like me. I found a copy of Erika Kates's (1991) study of welfare-funded college students in Massachusetts. The women in that document became my support group. Inspired by the work of Kates, I began my own case study. The flyers I posted at three colleges revealed that I, the researcher, was a former welfare mom. More than thirty women responded; most said they had come forward only because I was one of them. All but a handful of these women went to great lengths to hide their stigmatized identity from the college community; some hid it from neighbors, friends, and even family. There are few advocates for mothers on welfare in conservative Southern towns such as the one in which I lived. The very same welfare claimants who, with a measure of support, would be transformed into activists are instead women who practice the survival strategy of hiding their stigmatized identity, passing for respectable women. Because of the limitations of my circumstances, I was able to interview only twelve women. The interviews began in the fall semester of 1996, while Tennessee was in the first flush of welfare reform, and continued over a period of two years.

Much of welfare policy, reformed or otherwise, has the effect of "outing" welfare mothers and their children, or denying them the constitutional right of privacy. The mandate to get a job, or Workfare, requires documentation in the form of a letter from an employer rather than, say, a paycheck stub. It seems unlikely that mothers on welfare will pretend to have jobs so their benefits will be cut. A paycheck stub would both fulfill the required documentation and allow mothers and children some measure of privacy. Several of the women I interviewed were required to submit letters from landlords rather than rent receipts. Women who live in subsidized housing are subjected to Tidyfare. Officials routinely inspect the homes of poor women; if the homes fail to measure up to government standards of tidiness, eviction or homelessness is the penalty. A number of the women I interviewed spoke about the stress and intrusiveness that meeting government standards of good house-keeping added to their families' lives. But no provision was more offensive to these women than Learnfare. Learnfare is the welfare regulation that requires school attendance of children to be "monitored and enforced." Before visits to the welfare office, mothers are required to visit their children's schools and obtain signatures on forms documenting school attendance, which they must then present to the welfare office. Learnfare requires a memo from the school rather than a report card. A child who fails to attend school "regularly" will cost her family 20 percent of their cash benefits (Tennessee Department of Human Services 1996b, 18). Failure to comply with any aspect of the Personal Responsibility Plan can result in total ineligibility (Tennessee Department of Human Services 1996b). The mothers I interviewed were keenly aware of the dangers of such policy. As Nora (1997) pointed out, "Now that I have to go and let the schools know my children are on welfare, the teachers probably treat them differently, think less of them, expect that they won't be as smart or as well-behaved." The absence of privacy or confidentiality was a prevalent theme found in all the interviews. In Charlotte's words,

> Everyone has to know that you are on welfare. When you go to work, you have to tell your employer, "Well, excuse me, but I'm on welfare and could you write me a letter?" I could show them a paycheck stub, but that might allow me to have some dignity. And even that's not enough for them. Every time I get re-certified, every three months, I have to get someone in my children's schools to sign a piece of paper saying that my children are really going to school. As if I'd keep them home! So my children are stigmatized, too; everyone in the school knows they're on welfare. There is no such thing as confidentiality when you're on welfare. (Charlotte 1997)

Several of the women had entered college under official government programs of the pre–welfare-reform era and were consequently exposed as second-class college students by the requirement to obtain professors' signatures as proof of class attendance. Grade reports would not suffice. In my own case, the freedom to perform almost all of my studies at home made it possible for me to be both serious student and attentive parent. For a number of these women, the government's unfamiliarity with maternal thought and practice, as well as its propensity for surveillance, made this impossible. Instead, mothers were forced to study on campus, under supervision. A number of the women eluded the state's efforts to expose their stigmatized identity to the community. Two women hid their identity as college students from the welfare office; one forged her professors' signatures; and one responded to Learnfare by home-schooling her child. Three women hid their status as welfare mothers even from parents and family members. There were no economic gains to be had from any of these tactics. Rather, the women took these actions for the purpose of sparing themselves and protecting their children from a measure of the public humiliation that welfare policy seems designed to inflict.

Like the national welfare population, and in stark contrast to the welfare propaganda, the women in my study are diverse in terms of age, race, and socioeconomic background (McFate 1997). Five are African American; seven are white. Their work histories ranged from two to twenty-six years. Welfare reformers' insistence that poor moms are women who just will not work stands in stark contrast to the wealth of longitudinal studies that have "firmly established that the vast majority of both black and white recipients have had substantial experience in the labor force" (Edin and Harris 1999, 271). Substantial research reveals that when low-wage jobs fail to support women's families, or when the conflict between the demands of work and family threatens the welfare of children, women privilege the needs of children by returning to the welfare office (Edin and Harris 1999; Edin and Lein 1997). According to data issued by the state of Tennessee, at the outset of welfare reform, 90 percent of the state's welfare claimants had a work history (Tennessee Department of Human Services 1996a, 7). Moreover, the average welfare claimant was not a teenage mother. The average age of the Tennessee welfare claimant was thirty-two (Tennessee Department of Human Services 1996a, 7). The respondents' ages in my study ranged from twenty-one to forty-nine. Seven of the women were divorced, and five had never married. The educational level of their parents ranged from the eighth grade to the Ph.D; five had one or more parents who held college degrees. Before welfare reform dramatically reduced the welfare rolls, some 57 percent of the adult welfare population had a high-school education or better, and 13 percent of these had attended college (McFate 1997). Thus, 57 percent were at least minimally qualified for higher education.

Tennessee calls its brand of welfare reform Families First. Lest anyone doubt what kind of families are "first," Tennessee's variation of Bridefare stipulates that moms who marry may remain on welfare with a higher income than the more needy single moms (Tennessee Department of Human Services 1996b, 18). The state offers rewards to men who marry mothers on welfare: Child-support debts are forgiven. But if the marriage should end, the men are again subject to state prosecution (Tennessee Department of Human Services 1996b, 18). There is no provision for forgiving tuition dollars for women who would choose higher education over marriage as the path to economic self-sufficiency. For most of these women, marriage was the problem that brought them to the welfare office. Divorce law is such that "nearly 40 percent of divorced mothers end up in poverty" (Williams 2000, 115). For Nora (1997), "Domestic violence made marriage intolerable. I used welfare to escape a marriage with a controlling, intimidating, and violent husband." Charlotte also used welfare as a refuge from domestic violence. In her words, "Domestic abuse is no big deal to DHS [the Department of Human Services]. I was beaten so badly I had a broken hand, and my back was dislocated. I wasn't going to raise my children in a home like that, but I raise them in poverty. Which of these is the lesser of the two evils?" (Charlotte 1997).

The women talked at length about their commitments to and concerns about higher education. Expressing strong desires to pursue higher education as the path to jobs that would support their families, most said there was no time in their busy lives even for dating. In Sarah's words, "Women are the role models in my family. Women keep the family and kids together. I have these kids to raise and school to finish. I have no interest in marriage" (Sarah 1997). For most of these twelve women, college was a lifelong dream, but for Elizabeth it was never perceived as a possibility.

> I'm an honor student. Why did I make Cs and Ds in high school? I was up until 1 A.M. . . . studying, but my parents were telling me I was stupid and worthless. They wanted a boy. I heard it all my life, fought it all my life. I still hear it in my head, the voices telling me I'm stupid, worthless, and not wanted. Going to school and seeing that I can make these grades

helps to slow the remark down, I don't hear it so often. I never thought of going to college. I got married right after high school. I traded one hell for another. (Elizabeth 1997)

Elizabeth's husband struck her in the abdomen with his fist when she was seven months pregnant. She lost the baby but remained with her abuser because, "I couldn't think of anyplace to go." Eventually she would go to the welfare office. Although some welfare offices attempt to screen for domestic abuse and promise to offer supportive services, both the intrusiveness and the stigmatization of welfare have increased to such an extent that many women, like Elizabeth, will not "think of anyplace to go." As Ann Withorn points out, "The worse the system treats people the less they use it; women return to batterers, take jobs with hours that put kids at risk, move back to families whose earlier dysfunctions had already made them vulnerable" (Withorn 1999, 2). Six of the twelve women I interviewed had sought refuge in the welfare office from domestic violence. In a study of welfare-funded college graduates in Tennessee, 31 percent admitted to a history of domestic violence (Gittell, Gross, and Holdaway 1993).

The topic of discouragement, or even hostility, in the welfare office surfaced time and time again. Like the women in Kates's study, some of the women said that they had encountered helpful and kind caseworkers, but such encounters were presented as exceptional. Most were routinely rotated from caseworker to caseworker; they did not see the same worker for more than three visits. During my own years as a mother on welfare, I speculated that this is a practice designed explicitly to discourage workers from coming to care about the welfare of the women and children over whom they wield power. According to Nora:

> Since DHS found out I was in school, they have not been helpful in any way. One semester I only had classes on Mondays, so they scheduled all my appointments on Mondays. They send you a notice telling you when to show up. If you have something else to do, like go to class or work, well, too bad. The last time, I called to change the appointment because I was supposed to be at work and I got their voice box. They never answer the phone. I left a message. They didn't call me back; they never do. I haven't gotten a check for two months. (Nora 1997)

Two women reported that they had lost benefits for sixty days because they went to class or work instead of welfare appointments. One woman lost benefits for two months because her baby was not up to date on his immunizations. The infant was in the hospital, in a coma. Welfare literature issued by the state describes Families First as policy that aims to enhance self-esteem and build self-confidence (Tennessee Department of Human Services 1996a, 3). Yet in Nora's view, it is college rather than any version of welfare that enhances self-esteem:

> Welfare beats us down. I had to get counseling last year from the stress of being in school and moving twice in two months. They put us in the projects. When I was home my children and I were with the worst of society; when I was at school I was around the best of society. My driving force is the dream of getting a home for my children. College has taught me the value of community. (Nora 1997)

Time limits combined with work requirements ensure that few economically disadvantaged single moms will find their way to higher education. Tennessee welfare reform mandates an eighteen-month consecutive time limit and a lifetime limit of five years. When Families First was first implemented, college students were required to fulfill work requirements of twenty hours per week (many states require thirty to forty hours). Elizabeth's waged work and college schedule equaled a sixty-plus hour week, excluding time for family-care work. She lost her place on the honor roll, and her children, deprived of care, developed behavioral problems. Toward the end of the first semester of welfare reform, the forty-nine-year-old mother of three collapsed in exhaustion and was unable to go either to school or to her job. In response to complaints by professors, state officials implemented the policy of counting one hour of study per class hour as fulfillment of the work requirement, resulting in a work requirement of ten to twelve hours per week. But this policy varied from caseworker to caseworker and from semester to semester. Some of the women were subsequently required to fulfill a twenty-hour work requirement; others completed semesters in which they were free from the work requirement. Charlotte gives an account of her experience with the twelve-hour work requirement:

> You get home from school, you get the kids fed. You make sure they get their homework because you cannot put yourself first, you have to put the children first. Maybe you do some laundry, maybe you break up a fight. Then it's time for you to go to work. You get off at 9 or 9:30 P.M., you come home. When do you have time to study? When do you have time to spend with your children? You're worn out. You study until 2 or 2:30, and then fall asleep in class the next day. I pay the babysitter $10 a

night so I can work three hours a night at $4.75 an hour. I make $14.25; that leaves $4.25 to pay for the gas to and from work and to take the babysitter home. But hey, I'm working. I won't get thrown off the system! Welfare does not agree with education; they want to throw you into a dead-end job and get their statistics up. It's like this article in the *Tennessean:* "Further Drop in Welfare Rolls Pays Dividends." Yeah, but it doesn't say what it pays the children. (Charlotte 1997)

By the summer of 1998, six of the women had earned degrees and left the welfare rolls. Nora, who had juggled caring for a seriously ill baby with earning a master's degree, was employed at a beginning annual salary of $28,000. She bought her dream house. Three of the six were in graduate school and had replaced welfare grants with fellowships and assistantships. The remaining two were earning annual salaries of $20,000 and $24,000. This puts them in the same league with most full-time employed women, 60 percent of whom earn less than $25,000 a year (Williams 2000, 83). There was a general consensus among the women that if welfare reform had come along just a little sooner, they would not have realized their dreams of a college education. Of the remaining six women, four were still in school, and all but one were off welfare because their children had begun receiving the disability benefits for which they had long waited. One was a participant in a state-sponsored experiment and exempt from many regulations. As for the last two, one woman disappeared, and one quit school. Onerous welfare-reform regulations on top of poor health and the absence of social support, or even a supportive family, was Elizabeth's undoing.

The last time I spoke with Elizabeth she had been eliminated from the welfare rolls and was looking for a second job. Although the state offers a temporary or transitional child-care subsidy, the difficulty of finding reliable and safe child care—as well as paying for even a portion of the care for three children—is such that she planned to do what increasing numbers of mothers must do: let children fend for themselves. The provision of temporary child care seems to be based on the presumption that single mothers will soon be in a position to purchase child care on their own, or that a "push" off of the welfare rolls and into the labor market is all that women need, as it is "laziness" or absence of motivation that stands in the way of economic independence. Yet studies consistently find that women cycle between welfare and work because the low wages earned by the majority of all employed women do not support families (Edin and Harris 1999; Gittell, Gross, and Hold-away 1993; IWPR 1995; Spalter-Roth et al. 1992). Full-time employed mothers earn 60 percent of the wages of full-time employed fathers (Williams 2000, 2). Unlike fathering, mothering is a disability in the labor market, even to the extent of reducing women's wages, and this holds true "even after adjustments for prior experience" (Christopher et al. 1999, 8). Higher education is the surest path to closing this variation of the sex–wage gap.

Contrary to the premise of welfare reform, and in spite of a work history encompassing some two decades, Elizabeth has never gained economic independence from wage work. She has never earned a "family wage." Although higher education would vastly improve Elizabeth's ability to meet her family's economic needs, she is one of tens of thousands of mothers on welfare who have been forced out of school by welfare-reform policies that are seldom willing to acknowledge that either college or caring for families is work. Long before Elizabeth gave up on her dream of a college education, she worried that this event would come to pass:

> My children are why I'm here. I'm going to do my best to take care of them. It's like I told them. If they weren't here, I'd work a forty-hour job for [minimum wage]. I could live on that, but I can't support three children with a minimum-wage job. When they asked me to sign [the Personal Responsibility Plan], it was a slap in the face. I wouldn't be on welfare if I weren't a responsible mother. I eat one meal a day so that my kids can eat three. If I have to quit school and go to work at two jobs, who will raise my children? (Elizabeth 1996)

Elizabeth's pursuit of higher education was discouraged by both individual welfare workers and a welfare policy that is far more concerned with filling low-wage service-industry jobs than it is with supporting programs that will ensure the long-term well-being of families. Elizabeth, like the other women in my study, expressed anger and distrust toward a government that structures social support in ways that seem to express a determination to make single mothers fail in their aspirations to be both good providers and good mothers. As a full-time college student and solo mother to three, Elizabeth was overburdened by responsibility before welfare reform came along and added yet more hardship with the mandate of "personal responsibility."

All but those women forced to study on campus stressed that what they valued most about college was that it was family-friendly. They chose classes that would allow them to be home when children were home, they studied at home, and when children were not in school, they accompanied their mothers to classes. Higher education offers the perk of allowing single moms to buy time to care for young children. For by the time moms are ready to enter the labor market, children are four to five years older and thus far less vulnerable to the dangers of self-care or to the substandard child care generally available for poor children (Madsen 1998b). In fact, college-educated mothers serve as important role models for poor children. Few social programs offer the promise of alleviating the shamefully high U.S. child poverty rate that higher education for economically disadvantaged parents offers. As in the Kates study, a number of the women in my study spoke at length about the positive impact their own education had on their children. As Elizabeth explained, "That first semester I had a 3.9 average. I showed that [grade report] to [my children]. They said, 'Wow, you haven't been in school for twenty-five years and look at you!' [After that] their grades shot straight up" (Elizabeth 1997). Nora expressed similar sentiments:

> My children love school. My daughter is in the ninetieth percentile or above in the TCAP test and the ninety-ninth percentile in spelling. She is always sitting around reading. They see me studying. They know they are going to college; we talk about it all the time. It is just what they expect to do. Seeing me go to college makes them want to go. (Nora 1997)

CONCLUSION

Contrary to the stereotypes that paint mothers on welfare as lazy and inferior inhabitants of an alleged underclass, mothers have struggled valiantly to use welfare as a ticket to higher education for a minimum of some four decades now (Jensen 1995; West 1981). While political elites and poverty experts have gone about the business of spreading stories of immoral and idle Welfare Queens, untold numbers of mothers on welfare have quietly surmounted the arduous obstacles imposed by both poverty and welfare regulations to better the lives of their families through higher education. With the aid of a welfare check, poor mothers have transformed themselves into taxpayers with double and quadruple their former incomes. While welfare reform's work-first mandate forces women to leave welfare for low-waged jobs, higher education enables women and children to leave both welfare and poverty.

The transformative powers of higher education are certainly not limited to material gains; studies find that children's educational aspirations rise alongside the educational attainment of their mothers (Gittell, Gross, and Holdaway 1993; Kates 1991).

The national welfare law's restriction of education to one year of vocational education and insistence on the value of a job, any job, for a population made up almost entirely of mothers who care for children without adequate support from fathers, makes it all too evident that welfare policy has been created without so much as a thought to gender equity. A scant thirty years ago, the gender order was such that women were routinely denied jobs because they were mothers of small children. Times have changed, and today welfare reform mandates that poor mothers of children as young as three months old report to jobs. Yet the law does nothing to protect mothers from losing jobs because of sick or needy children's unrelenting demands for attentive parental care. Jobs that offer the family-friendly benefits so necessary to the health and well-being of women's families are invariably jobs that require a college education.

Today welfare reform has emerged as the greatest of obstacles to the efforts of poor women to attain economic independence through virtually the only path available to women: the pursuit of higher education. Time limits and wage-work requirements have made the once difficult task of succeeding in college—in spite of poverty, family responsibilities, and intrusive welfare regulations—well-nigh impossible (Madsen 1998a). Welfare law's insistence that single mothers must balance college and family work with wage work is policy that forces women out of higher education and condemns their families to lifetimes of poverty. The discouragement of higher education is, in fact, policy that undermines welfare reform's own goal of economic self-sufficiency.

Despite the stereotypes, untold numbers of "mothers have not yet been permanently damaged by the psychologically abusive assaults on their character inherent in welfare policy. Many still have the confidence, intelligence, motivation, and perseverance required for higher education" (Madsen 1998a). We may never know how many of the hundreds of thousands of mothers on welfare who were enrolled in higher education when welfare reform hit have been forced to give up the dream of higher education and, with it, the possibility of offering their children lives free from poverty. Certainly, there are vast numbers of worthy women who have never glimpsed the opportunity to set foot into the citadel of higher education merely because they are mothers rather than fathers. My own mother was one.

I am what welfare reformers like to term an intergenerational single mother. While my father went to college on the GI Bill, my mother aided and supported him by working for women's wages outside the home and working at women's unwaged work inside the home. As luck would have it, the government subsidy went to the wrong parent. My mother did not get a return on her costly investment. After years of domestic abuse, she traded in her socially approved status as wife for a status that in her day was stigmatized to a degree rivaling that of today's welfare mother. She became a divorcee. Although my father quickly remarried, my mother did not view marriage as quite the bargain that he judged it. She preferred her independence, even at the cost of poverty and stigma. Without any aid from my government-subsidized, college-educated father, she raised her children on women's wages. She never experienced the humiliation of welfare. Instead, she spent a lifetime in the pink-collar workforce earning poverty wages and training men, one after another, for the job of being her superior.

My mother had precious little time for the important and thoughtful work of mothering. She is white. If she had been black, she most certainly would not have held that particular job in our Southern town; her work would have been harder and more thankless, and I would have received even less parental care. It is this long and remarkably unacknowledged legacy of gender, class, and racial oppression that lies behind what welfare reformers like to point to as the intergenerational poverty of single mothers. They say we make "poor choices." My mother's poor choice was that of bowing to custom and following the traditional script of forgoing her own dreams of higher education and meaningful work and instead assuming the wifely virtue of privileging and supporting the dreams and aspirations of her husband. More often than not, the poor choices made by mothers on welfare are much the same as the "choices" presented to my mother. Our poor choices are merely the consequences of a long legacy of sexist, racist, and classist oppression. My economically disadvantaged white mother was every bit as locked out of the citadel of higher education as were the elite white women of the nineteenth century. Welfare reformers seem bound and determined to continue this tradition.

Virginia Woolf spoke of the connection between women's long history of economic poverty and educational deprivation, observing that, "Intellectual freedom depends upon material things.... And women have always been poor, not for two hundred years merely, but from the beginning of time. Women have had less intellectual freedom than the sons of Athenian slaves" (Woolf 1957 [1929], 108). The intergenerational poverty of women is, of course, rooted in this long tradition. As Woolf observed, throughout all of history, mothers have rarely been in a position to bequeath wealth to daughters. Instead, they have inherited and bequeathed a status that is the consequence of a systemic oppression that has long awarded higher education and its fruits to fathers rather than to mothers, to whites rather than to racial or ethnic minorities, and to the wealthy rather than to the economically disadvantaged. The axes of race, class, and sex oppression interlock nowhere quite so well as in the welfare mother.

My mother followed the path so esteemed by welfare reformers—that of personal responsibility, or a lifetime of low-wage work and educational deprivation. The only responsible parent I ever knew, she was unable to bequeath to her children the fruits of higher education. Without the aid of welfare, I would have done little more than follow in her path. The lessons learned from the experience of being a stigmatized U.S. welfare mother on one hand and an esteemed college student on the other are enough to empower the most oppressed among us. Educating welfare mothers is the stuff of revolutions; it is the work of building a just and humane society, a society that truly values and respects the potentiality of all life. Promoting access to higher education for the mothers of poor children will surely hasten the day when this nation will look back on an era in which one out of every seven Americans lived in poverty with a horror akin to that with which we now view the days when women were chattel, black people were slaves, and only the propertied class of white men held citizenship rights. Mothers on welfare need and deserve support and encouragement to pursue higher education. As long as it is mothers who are the primary caregivers for poor children, educating mothers will remain the most prudent of paths toward the elimination of poverty and the elevation of the species.

REFERENCES

Charlotte (pseud.). 1997. Interview by the author. Tape recording. Murfreesboro, Tenn., 20 March.

Christopher, Karen, Paula England, Katherine Ross, Tim Smeeding, and Sara McLanahan. 1999. "The Sex-Gap in Poverty in Modern Nations: Single Motherhood, the Market, and the State." Working paper no. 3, Joint Center for Poverty Research, 12 November.

Coffield, C. Ditmar. 1999. "'Manpower Placement' and 'Comprehensive Training': The Impact of a 'Work First' Model." Paper presented at the 29th Urban Affairs Association Annual Meeting.

Congressional Record. 1994. 103rd Cong., 2nd sess., Vol. 140, pt. 35.

Edin, Kathyrn, and Kathleen Mullan Harris. 1999. "Getting Off and Staying Off: Racial Differences in the Work Route off Welfare." Pp. 270–301 in *Latinas and African American Women at Work: Race, Gender, and Economic Inequality,* ed. Irene Browne. New York: Russell Sage Foundation.

Edin, Kathryn, and Laura Lein. 1997. *Making Ends Meet: How Single Mothers Survive Welfare and Low-Wage Work.* New York: Russell Sage Foundation.

Elizabeth (pseud.). 1996. Interview by the author. Tape recording. Murfreesboro, Tenn., 16 November.

———. 1997. Interview by the author. Tape recording. Murfreesboro, Tenn., 8 February.

———. 1998. Interview by the author. Tape recording. Murfreesboro, Tenn., 2 May.

Gittell, Marilyn, Jill Gross, and Jennifer Holdaway. 1993. *Building Human Capital: The Impact of Post-Secondary Education on AFDC Recipients in Five States.* New York: Howard Samuels State Management and Policy Center, City University of New York.

Gittell, Marilyn, Margaret Schehl, and Camille Fareri. 1990. *From Welfare to Independence: The College Option.* New York: Howard Samuels State Management and Policy Center, City University of New York.

Herrnstein, Richard J., and Charles Murray. 1994. *The Bell Curve: Intelligence and Class Structure in American Life.* New York: Free Press.

Institute for Women's Policy Research (IWPR). 1995. *Welfare to Work: The Job Opportunities of AFDC Recipients.* Washington, D.C.

Jensen, Rita Henley. 1995. "Welfare: Exploding the Stereotypes." *Ms. Magazine,* July–August, 56–61.

Kahn, Karen. 1998. "Workfare Forces Single Mothers to Abandon College Education." *Sojourner: The Woman's Forum* 24, no. 2: 31–33.

Karier, Thomas. 1998. *Welfare Graduates: College and Financial Independence.* New York: Jerome Levy Economics Institute, Bard College.

Kates, Erika. 1991. *More Than Survival: Higher Education for Low Income Women.* Washington, D.C.: Center for Women's Policy Studies.

Madsen, Sandy Smith. 1998a. "A Welfare Mother in Academe." *Chronicle of Higher Education,* 31 July, A44.

———. 1998b. "Education Ends Welfare." *New York Times,* 26 July, A14.

McFate, Katherine. 1996. "Struggling to Survive: Welfare, Work, and Lone Mothers." In *American Women: Where We Stand, Women and Work, 1996–1997,* ed. Cynthia Costello and Barbara Krimgold. New York: Norton.

Murray, Charles. 1984. *Losing Ground: American Social Policy, 1950–1980.* New York: Basic Books.

———. 1988. "What's So Bad about Being Poor?" *National Review,* vol. 40, no. 21, 28 October, 36(5).

Nora (pseud.). 1997. Interview by the author. Tape recording. Nashville, Tenn., 2 May, 14 June.

Sarah (pseud.). 1997. Interview by the author. Tape recording. Nashville, Tenn., 4 March.

Schmidt, Peter. 1998. "States Discourage Welfare Recipients from Pursuing Higher Education." *Chronicle of Higher Education,* 23 January.

Spalter-Roth, Roberta, and Heidi Hartmann. 1991. *Increasing Working Mothers' Earnings.* Washington, D.C.: Institute for Women's Policy Research.

Spalter-Roth, Roberta, Heidi Hartmann, and Linda Andrews. 1992. *Combining Work and Welfare; An Alternative Anti-poverty Strategy.* Washington, D.C.: Institute for Women's Policy Research.

Tennessee Department of Human Services. 1996a. "Families First: Tennessee's Welfare Reform Plan." Brochure, Nashville, September.

———. 1996b. "Welfare Reform in Tennessee: Families First." Brochure, Nashville, September.

U.S. Bureau of the Census. 1998. "Educational Attainment in the United States: March 1998" (online). P20:513. Available at: <http://www.census.gov/dcmd/www/embargo/embargo.html> (viewed 15 September).

Urban Institute. 1999. "TANF Income Calculator" (online). Available at: <http://newfederalism.urban.org/incalc2/ICStep1.cfm> (viewed 12 October).

West, Guida. 1981. *The National Welfare Rights Movement: The Social Protest of Poor Women.* New York: Praeger.

Williams, Joan. 2000. *Unbending Gender: Why Family and Work Conflict and What to Do about It.* New York: Oxford University Press.

Withorn, Ann. 1999. "This Is an Emergency: Welfare Reform, the 'Shame on Cellucci Eight,' and What I Learned in Prison." *Sojourner: The Women's Forum* 24, no. 5: 22–23.

Woolf, Virginia. 1957 (1929). *A Room of One's Own.* San Diego: Harcourt Brace.

LETICIA ALMANZA

10   Seven Years in Exile

A Saint broken in half
A yelping dog with ribs protruding
A candle burning its last breath
A siren sound awakes the dead.

"A SIREN SOUND AWAKES THE DEAD" echoed through the room. I had just finished the reading of my poetry at the university, and I had carefully selected this ending to my reading. The echo lured me like Odysseus into a juxtaposition with today's siren sound, alerting me of danger. It is a danger in our society to come out and expose your Otherness. It is a danger to rub against the grain. I am a Mexican American woman who was raised in intergenerational poverty. All my life I have lived under systems of oppression that have stifled me, that have inscribed on me the label of Other. I have been trapped in the dichotomy of Western thought, the ideology that has refused to embrace differences, separating itself through an imposition of superiority in white and privileged America.

To be Mexican, to have the Mexican accent, to be poor, to be a woman—all shake the walls of the hegemony that sustain its power. This structure makes it imperative to suppress and oppress in order to buttress the superstructure. With reason, Gloria Anzaldúa exhorts in *Borderlands/La Frontera: The New Mestiza,* "The dominant white culture is killing us slowly with its ignorance . . . we have never been allowed to develop unencumbered" (Anzaldúa 1987, 86). In elementary school, my native Spanish tongue was deemed unfit. I was branded retarded. I was considered to be a slow learner because of my inability to speak the language of the dominant culture. This supposed connection between speaking English and intellect is an endemic notion in America, certainly one that thrives in the Southwest. I am also a Native American, yet a non-native American, because I was born in Mexico, another suppression. I was born poor to migrating parents. There were times that I wore rags and torn shoes to school, dragging my leg across the pavement, like a wooden leg, to keep the broken soles of my shoes from flapping. Yet, I must pretend that my poverty is nonexistent because I live in a wealthy country. We Americans freely criticize every economic system but refuse to break through the mirror and see our own people, the poor, with the excuse that there is a welfare system, which is really only a pat on our backs to make us feel better about our own exploitation of others. Once a professor of economics told our class, "You have to admit, [capitalism] is still the best economic system in the world." Yes, it is, if you are not the one dragging your leg across the pavement.

I have been imprisoned even by my own Mexican culture, where cycles are repeated in the subjugation of women. The job of *la mujer* is to reproduce, take care of the man, nurture him, *dandole teta*. All these suppressions began to surface that day I read my poetry aloud at the university. I found an avenue, academe. But I also began to realize the ways that academe had shut the doors on this poor Mexican woman, the ways that my breath had been strangled, the ways that my voice had been silenced. I was kept in the desert, marginalized, castigated for being different because of their "ignorance."

We find ourselves trapped in the imprisoning dichotomy of Western thought. Through education I was given a ticket out; I was shown another option. That is, I began to see that I could abandon the erroneous ideology that reinforces hierarchies, which, simply put, is the deeply engraved institution of Western thought rooted in prejudice against anything different. But I was different. I was inscribed as different. I had been crossing borders literally and figuratively all my life. But when the borders can no longer define, a new discourse emerges that eliminates the boundaries, transcending duality, creating what Anzaldúa terms a *mestiza* consciousness. Speaking about *la mestiza*, she says: "She learns to juggle cultures. She has a plural personality, she operates in a pluralistic mode ... [because] she has discovered that she can't hold concepts or ideas in rigid boundaries. . . . Rigidity means death" (Anzaldúa 1987, 79). In essence, *la mestiza* is a deconstruction; she is the master and the slave, the synthesis of duality that can deliver the prisoner from dichotomous Western thought. I am bringing something back from the desert, a call to restoration through the juncture of my severed parts.

I always wanted to be a messenger. I was a middle child in a poor Mexican family of seven children. My mother was from the city and my dad from the *rancho*. When I was ten years old, we migrated to the United States, crossing borders once or twice a year to visit relatives, which somehow marked my psyche in a twofold way. There was the degrading, dehumanizing way in which I had to produce some magical papers that were supposed to grant me access back into the United States. And there was also the uncertainty of the borderline, the blurry, murky waters of the Rio Bravo, which most people know as the Rio Grande. It was normative for me to juggle cultures.

So when I began school in the United States unable to speak a word of English, I found adaptability to come quite naturally; disarray was my way of life. In spite of public humiliations—branding me as a slow learner, stupid, a waste of education dollars—I managed to learn the language and compete academically with the rest of the student body. I think, in fact, that I saw the adversity as an assurance that I was on the right track. I made it my goal to prove to the "ignorant" forces around me that I was not "retarded."

In the culture of the Mexicans in America, the "ignorant" forces extend to our families, especially regarding women. This force is a system that is intended to keep women tractable, subjugated to a patriarchy locked in traditions and cycles. After seeing my older sisters drop out of school, my dad seemed almost pleased. They could now help around the house, perhaps even work at some minimum-wage job to help the family financially. My sisters were married before they were nineteen. Dad was just waiting for the day I would follow suit, in my wedding dress, repeating the vows. But when that did not occur, and I concentrated on schoolwork instead, my dad developed an animosity toward me. To point out a marking instance, when I graduated from high school, my parents did not attend the ceremony; only my two younger sisters came to witness my success. In fact, my dad had us walk alone to the ceremony and back, in the dark. That ceremony came with a price. It represented the many times I had steered away from my dad to complete homework assignments surreptitiously with the bathroom light as my only witness. I was preparing myself for my college venture, a goal that came as a huge blow to my father, a blow that seemingly hit him from the back—or, rather, from the inside.

The constraints and restraints—or better said, *la rienda*—on a Mexican woman have been well established, cemented with tradition. The woman serves the man. Her purpose is to reproduce and to nurture the man, take care of the children, take care of the home—domestically, of course. Thus, I do not know how the idea entered my head of going away to college. But it did. It is critical to understand that, in my culture, for a woman to leave the house means that she is getting married. Daughters do not leave the house to live somewhere else unless it is under the protection of another man—at least, it had not happened in my family until I did so. If I left the home outside marriage, I could easily be considered a *wila*, a woman of the street. It took everything from me to stand before my father and declare, "I am going away to college." I knew that I was refusing the rules of our culture, challenging its authority and its premise. It was my own form of civil disobedience.

However, one of the pluralistic forms that splits *la mestiza*, is that, although we are in the business of breaking paradigms, we feel the pain in the splitting process. My dad's resistance to education had its grounding somewhere. Together, my father and mother amalgamated seven years of education in Mexico and worked at minimum-wage jobs here in the United States. They experienced degradation on a daily basis. I, with my books and my cap and gown, represented the same people who oppressed them. My dad had been knocked down so many times by our class system that he had resigned himself to looking at it from the bottom up. Every day, my dad returned home from work angry, filthy, muddy. I could read in his eyes, "wretched existence," and I would wonder, "who disparaged him now?" He was made to feel small and inferior, and he brought that home with him.

Once, my dad told my mom that some kid had called him a wetback. On that day and many to come, he was angry with the world. To my father, who was literally in the hole he had excavated—muddied, unable to speak English and fight back, in essence mute—the word represented him as a dehumanized commodity: the forgotten, the poor, the trampled, *el mojado, la burla de nuestra nación* (the wetback, the scorn of our nation). Thus, unable to channel the source of his grief, my dad wore pain like a girdle wrapped around his heart, unaware of how to release it. He tightened it even more by inflicting pain on the people he loved the most, *su familia.* The episodes of our dramatic home life bolstered my resolution to continue my education.

The familial forces were not the only ones that hindered my path to academe. In "A Room of One's Own," Virginia Woolf asserts: "A woman must have money and a room of her own if she is to write fiction" (Woolf

1993 [1929], 1927). I had neither. Yet I was granted admission to one of Texas's best universities. I thought that I was receiving sufficient financial aid to cover my costs. When I marched up to the university, I had only $300 in my pocket, my financial aid letters, and a bag of clothes—only to be ejected because I could not financially afford my higher education. I had gone to the university under the presupposition that a Pell grant awaited me. I would not have been there otherwise. However, I was apprised on arrival at the financial-aid office that my parents had made too much money the previous year and that I consequently did not qualify for the Pell grant. I still find this hard to believe. My parents held minimum-wage jobs to support four children; my father was a ditch digger for the Bay City Gas Company and my mother a janitor for the Bay City Country Club. My family's income was below the federal poverty level for a family of six, and I could not get a Pell grant.

It is regrettable to admit—to come out, if you will—that being the first in my family to venture out in this lonely college journey, I found myself sensing and experiencing alienation. I was entering a world I did not recognize. My mother had dropped me off and left me there. Alone. I had never set foot on a college campus before; I did not know how the financial-aid program worked. In my ignorance, I thought that all I needed to do was show the people in the financial-aid office my green-colored papers and I would be let in through the gateway of higher learning. Showing green papers was a well-established custom for me. I had been crossing borders since I was ten years old, showing the green card that certified my Texas residence. This time, though, the papers were not enough to grant me access to academe. The attendant in the financial aid office, knowing (because I had already explained my circumstances to him) that my mother had dropped me off and that I had nowhere to go, did not volunteer any information about how I would be able to afford college without aid. I did not know anyone there and had no one to turn to for guidance. I escaped from the office with a minimal loan to pay for my tuition and some of my books.

The waters are murky, imperceptible, when the line that divides is unclear. When I turned eighteen (one has to be eighteen to apply for U.S. citizenship if the parents are not U.S. citizens), I made haste to the Immigration and Naturalization Service to apply for my U.S. citizenship. I was called in for testing, then I was directed to the courthouse to be sworn in, to abandon my country of origin. The subject (me) is not declared a U.S.

citizen until the paper (shall I say the proof?) indicating naturalized citizenship is provided by the government. This comes much later, when one is called in to attend a formal ceremony. When I arrived at the university and during my application process, I was sandwiched between these two states of being. Was I a U.S. citizen or not? Even during the time I managed to stay at the university, which was two semesters in total, I was straddling two worlds. Fall semester, I did not have the paper that branded me a naturalized U.S. citizen. However, by the spring semester I had the piece of paper in my hands. Federal financial aid is not granted to non–U.S. citizens, I recently discovered. I am not sure whether I was denied aid on this basis or not, because no one addressed that issue at the financial-aid office. Truly, had I been under inquisition, I would not have known how to respond. I was not sure what I *was*.

My grades suffered during my stay at the university, and those poor grades played a critical role in keeping me away from academe for seven years. There are two dominant reasons for my failure, I now recognize. I was away from my family, and I was poor. My family is an integral part of my life. Regardless of how crazy and wild my dramatic home life was, I craved that chaos; it was my rooting, my grounding. "You belong with us," their voices called me from a distance. In this university surrounded by the privileged, I was the outcast. Oh, I tried to pass as one of them by wearing a mask, attending Latin parties among the privileged international Latinos, but that was not me. There was no celebration in my heart without my family around. We had our own carnival we lived, the one that involves poverty, love, anger, laughter, and more love; the one that reminisces about the days we dragged our legs across the pavement because our shoes were torn and an ambivalence of painful laugher erupts. I longed for my sister's storytelling about "when Mom was at a school party with her country club uniform on and had a red stain on her white shirt, and how the rich mothers had come to the school party all decked out. They looked at Mom in a funny way and stayed away from her as if she was contagious." We all hugged and cried. That was the real me. She was nowhere to be found on that college campus, and my grades suffered. College is for the privileged, I resolved, and I stayed away from that world for seven years.

It is difficult when one finds no connection with the new world. But I kept trying to bring it together, the old and the new. Seven years later, after my disastrous stay at the university, I gave academe a second chance.

I was afraid that I would not do well academically because of the stain on my transcript from the previous university, but I gave it a second try. Intuitively knowing that something was left unfinished, I enrolled in a junior college twenty-eight miles from home. However, this time I was at home in my hometown, near my family. And when I say family, I do not mean my husband and children alone. When I say family, I extend it to include my mother, father, and siblings—even cousins, uncles, and aunts, and grandparents—who lived in the Rio Grande Valley.

While at the junior college, I performed remarkably well academically. But unlike the university I had attended seven years earlier, this junior college had a diverse student body: racially integrated, poor and rich, and the young and old. I felt at home. Through the study of literature, the carving of the words, I found my fortress. My quest to find the answers to the riddles and to retrieve the pieces of my life began at this college in my world literature class in the fall of 1996. I had a great professor who encouraged me to voice my thoughts. Odysseus was not so different from us poor Mexicans: Fate had dealt him a hard hand. (I began to feel the winds carry me on the direction of literature and writing.) This same professor provided me with an opportunity to explore my writing by allowing me to become a character found in the literary works through essay analysis. With a natural ability, I lived the roaming spirit of the Ancient Mariner and the angry soul of Jane Eyre. But where life would carry me, I would never have imagined.

On my road to recovery, there was a stumbling block. After the junior college, I transferred to a nearby four-year university, where I experienced an alienation similar to the one I had lived through during my first trip to higher education. This time I was still around my family. In fact, my sister was going back to college with me. We both fled after the first semester. We were taking a linguistics course, and the professor asked whether there were any non–native-English speakers in the class. My sister and I publicly and proudly admitted that Spanish was our native tongue. The professor proceeded to inform us that this class might be "a little more difficult" for us. But when we proved her wrong by making the highest grades in the class on the first exam, we were branded "exceptions." Having been well nurtured at the junior college and unwilling to relinquish my pursuit of an English degree, I managed to escape the brutality there to find fertile grounds at a very diverse university where to be Other is normative.

In the spring of 1999 at this university, two semesters before graduating, I enrolled in a Mexican American studies course—the search for identity course. I think this was one of the most important rotations in my life. How appropriate—an identity search. Wasn't that in fact what I had been dealing with all of my life, and now I had a ticket to the carnival, a reason (should I say, an excuse?) to meet the Mexican woman behind the mask. My professor, with the gravity of the moon, led her students on the expedition. Using disparate sources such as poetry, novels, and theoretical essays, we were going to uncover the mysteries buried in *la mestiza* consciousness. All the probing and tilling of the ground germinated nostalgia in me about my indigenous heritage, the part of me that had been suppressed.

Thanks to this course and my nurturing professor who encouraged my writing, I did manage to tap the waters of my literary heritage, awakening an ancestral spirit of poesy. I wrote a piece of fiction titled "Pieces of the Shattered Mirror," which was published in the *Bayou Review* and awarded a prize for Outstanding Contribution by that journal. I also wrote poetry echoing my Corn Mothers, *mi familia*, my ancestors, and the *barrios,* and was honored with an invitation to read at a poetry reading during the university's Women's Month celebration. For the first time in my life, I realized how advantageous it is to be a Mexican, bilingual, a member of the indigenous groups of the Americas, a group of people with much culture and heritage still awaiting exploration. Treasures lay unearthed in inscriptions imploring a gentle stroking, a burnishing hand, to rub away the friction and find our own reflection. I graduated planning to attend graduate school and focus on Mexican American studies to search for answers in the inscriptions of my people and to chant them to the world so that we can celebrate our diversity as a human race. Instead, life took a surprising turn when I found myself suddenly single with two young daughters. I decided to teach English at a largely Hispanic inner-city high school. Most of my students are from disadvantaged and poor backgrounds. As it did for me, for most of these kids college appears unattainable. But in teaching them, I exert a leave-no-child-behind philosophy and have learned the aesthetics founded in the *mestiza* consciousness.

The road to academe has been one of *espinas y nopales,* thorns and cactus, for me. From the small child who did not speak the English language to the English major, magna cum laude college graduate, I am working against a dominant culture that suppresses and oppresses the difference that is threatened by the Other. I cannot abandon my class roots, nor do I want to. I am poor and will always be poor. I do enjoy visiting my dad and conversing with him. I find pleasure in talking to my older sisters, who have accumulated only eight years of school. I am that woman. I do not wince when I hear someone with an accent. I do not cringe when I see someone wearing a stained uniform. Through all of my crossing of borders, I can no longer distinguish the line.

I'M THAT WOMAN OF THE DESERT

Tierra desolada, abandonada,
Empty land, dry land, forgotten land,
Ignoble nature.

The drought rewards
You with *nopales*
Thorns that protrude,
A strangled breath.

Spikes ready to do battle
With the first human that
Attempts to get close.

Shooting from every direction
Piercing the skin of its intruders
Receives the shower of blood.

Those that can conquer you
Will disarm you
Shaving away at our skin to
Reach the slimy substance,
          Water left too
Long in a tank unattended

Cut into a thousand pieces
The slime stretches from
The knife to the table.

What lies behind your
Prickly body *nopalitos*?

REFERENCES

Anzaldúa, Gloria. 1987. *Borderlands/La Frontera: The New Mestiza*. San Francisco: Aunt Lute Books.

Woolf, Virginia. 1993 (1929). "A Room of One's Own." Pp. 1926–86 in *The Norton Anthology of English Literature*, vol. 2, 6th ed., ed. M. H. Abrams. New York: W. W. Norton.

III. POLICY, RESEARCH, AND POOR WOMEN

Sandra L. Dahlberg

11 Families First—but Not in Higher Education

Poor, Independent Students and the Impact of Financial Aid

When we open the doors of college, we open the doors of opportunity; we give people the chance to live out their own dreams. And in the process, we strengthen our Nation and our ability to contribute to the progress of the entire world.

—William J. Clinton

Most [Americans] believe that government can and should play a central role in providing both the means for individuals to better themselves and a cushion for times *when individuals' own efforts are not enough.*

—Martin Gilens

FINANCIAL AID, once the promise of affordable access, is quickly becoming the welfare of higher education. I am a professor at a public, open-admission university at which the majority of students are first-generation college students from poor and working-class backgrounds, two-thirds of whom are non-white, and more than 53 percent of whom are independent. For the past three years, I have worked with the university's financial-aid department as a member of various scholarship committees. For four years, I served on the Financial Aid Advisory Committee at a large, public research institution, while at the same time, as a poor single mother, I was a financial-aid recipient and experienced firsthand the ramifications of these policies. I focus on the neediest students at public institutions to separate myth from reality in terms of financial-aid policy and its effects on the poorest students, presenting what I experienced as an aid recipient and the ways that I have seen these policies affect my students.

An increasing stigmatization advanced by the media and accepted by politicians portrays some students as deserving and poor independent students as getting something for nothing, thereby draining the public's coffers. The philosophy of affordable access that long guided financial-aid legislation has been replaced with an "opportunity with responsibility" ideology that replicates welfare reform's "work-first" and "personal responsibility" mandates.[1] According to Patrick Healy and Sara Hebel (1999, 36–38), "Education Department officials said that the intent of the Higher Education Act [of 1998] was clear . . . and represented a watershed in federal financial-aid policy: Students are now required to 'earn' their aid." Higher education as a means of self-empowerment through social mobility and as a recognition of academic merit—as tenuous as those concepts may have been in the past—are sorely at risk today. With those concepts at risk, we jeopardize not only the lives of poor students in America, but the future of the country, as well.

The pejorative rhetoric of welfare—rhetoric that pits the "deserving" poor against the "undeserving" poor—is mirrored in academe in "opportunity with responsibility" financial-aid policies. The pointedness with which this legislation requires that aid be earned in effect alleges that aid was not earned or "deserved" under previous aid policies. Aspects of this "earned" aid policy presume fraudulent intentions in poor students and mandate correctives that will inhibit genuine fraud, but these measures will also impede access for the poorest, most at-risk students. These "earned" aid policies countermand the premise that shaped federal financial-aid policy for nearly five decades: that affordable access to higher education is an American right and a social necessity.

Notions of U.S. higher education as a meritocracy are disrupted when "deserving" and "undeserving" are measured in terms of personal and familial income and not on the basis of the student's ability to succeed in college. As the real value of grant aid for the poorest U.S. students declines, education analysts and observers are beginning to ask whether we are seeing the end of affordable access. An article in *U.S. News and World Report* raises the question, "Will colleges reject [an applicant] if they think [she] need[s] too much money?" The answer is not reassuring: "They shouldn't, because most schools claim they keep a wall between admissions and financial aid. But they might" (Comarow et al. 2000, 86). Julie Blair (1999, 21) says that "a growing number of colleges are dropping their 'need blind' approach to admissions. Instead of accepting all applicants without regard to their financial status, they are now taking students' ability to pay into account."

It is a common American perception that meritocratic access to public universities exists for those who have academic ability, regardless of income. Increasingly, however, at many public schools the most "deserving" students are those who can afford to pay the costs to attend without aid; the "undeserving" are those students who receive need-based financial aid. The best of the "undeserving" are those high-ability traditional students whose only "fault" is having poor parents. The least of the "undeserving" are those students whom the institution views as having made "mistakes" by having children before obtaining a college degree, regardless of the student's age and without regard to why a college degree was not earned or attempted earlier in life. I have heard administrators, professors, and regents question students who received financial aid, and who had children, about the "mistakes" that resulted in parenthood, deferred education, and poverty. It was the financial-aid–need status that created the assumption of error, as financially secure student-parents were not subjected to this interrogation. Most of the high-need independent students subjected to this inquiry were from poverty-class or working-class backgrounds; most were single mothers.

Financial-aid analysts recognize that socioeconomic status greatly affects access to higher education. John A. Gardner (as quoted in McDonough 1997, 2) found "among the highest-ability students, 60 percent of the lowest [socioeconomic status] students attended college, while 86 percent of the highest [socioeconomic status] students attended. Students of color and poor students are less likely to start or finish college" (McDonough 1997, 2). According to Joni Finney and Kristin Conklin (2000, A68), U.S. Census Bureau statistics from 1998 show that "65 percent of students 18 to 24 from families with incomes greater than $75,000 enroll in college. In contrast, only 26 percent of students in the same age group from families with incomes less than $25,000 attend college." The figures differ in these studies, but both studies clearly show a gap in college enrollment based on socioeconomic status. Enrollment, in most studies, is measured during the "standard college age" of 18–24 years of age. Many poor people, myself included, delay enrollment or enroll for a term or a year, but are unable to secure the necessary funding to continue. Lower–socioeconomic-status students are often unaware of financial aid to make access affordable, or the level of aid offered may be insufficient, or they lack knowledge about college procedures. When the poor seek access to higher education later in life, they find a less sympathetic reception than the concerns about socioeconomic-status–based exclusion indicate.

Hand-wringing about the under-enrollment of lower–socioeconomic-status students becomes an empty gesture when these same students are not given affordable access when they do enter the university, and when they are faulted for not attending during their youth. It is rarely considered that the poor, independent student with children was once one of Gardner's 40 percent (or Finney and Conklin's 76 percent) of poor dependent students for whom sufficient support was not provided during youth. This myopia reinforces the idea that a college education must be obtained according to a middle-class time line. For one in three undergraduates in the United States, the "standard" college time line is contradictory to their experiences and an ineffective measure of lower–socioeconomic-status college attendance. As a result, aid policies, which are based on this model, are ineffective for poor and independent students. High-need traditional-age students fare better under the financial-aid system, but the correlative gaps between enrollment levels and socioeconomic status demonstrate that all poor students must negotiate a financial-aid bureaucracy that, like welfare, is often implemented in ways that facilitate the failure of the aid recipient.

There are two categories of high-need students; my emphasis is on the high-need independent student population, most of whom are women. Independent female students are entering higher education at increasing rates but are seldom addressed in terms of policy needs. According to Paula Wolff (2001, B20), "Between 1970 and 1995, the rate of women older than 25 entering college was roughly three times that of women younger than 25 or males of any age." By definition, independent students have legal dependents; are married, veterans, or wards of the court; or are older than twenty-four.

According to the U.S. Department of Education, by 1995 non-traditional students represented 30.6 percent of the national undergraduate student population (Lee 1999, 13). When financial-aid policies are developed and analyzed, however, the focus is on the larger dependent (traditional) student population, thus erasing high-need independent students from the picture—and, too often, from the policies seemingly designed to help all poor students gain access to and afford higher education. Thomas J. Kane concedes that "the financial aid system was not designed with 'non-traditional' students in mind" and that "the same rules designed for the traditional college student do not work very well in determining the need of independent students" (Kane 1999, 33). John B. Lee (1999, 12) asserts that it is more expedient to use as examples traditional high-need students, "because their circumstances provide an easily defined relationship between family income and student financial aid." Unfortunately, this expedient example also allows for an elision of the circumstantial complexity of high-need independent students, a move that reinforces negative societal perceptions of the poor, independent student as unworthy of serious legislative and analytic consideration.

The concentration on dependent students for analytical ease becomes particularly problematic when Lee insinuates that many high-need independent students elect to place themselves in a high-need category for financial aid by asserting that "full-time independent undergraduates received a larger share of student financial aid than full-time dependent undergraduates. In part, this is because many full-time independent undergraduates gave up full-time jobs to attend college, which lowered their income substantially and made them eligible for student aid" (Lee 1999, 13). In assessing U.S. Department of Education data for 1995–96, Lee notes that independent undergraduates received 36.3 percent of grant aid but represented only 30.6 percent of the undergraduate student population. This concept of a "chosen" poverty that resulted in high need is presumably meant to explain the 5.7 percent "over-allocation" of grant resources awarded to independent students. Such assertions, whether intentional or not, effectively reify stereotypes that portray high-need, independent students as "undeserving" ("gave up full-time jobs") and evoke images of Welfare Queens defrauding the aid system by getting more than they "deserve" and thereby limiting resources for more deserving, or "real," students.

Sustained omission regarding the complexities associated with independent high-need students in policy analysis re-inscribes class prejudice in the only arena to which the poor can turn to alter their lives permanently—higher education. Most high-need independent students did not choose to make themselves need-eligible; many were already poor, and the impoverished existence of high-need independent students is anything but comfortable. But financial aid *does* offer hope to those who desperately want to change their lives and the lives of their children. Some of these poor, independent students are single parents who are (or were) on welfare, and college offers the means to break cyclical or generational poverty. Some poor, independent students are enrolled in college as a result of divorce or spousal death because they are unable to support themselves and/or their children without an education. Other high-need independent students are jobless due to corporate restructuring and need an education to re-engineer themselves for the job market. But to assert that it is just easier to study the situations of high-need dependent students, as Lee does, or to avoid in-depth analyses of these high-need independent students in the examination of financial-aid policies, as do most analysts, reinforces the perception that the dependent student is in some way more "deserving" than the poor, independent student. As much as our society touts the bootstrap myth, it is clearly a disadvantage to be marked a poor women in higher education, which the essays in this volume demonstrate. Our cultural schizophrenia regarding the poor is perhaps most evident in higher education, where "deserving" and "undeserving" are increasingly based on income, age, and parental status, without regard to students' efforts to "bootstrap" themselves out of poverty. As a result, this schizophrenia negates the long-term, tangible contributions made by poor students in the form of loan indebtedness and increased employment—at least, in the media and in political spheres.

The fact is that poor, independent students—as individuals—usually pay a greater proportion of their educational expenses than do dependent students, particularly middle- and upper-income students whose parents pay some or all of the student's educational expenses. The substantial loan debt and a significant weekly work expectation incurred by high-need independent students are seen as potentially burdensome to dependent (and middle-income) students and problematic in terms of educational retention (Redd 1999, 85–86). The poor, independent college student faces these challenges, working harder and longer, earning less respect, and garnering less benefit. Without doubt, it is far easier to obtain and complete an education without concurrent obligations to children or the additional personal and financial burdens carried by most independent students. However, even as they overcome the cumulative effects of multiple obstacles, high-need independent students face scrutiny by administrators who often assume they are "failures" because they are attending college later in life while balancing other commitments. The irony is that the first federal financial-aid program specifically targeted older, independent students, and its success fostered the programs now considered the domain of dependent eighteen-to-twenty-four-year-olds.

AFFORDABLE ACCESS

The intent of the first federal financial-aid policies was to extend the social benefit U.S. society realized with the post–World War II GI Bill (used mainly by men). The GI Bill was the "single largest merit-based student aid program in United States history," with the veterans considered "meritorious by virtue of having served their country in the military" (Creech and Davis 199, 123). The veterans who transformed the demographics of higher education, and their subsequent impact on U.S. productivity and technological advancement, reassured a skeptical public that "broadening access to higher education was a more attractive and feasible goal for higher education than many observers had thought earlier" (McPherson and Schapiro 1998, 6). The GI Bill was the forerunner of the Johnson administration's federal financial-aid policies designed to improve the U.S. workforce in the face of Cold War challenges and address the growing need for post-secondary education as the Baby Boom generation entered college (Creech and Davis 1999, 124).

In the 1960s and 1970s, there was much public support for financial-aid programs to eliminate segregative educational policies and to address access issues in terms of race, gender, and social class. Americans believed that such inclusion would benefit society (Creech and Davis 1999, 123; McPherson and Schapiro 1998, 7–8). In the face of deficits, inflation, and declining federal and state budgets in the 1980s, some of this support waned, but still the public supported the ideology of affordable access to higher education. In the 1990s, growing public resistance to government spending resulted in further tightening of state and federal budgets and less funding for higher education, which fueled tuition increases (McPherson and Schapiro 1998, 27–30).

Between the mid-1980s and the mid-1990s, colleges faced diminished federal and state subsidies while simultaneously experiencing a decrease in the number of high-school graduates necessary to generate tuition revenues and maintain stable program levels (Creech and Davis 1999, 126). Kane notes that "between 1975 and 1995 the population of 18- to 24-year-olds declined by roughly 11 percent nationally" and more

than double that in the Northeast (Kane 1999, 139). As a result, institutions began to recruit independent students and enroll them in greater
numbers than before (Creech and Davis 1999, 126). The recruiting of
independent students stabilized enrollment figures and enabled public
colleges to justify requests for sustained public funding at a time that
"colleges and universities were forced to prove their worth to maintain
their share of the budgetary pie" (Blair 1999, 20). On the campus at
which I was enrolled during most of this period, nontraditional students were the university's "dirty little secret," as officials in financial-
aid, housing, and academic programs—even members of the board of
regents—reminded us that we were poor substitutes for "real" students,
that we were pawns and placeholders to sustain the university until the
"real" student population rebounded. When the traditional student population began to rebound, and middle-class pressure for available financial aid intensified, changes in financial-aid policies were enacted to
"protect" the needs of the traditional high-need and middle-income
students against the drain of poor, independent students. Politicians
responded to middle-class demands to make college more "affordable"
by passing the Taxpayer Relief Act of 1997 and through the 1992 and
1998 reauthorization of the Higher Education Act. These legislative acts
effectively reinforced aid as a program for dependent students, and colleges matched the legislation by escalating the use of institutional aid
(usually reserved for the neediest students) to attract upper- and middle-income traditional students with "merit" aid.

In recent years, the U.S. taxpaying public has demanded greater
accountability for government programs—including financial aid—
while asking that financial-aid programs offer more aid to middle-
income students and their parents, preferably in the form of merit aid.
The problem is that the move from need-based aid to merit aid dispro-
portionately benefits affluent students who would attend college regardless of aid offered. Claire L. Gaudiani (2000, 19) reflects that "the consensus for need-based aid has broken down. . . . The trend . . . is toward
deceptively named 'merit aid' that actually reduces access for poor and
middle-income students." The increasing trend toward using enrollment management and tuition discounts to control student populations,
through the distribution of "merit aid," decreases the pool of need-
based aid. Ben Gose (2000) explains that "discounting means using
financial aid in a strategic way to achieve an institutional goal—like

enrolling a bigger, smarter, or more diverse class. That idea bothers many educators, who would prefer to see aid go to needy students." These educators and aid administrators also "expressed frustration and anxiety over the current aid environment, in which an increasing proportion of scholarships goes to students from middle- and upper-middle-income families" (Gose 2000). Institutional use of aid money to "sweeten" admission offers hinders the affordable-access philosophy by reducing funds necessary to retain poor students who are profoundly affected by educational costs, tuition increases, and shrinking aid resources.

Affordability, however, is further complicated for the high-need student. The arrival of the poor student in academe is very often accompanied by fear of failure and a sense of alienation. External merit scholarships that recognize outstanding academic achievements effectively announce acceptance. Academic acceptance is of particular importance to the poor student because such awards affirm that she "belongs" in college. It also promises that financial strain will be eased by the scholarship amount. Unfortunately, this promise is empty. Political pressure to provide more aid to middle-income and affluent students, presumably on the basis of merit, collides with need-based aid programs when high-ability, high-need students earn external scholarships.

I define external merit scholarships as those for which the student has individually applied and which are awarded by organizations or academic departments on the basis of academic achievement. When I obtained external merit scholarships, I learned that I could not lower my educational costs by the awarded amount, as I had assumed. I have simplified my experience to demonstrate how an institution can prevent a poor student from securing any financial benefit from external scholarships, in large part so that the institution can reallocate the amount of the poor student's gain to promote tuition discounting for affluent and middle-income students.

I was a high-need student who received a financial-aid award that included grants totaling $4,000. I was also awarded $6,500 in (subsidized federal and Perkins) loans.[2] As a divorced single parent, I had no assets that could be applied to educational costs, and my income was well below the poverty level. My total award consisted of $4,000 in need-based grant funding that did not have to be repaid and $6,500 in loans. A federal work–study award of $2,000 completed the aid package. The amount of aid offered equaled the college's educational budget of $12,500, so I had no unmet need.

My cumulative college grade point average was 3.9 on a 4.0 scale, and I earned a $2,000 scholarship in recognition of outstanding academic achievement. The financial-aid office was notified of my success. Yet because I received full financial aid, it was the college, not I, who controlled the application of those funds to my aid package. What happened, therefore, is what often happens: My institutional grants were reduced by the scholarship amount. (Pell grants, a federal entitlement determined by the Federal Methodology, or FM, are unaffected by this practice.) I had hoped to reduce my loans, which would have lowered the actual *cost* of my education. For my hard work, no discernable benefit was provided other than I earned the ability to claim the scholastic honor on my résumé and on future scholarship applications. In contrast, when a similar academic award was given to a student with no financial need, the no-need student found the entire $2,000 credited to her student account, reducing her educational costs by that amount.

In addition to being an intense disincentive for poor students, this policy promotes institutionally (and legislatively) sanctioned class-based discrimination because non-need students are able to profit from their scholastic efforts in a manner that poor or high-need students are not. This establishes a clearly demarcated two-tiered, separate-and-unequal economic system in academic institutions: High-need students who *need* the financial gain promised by scholarships are denied its benefit; instead, that gain is realized by their affluent peers. It is easy to understand why the high-need scholarship recipient feels violated by the policy. It is an egregious negation of the student's success, and it undermines the intent of the body granting the external scholarship. This violation is exacerbated when public universities that purport to be need-blind and class-blind in the promotion of public interest nevertheless participate in the redistribution of scholarship funds that result in the very poorest of high-ability students subsidizing their more affluent peers.

TWO-TIERED AID POLICIES

A two-tiered system erodes the philosophy of affordable access, and financial-aid practices that reinforce class stratification limit the access of poor students to higher education. Blair argues that the use of "merit" aid to attract non-needy students (and provide institutions with more tuition dollars) "serve[s] primarily the accomplished middle and upper classes and divert[s] money from the truly needy. Merit aid, [aid analysts and critics] contend, will result in an elite system of higher education and perpetuate an economically stratified society" (Blair 1999, 20). Increased stratification as implemented in merit discounts at the expense of high-need students, according to Travis J. Reindl of the American Association of State Colleges and Universities, has "a lot of political implications that people have not thought through . . . and we are going to see some of the uglier aspects of these political dynamics when the well gets a little dryer than it is today" (as quoted in Schmidt 2000). McPherson and Schapiro (1998, 40–41) argue that state funding of higher education constitutes a subsidy for middle-income and affluent families, whose college-attendance rates are greatest, and that "price sensitivity" to the rise in public tuition rates "is concentrated among low-income students, with little or no price response observed among higher-income students."

The two-track system will be more destructive if pending legislation is passed to give middle-income students access to Pell grants. According to the *Chronicle of Higher Education,* there is a great deal of political pressure to have Pell grants "encompass a 'small amount' of middle-class people" (Hebel 1999, A32). In the *Chronicle* article, Professor Tom Wolanin, who was a top aide to former House Education Committee Chair William D. Ford, notes the disturbing trend toward a "two track system for student aid," acknowledging that "if you have a poor system and a middle-class system, the middle-income people win" (as quoted in Hebel 1999, A32). The losers are the poor students for whom these aid programs were initially devised. The Catch-22 for financial-aid advocates is that "the Pell program could be jeopardized politically if eligibility were limited for a key constituency: middle-income Americans, who vote more steadily and contribute more to campaigns than do poor Americans" (Hebel 1999, A32).

The generational damage of this trend will be devastating if it is not reversed through revised legislation. Colleges and universities that once recruited independent students to fill enrollment gaps may no longer need these students, but these students still need affordable access to higher education. Welfare reform, coupled with the rise in the number of single-mother households and the lag in real wages that undereducated women can expect to earn, means that more and more poor women will seek an education as a way out of poverty. It is important to recognize that attending college as a poor single mother is difficult in ways that are unimaginable for the traditional student. For one thing, the poor woman in higher education must be proactive in her efforts to obtain access and maintain her family, and students receiving welfare benefits are particularly courageous, because college enrollment often removes the safety net that welfare benefits offer the children. Yet when these poor women enter the academy as potential scholars, they encounter aid policies enacted in response to anecdotal images of aid recipients as "undeserving" because poor women are statistically "less successful students" than are traditional college-age, middle- and upper-class students (Macy 1999; Wolff 2001). The emphasis on "standard college-age" studies and statistics erases the successes of students whose parental responsibilities and employment requirements prevent them from graduating within five years, without tracking actual graduation rates. Their rates of graduation fall outside the "normal" range used for college rankings, and the extended time it takes to move from initial enrollment to graduation is portrayed as a negative college characteristic, and hence "less successful." It is necessary to examine the ways that traditional college reporting of retention and enrollment contribute to the perception that these poor, independent students are "less successful " and therefore "undeserving." It is time to re-examine the efficacy of a reporting system that works for only the youngest 70 percent of the college population and to the disadvantage of the other 30 percent of college students.

REMOVING SAFETY NETS FOR POOR STUDENTS

Congress enacted the Return of Title IV Funds Policy in the Higher Education Act of 1998 in response to public concerns that high-need grant recipients were misusing public aid funds. The Return of Title IV Funds Policy requires that all Title IV loans (FFEL, FFEL PLUS, and Direct PLUS) and grants (Pell, SEOG, and LEAP) be retained in proportion to the amount "earned" by the student until the student completes 60 percent of the term, at which point full aid is "earned." If the student withdraws—for any reason—before reaching the 60 percent mark, the "unearned" aid must be repaid, and future enrollment and access to aid is blocked until the "unearned" aid is paid in full.[3] The policy was enacted to prevent the misuse of financial-aid money by people who obtained aid money but did not attend school with the intention of completing the term. The problem with this policy, as written, is that it offers no palliative for students forced to withdraw as a result of extreme or catastrophic circumstances before the 60 percent point in the term.

My first encounter with this policy was through Melinda, a bright student in my freshman course.[4] She was a solid B-plus student; she was also a high-need, independent student who received financial aid. At midterm (the 50 percent point), Melinda was in a car accident and underwent surgery, the recovery from which prompted her to withdraw from classes. She plans to re-enroll for the next term, but before she can do so she must pay for any "unearned" aid she received. Now her ability to obtain an education depends not on her need status or on her academic ability but on her ability to repay the "unearned" portion of her aid. This repayment mandate may bar a very capable and dedicated student from further access to the education she needs to succeed in life. Under this policy, misuse or fraud is assumed, and no mercy is given.

The federal Return of Title IV Funds Policy is understandable in terms of accountability: The public wants to insure that money is properly applied. Yet the Melindas are cases for which no allowances are provided. Melinda could do nothing to prevent her withdrawal. She did not intend to defraud the public. Rather than recognize that true hardships are beyond the control of aid recipients, this legislation is mired in the "personal responsibility" philosophy of welfare reform. Absent any corrective for hardship, the policy implies that withdrawal is a result of fraud. Hardships can happen to anyone, but the current policy makes continued affordable access to higher education contingent on one's ability to forestall the unforeseen—which is an impossible task. It is more difficult for those with the fewest personal resources to overcome hardships, and this policy intensifies the financial impact of the hardships by creating an additional barrier that may prove impenetrable.

The Return of Title IV Funds Policy also affects the administration of financial aid. Before it was enacted, the mission of financial-aid officials was to determine need and distribute the aid necessary to insure affordable access to higher education. Congress's Return of Title IV Funds Policy requires aid officials to act as collection agencies, as well. Lisa Beaudo, director of the Office of Scholarships and Financial Aid at the

University of Houston–Downtown, says that she finds the new regulations "philosophically and emotionally damaging for my staff and the students I serve" (Beaudo 2001). Beaudo says, "I never envisioned myself having to take money away from students in this manner. The current environment is just ugly, ugly for everyone, myself included." Like most financial-aid administrators, Beaudo is sympathetic to the intent to control the misuse of funds by students who obtain aid money and then withdraw. The problem is that she believes that cases of actual misuse are rare and not in proportion to the number of hardship students who will be hurt by the policy. The severity of the policy—its inability to recognize true hardship or emergency circumstances beyond students' control—was made visible in the wake of the September 11 catastrophes. Federal directives were issued immediately to exempt from this policy the military reservists and active-duty service personnel deployed after the attacks. Victims of the disaster, however, did not qualify for such an exemption.

FAMILIES FIRST, BUT NOT IN HIGHER EDUCATION

Before financial-aid reform in 1992, child-support payments were routinely isolated from educational budgets or applied to offset support calculations for the dependent children. This was actually a way to recognize the "income" but not appropriate the support. Under the 1992 re-enactment of the Higher Education Act, politicians responded to powerful middle-class voters (alarmed by the rising costs of higher education), who charged that higher budgets gave student-parents an unfair advantage and left traditional and middle-class students with fewer resources. In an effort to create a more "equitable" distribution of aid funds, the 1992 financial-aid reform disallowed the consideration of dependent children in the calculation of student budgets, except to cover child-care costs. These same policies, however, considered child support received by the custodial student-parent as personal income levied against the educational budget of the student-parent, as if the children did not exist. The regulations provide a degree of institutional interpretation so that the implementation of these regulations varies from school to school and state to state.

Politicians were also reacting to reports of flagrant fraud perpetrated by affluent parents who manipulated the independent-student status to obtain aid for their children (Burd 1997, A29), and in 1992 Congress clearly defined independent-student status. Ironically, in the efforts to reduce fraud (committed by the affluent) and make the distribution of aid "fair," child support came under the purview of student income, and the poorest student-parents were hurt the most by the reforms. The reforms were reported as neutralizing aid-distribution policies so that all students would be treated equally. Coincidentally, perhaps, these regulations were enacted just as the traditional student population was rebounding, and enrollment management refocused on the recruiting of traditional students. The confluence doubly affected independent students in terms of governmental and institutional policies.

In 1992, I was issued by court decree a child-support payment of $505 for my two children, age seven and ten. I was the custodial parent; I was in graduate school; and I had limited employment. Under the 1992 congressional mandate, financial-aid policies can consider only the modest needs of a single student, so the budget for my living expenses was based on the cost of renting a one-bedroom/studio apartment; food for one adult; and the clothing needs and medical expenses and insurance for myself only. I lived in on-campus family housing, but my educational budget could not incorporate added costs for the three-bedroom apartment required by the university's housing policy when children are not of the same gender. There were no allowances for food, medical care, or clothing for my children because they were simply removed from the equation. Yet my child support was considered income that decreased my need level, and I was eligible for less subsidized aid and fewer institutional grants. The educational budget may have been modest indeed for a single student, but for a family of three it meant abject poverty. The result was that I had to increase my indebtedness to recover money that the courts (and the children's father) provided to feed, house, and clothe them.

I was in graduate school for almost six years. The amount in loan debt I incurred to replace child support was more than $36,000, to which were added educational expenses paid through even more loans and interest paid over the life of the loan. The university—in this case, a public university—in effect confiscated the child support awarded to my children by the same state's courts. The silence surrounding this grievous policy works to marginalize poor student-parents further as they find themselves penalized for seeking access to higher education and without recourse to contest the redistribution of court-ordered child support. The damage is compounded because these financial-aid policies can be executed in ways that seriously threaten custody provisions in divorce situations and place families at risk. The court (and the support-paying, non-custodial parent) can legally demand an accounting of how child support was spent, and if that money was not spent on the children's needs, then the custodial parent can lose custody on the basis of negligence. Rather than risk custody, most student-parents in this position do as I did: They keep silent regarding the appropriation of their child-support funds and borrow to cover the loss. They assume the burden of additional indebtedness so that economic advancement—in real terms—is largely unrealized until years after the children are grown.

In the case of child support and financial aid, the rhetoric of personal responsibility as developed in public aid policy becomes punitive and hypocritical—if not illegal. Certainly, it is unethical. I was exerting personal responsibility by making that modest budget for one stretch to cover three. My ex-spouse responsibly paid child support and thereby prevented our need for public assistance. I was responsible in my efforts to secure the necessary education to support myself and my children above the poverty level and to raise my children to see themselves as productive citizens. Yet the institutional elasticity in the Federal Methodology (FM) promoted the willful disregard of my children and was a barrier to sustained family solvency and true affordable access. Although it is illegal for a custodial parent to misappropriate child support in ways that neglect the children's basic needs, it is evidently not illegal for a public university to do so. Families are not first in higher education, except as the first heirs to legislatively sanctioned impediments. It is very difficult to see how this legislation is in any way "neutral" or a means of "fair" access. Certainly, not all schools interpret and deploy policy in this manner, but that they *can* is disturbing.

The student who receives welfare benefits faces a doubly injurious penalty for receiving scholarships and financial aid, even loans. President Clinton's vow to "end welfare as we know it" did just that, but that legislative mandate collided with his statement that "the doors of college ... [are] the doors of opportunity ... [that] strengthen our Nation" (Clinton 2000). With the 1996 passage of the Personal Responsibility and Work Reconciliation Act (PRWORA), educational opportunity for welfare recipients was replaced with the opportunity to "work first" in a minimum-wage or sub–minimum-wage job of twenty to thirty-five hours a week (Adair 2001). If a woman can manage to attend school and maintain the necessary levels of employment, then she can retain Temporary Aid to Needy Families (TANF) benefits that include wage and child-care subsidies, medical coverage, and food stamps. However, her work requirements may dictate college enrollment on a "very-part-time basis," which may in turn limit her access to aid (Wolff 2001). According to Wolff, "A 1995 study from the National Center for Educational Statistics reported that only 7 percent of part-time students received aid. And a smaller percentage of very-part-time students obtains such financial assistance." In post–PRWORA America, education as a way out of poverty is no longer privileged. Before 1996, Aid to Families with Dependent Children (AFDC) policies more readily recognized education as a way to end poverty, but that did not mean that individual social workers routinely supported education for the women whose cases they managed. At the welfare office, women who received AFDC payments had to be assertive in their efforts to attend school and retain benefits. At the college, affordable access to higher education for AFDC recipients was further complicated by institutional ignorance, if not malice, regarding AFDC regulations and their potential to interact negatively with financial-aid policies.

In the calculation of financial need, for instance, the welfare benefits to maintain dependent children in the absence of child support can, like child-support payments, count as the student-parent's income without regard to the children's needs, which are outside the scope of the educational budget. While external merit scholarships reduce the welfare mother's access to institutional grants and leave loans in place, students receiving welfare benefits must justify to welfare workers the receipt of external merit scholarship funds, which welfare workers see as cash assets to replace welfare grants. For the welfare recipient, external merit scholarships can simultaneously result in the loss of welfare benefits *and* a significant reduction in her financial-aid package. As the frenzied student works to placate these two cadres of aid workers—which means literally hours spent waiting to speak to the officials who hold the woman's future in balance—professors question the student's "dedication" to her studies.

The promise of access is empty at best when social and educational policies are mired in extreme disincentives. The poor woman who wants to earn a college degree must now weigh her chances for future financial success against the burden of student-loan debts that may restrict the educational advancement of her children. At the same time, without a college education, the poor woman cannot provide a stable income for her children or herself. When the woman's child wants to attend college, the mother's student-loan indebtedness (which can be a significant portion of the monthly income) cannot mediate the Expected Family Contribution.[5] The debt simply does not exist for the FM. Student-loan indebtedness is ignored, as is consumer debt—and for the same reason. The FM assumes that debts represent poor financial choices made by the parent. Ironically, had the woman not made the "poor choice" to earn an education, and had she remained on welfare instead, her dependent child most likely would have qualified for full aid. In her effort to become a productive citizen and taxpayer, the woman reduces her child's access to higher education and nullifies her hope of ending cyclical or intergenerational poverty.

In *Why Americans Hate Welfare*, Gilens examines the role of media in shaping public opinion, and the persistence of public support for self-help programs in spite of "misguided" and misleading negative media portrayals of poverty. His finding: that Americans support "government aid for those who are trying" to obtain self-sufficiency through education and work (Gilens 1999, 63). According to Gilens, 96 percent of Americans support government-funded educational support or job training for welfare recipients as a way to end cyclical or long-term poverty (Gilens 1999, 188). Contrary to media claims, Gilens's research demonstrates that "most middle-class Americans, hard-pressed or otherwise, want to boost, not cut, assistance to the poor" (Gilens 1999, 212). The middle class may want to reduce its taxes and obtain more college aid, but not at the expense of the nation's poorest citizens. In fact, Gilens discovered that 56 percent of Americans would increase their tax obligations if such money resulted in more aid to the neediest Americans. This desire to fund the poorest of students and citizens, however, does not remove the perceived need middle-income parents express in terms of financial-aid access. So because the poor are less likely to vote than are middle- and upper-income Americans, and they are less likely to be involved in politics at any level, it is easier for politicians to accept as fact "misguided and distorted" media claims regarding public support for aid programs (Burd 2000). It is more expedient to create and use a rhetoric that pits middle-class voters against the poor than to address the real issue: the need for increased funding of higher education, especially for the poorest Americans.

Another avenue by which poor women gain access to higher education is military service. Since the 1970s, an increasing number of poor women have opted for military enlistment and the GI benefits intended to make college more affordable. Many women use these benefits after they find themselves the sole providers for dependent children. Female veterans first face erasure because they are women in programs perceived to be composed of men and for men, even though the number of female veterans increases annually. Then, after these women enter the university, they discover that veterans' tuition-reduction benefits (for Vietnam-era veterans and Gulf War veterans, for instance) can be treated in the same manner as the external merit scholarship and used to reduce the level of institutional grant aid rather than that of loans. In many states, veterans' tuition-reduction benefits are provided in the form of reduced tuition at public institutions. The cash benefits of the GI Bill or Montgomery GI Bill understandably apply toward student income, but tuition-reduction benefits are not a cash asset. Tuition-reduction benefits were intended to reduce the actual cost of the veteran's tuition to make higher education accessible for even the poorest veterans.

Interpretive flexibility allows institutions to calculate the "value" of the tuition-reduction benefit as if it were cash added to the aid package, thereby increasing the level of aid offered. For instance, if tuition is $4,000 per year and the tuition rate the veteran pays under the tuition-reduction program is $1,500, then the value of the benefit is $2,500. For high-need veterans, the value of the tuition-reduction can result in a negative unmet need amount. Negative unmet need indicates that more aid is offered than the budget warrants. Because aid may not exceed need, institutional grant aid is reduced, followed by loan aid, until the unmet need is zero—without decreasing the high-need veteran's actual educational costs. The veteran who has no financial need is able to profit from legislatively enacted tuition-reduction programs, and her educational expenses are $2,500 lower than those of her high-need counterpart. This is another example of how the two-track financial-aid system undermines benefits provided for the neediest students. Institutions use loopholes in aid policy to act first in their own self-interest and do so at the expense of the poorest students. By appropriating the benefit, the university has $2,500 more that it can award to another student, not necessarily a needy student. The public—and, perhaps, some politicians—remain unaware of the extent to which these policies are being used to repress the poor students they were intended to help.

The public also remains unaware that some financial-aid legislation, presumed to benefit the neediest students, in fact offers far more lucrative benefits to the institutions. One of the most obvious forms of institutional support under the mantle of student financial aid is the work–study program. High-need students are awarded amounts that they can earn from work–study employment to apply toward their college expenses in a given academic year. Although work–study jobs need not be performed at the student's academic institution, the vast majority of work–study positions are with the college. For students—especially overburdened, poor, single-parent students—the primary benefit work–study offers is on-campus employment. On-campus work–study eliminates the need to secure transportation to and from an off-campus job, so the student can spend more time at her studies. Work–study allows the student to schedule work hours to complement classes in ways that off-campus work cannot. This is indeed a great benefit. Work–study students are paid at least the federal minimum wage; they are not eligible for health benefits, and the amount they earn is determined by the aid awards. The students must report income received through work–study to the Internal Revenue Service and pay the applicable taxes, but the earnings are not declared as income on the Free Application for Federal Student Aid (FAFSA). Work–study income does not accrue any Social Security benefit.

The poor student's college or university receives a more tangible benefit from federal work–study. Student aid awards for work–study provide colleges with federally subsidized labor on which many institutions rely to reduce operational expenses. Federal work–study pays 75 percent of the cost to hire a student; the school assumes the other 25 percent. In other words, if a work–study student earns $5.50 per hour, the financial aid award "to the student" reduces the hourly institutional labor cost to $1.38 per hour. The federal government subsidizes the other $4.12 of the hourly wage. Large universities employ thousands of work–study students for ten to fifteen hours each week and thus realize quite a reduction in labor costs. Private institutions benefit most from this funding, as 62.5 percent of work–study money in 1995–96 went to private four-year schools that enrolled only 24.3 percent of the students eligible for work–study (U.S. Department of Education, as quoted in Lee 1999, 23).

Work–study, as the name implies, was designed to provide students with a way to earn part of their college costs. Because the students were paid wages for their work, these funds were generally applied to the personal-expense section of the educational budget. Independent students, for instance, are unlikely to live in dormitories or participate in meal plans. Work-study money could cover such essentials as food and rent. Before 1998, the student was always *paid* for work performed—and the student had discretionary control over the use of work–study dollars that her labor earned. The same 1998 Higher Education Act that requires aid be "earned," however, allows colleges to "automatically use work–study funds to pay institutional charges" (Healy and Hebel 1999). Using the "earned aid" policy to deny students access to earned wages impedes the legal and fiscal autonomy of work–study students. Their wages in effect can be garnisheed without a prior hearing before a fair and impartial judge. Work–study students become one of the few categories of individuals in U.S. society denied the right to control wage income. (Prisoners are another such category.) Poor students should not be subjected to regulations that are not evenly imposed on non-need students. If a non-need student has a non-work–study campus job, for instance, those funds cannot be withheld by the institution without a legal hearing at which the student employee can contest the garnishment. As politicians and society demand accountability and personal responsibility in return for public aid, should some protective measures not be enacted to protect poor students, rather than assuming that the public needs to be protected from them? We must create policies that protect both parties, including policies that recognize how the public trust and poor students can be abused by colleges and universities.

At the other end of the financial-aid spectrum is student-loan debt and its repayment. When a prospective (traditional dependent) student applies for financial aid at an institution, family economic factors (the parents' finances) that are taken into account include exceptional medical expenses, tuition paid for siblings in school (at any level), and parental retirement needs. However, in the FM used by public institutions, parents' student-loan debts are not considered a mitigating expense—regardless of the parents' level of indebtedness or the number of years since the parents' graduation from college. Some private institutions do consider such factors as parental educational indebtedness, but those schools usually require an additional application processed through the College Board, and the cost of multiple applications can be prohibitive for financially strapped families.

In the past two decades, the fastest growth area in financial aid is in student loans, which shift an increasing proportion of the educational cost onto the student. The growth in student loans has resulted in such a high level of student-loan indebtedness that the federal government extended the loan-repayment period. Until recently, student loans were repaid within ten years; now borrowers may take up to thirty years to repay their loans. This extension was provided to avoid increased default rates and to make the significant debt loads more manageable for borrowers.[6] Realistically, the thirty-year repayment nearly triples the cost of the loan. The full impact of this long-term student-loan indebtedness will not be fully evident to our society until currently enrolled traditional-age graduates with student-loan debts try to buy homes and raise children and find those efforts thwarted due to loan debt. Many of these thirty-year borrowers will find their children's access to higher education diminished by their own indebtedness, sometimes to the very school to which the child seeks entry. When politicians increased loan levels and extended repayment periods, no provision was made to the FM to ameliorate the impact of those loans on financial-aid calculations when the children of those students begin college. Excessive reliance on loans does not increase affordable access for the poor, but according to many analysts, it does make paying for college more convenient for middle-class and affluent families (McPherson and Schapiro 1998).

Politicians increased borrowing levels for independent students as a cure-all for the shortage of aid funds without considering that older students will see less of a return on their investment because they have a reduced "lifetime" in which to realize the financial gains offered by the degree. Older college graduates also face ageism and classism when they re-enter the job market, which slows their financial advances. This in large part is due to poverty-class and working-class work histories. Non-traditional students often have lengthy work histories in the "wrong" economic sector: menial or manual labor, union jobs, clerical or blue-collar employment. Society, however, is a beneficiary of the woman's educational efforts. As poverty-class and working-class women move from repetitive physical labor into degreed professional and managerial positions, they transform a limited work life of low earnings into careers that are longer and more productive. As our population ages and strains the Social Security system, it is shortsighted not to invest in these students who, with college degrees, will be able to work longer at increased public benefit than their previous employment would have afforded.

Conclusion

It is essential to re-envision the poor woman's place in higher education by recognizing the contributions that such students make to the educational environment, the institution, and to society—by implementing policies to support these students and by actively refuting misguided and false stereotypes. First, society and the higher-education community must recognize that many poor, independent students are diligent scholars who reinforce diversity in the classroom and enhance the institution's scholastic status. According to Wolff (2001), "Almost 30 percent of [independent students] over 40 earn 'mostly A's' in their courses, compared with about 7 percent of 19-to-23-year-olds students." Clearly, these students are academically successful in ways that statistically augment institutional rankings. They may not be as "successful," however, when they try to obtain the same institutional support as middle-income aid recipients or high-need dependent students until stigmatizing policies are replaced with policies that treat these women as academic equals. Without sufficient support, academic success and access are impaired. Academic administrators and university personnel cannot be expected to change their attitudes unless significant changes are made to financial-aid and higher-education policies. If college staff and administrators must enforce punitive policies that presume the poor student is "undeserving" or will attempt to defraud the university, then these poor students will always be perceived as "less than" their middle-class peers and somehow suspect.

Second, financial aid as a means of affordable access for all Americans must be examined in a way that recognizes and supports all students, including the 30 percent who are independent. Policy alone will not alleviate the stigmatization of the poor who use financial-aid funds unless the pool of available aid is increased. Increased access to loans is not sufficient, especially for poor, working-class, and lower-middle-class students. The shortage of available aid funding, and the subsequent vilification of poor students, undermines the acceptance of poor students at the university by stigmatizing their need for aid. At the same time, middle- and upper-income Americans increasingly are encouraged to view aid as an entitlement that is threatened by higher-need students. The result is a two-tiered system that results in the denigration of the lowest tier—and assertions of "undeservedness." More effort needs to be exerted to show politicians, seemingly influenced by distorted media images rather than by the successes of poor, independent students, that they are squandering opportunities to have a positive impact on the remediation of poverty through affordable access to higher education.

Finally, federal aid policies must be reformed to remove the existing disincentives that inhibit poor students' access. Policies need to be written and implemented that dismantle the existing two-tiered system whereby poor students are not granted the same benefits as are non-need students in the same circumstances. Policies must be enacted to protect the interests of the individual poor student against institutional self-interest. When financial-aid regulations can be applied inequitably based on income, age, and maternity, then these regulations infringe on the rights of all. When need-based aid can be used to divert money from truly needy students to affluent students, everyone loses.

Americans understand that we, as a society, cannot condemn poor women to the prison of low-wage underemployment and still claim to be a meritocracy if we do not provide the financial support that gives access to higher education to those so inclined and able. Neither can we blame poor, single mothers for "promoting" intergenerational poverty when we do not provide the means for real economic change. A college education provides this opportunity. Investing in poor women who want to attend college is economically and politically prudent. It is essential that educational investment take the form of increased grant aid, financial-aid policies that alleviate the existing disincentives, and revised welfare regulations that recognize the work value of attending college. Educators need to recognize that if nothing is done to eliminate the disincentives that deny poor students access to their scholarship awards, child support, and veterans' benefits, then higher education becomes openly complicit in the advancement of intergenerational poverty and class-based discrimination. The philosophy of affordable access has been integral to the alleviation of cyclical and intergenerational poverty, and it can be so again with legislation that allocates sufficient funds to make college truly affordable and accessible to the poorest of Americans, regardless of age, gender, race, or parental status. It is essential to reaffirm affordable access for all poor families, whether the students in the families are dependent or independent students. Finally, access must be accompanied by attitudes that recognize and support the high-need independent student for what she is: a hardworking, viable scholar and a valuable member of the academic community.

NOTES

Epigraphs: Clinton (2000, 1825); Gilens (1999, 2); emphasis added.

1. Burd 1999.

2. These are not my actual award figures. They are rounded numbers provided as an example based on my experience.

3. University of Houston-Downtown 2001, which is based on the Code of Federal Regulations. Unearned aid is calculated by dividing the total number of days in the term (excluding breaks of more than five days) by the number of days completed by the student. Institutions are responsible for returning aid funds to the federal programs by calculating the total institutional charges multiplied by the percentage of unearned aid. When unearned aid exceeds that returned by the institution, the student is required to return this excess to the federal government within forty-five days or the debt is referred to the federal government for collection.

4. "Melinda" is a pseudonym.

5. The assessment of the Free Application for Federal Student Aid (FAFSA) and FM in regard to student-loan debt is based on my experience when my daughter began college and I applied for financial aid at several private and public institutions.

6. In a 14 August 2000 speech, Bill Clinton announced that student-loan–default rates had dropped from 22 percent to 9 percent under his tenure. He cited the extended payback option as the reason for this lowered default rate. He did not mention the economic vibrancy that contributed to the decrease in loan defaults and the effects that an economic recession may have on those rates (Clinton 2000).

REFERENCES

Adair, Vivyan C. 2001. "Poverty and the (Broken) Promise of Higher Education." *Harvard Educational Review* (Summer): 217–39.
Beaudo, Lisa. 2001. Interview by the author. Houston, Tex., 23 March.
Blair, Julie. 1999. "More College Aid Going to Top Students." *Education Week* 18, no. 23 (17 February): 1, 20–21.
Burd, Stephen. 1997. "Students Who Lack Funds from Parents Say Federal Aid System Is Unfair.: *Chronicle of Higher Education,* 20 June, A29–30.
———. 1999. "Proposed Federal Rules May Increase Paybacks of Financial Aid." *Chronicle of Higher Education,* 3 September, A62–64.
———. 2000. "Senators Urged to Make Grants an Entitlement." *Chronicle of Higher Education,* 25 February, A41.
Clinton, William J. 2000. "Remarks in a Roundtable Discussion on Higher Education in Chicago, Illinois." *Weekly Compilation of Presidential Documents* 36, no. 32 (14 August): 1825–31.
Comarow, Avery, Ted Gest, and Jeannye Thornton. 2000. "Here's the Deal on Aid: Whatever You've Heard, a Lot of It Is Just Plain Wrong." *U.S. News and World Report,* 18 September, 86–92.
Creech, Joseph D., and Jerry Sheehan Davis. 1999. "Merit-based versus Need-based Aid: The Continual Issues for Policy Makers.: Pp. 120–36 in *Financing a College Education: How It Works, How It's Changing,* ed. Jacqueline E. King. Phoenix: Oryx Press.
Finney, Joni, and Kristin Conklin. 2000. "Enough of Trickle-Down: It's Time for a Flood of Aid for Needy Students." *Chronicle of Higher Education,* 5 May, A68.
Gaudiani, Claire L. 2000. "The Hidden Costs of Merit Aid." *Change* 32, no. 4: 19.
Gilens, Martin. 1999. *Why Americans Hate Welfare: Race, Media, and the Politics of Antipoverty Policy.* Chicago: University of Chicago Press.
Gose, Ben. 2000. "Tuition Discounting May Rankle, but It Has Become Widespread." *Chronicle of Higher Education,* 18 February, A62.
Healy, Patrick, and Sara Hebel. 1999. "New Regulation Will Require Dropouts to Repay Some of Their Federal Aid." *Chronicle of Higher Education,* 12 November, A36–38.
Hebel, Sara. 1999. "New Tax Credits Are Changing the Economics of Student Aid." *Chronicles of Higher Education,* 21 May, A30–33.
Kane, Thomas J. 1999. *The Price of Admission: Rethinking How Americans Pay for College.* Washington, D.C.: Brookings Institution Press.
Lee, John B. 1999. "How Do Students and Families Pay for College?" Pp. 9–27 in *Financing a College Education: How It Works, How It's Changing,* ed. Jacqueline E. King. Phoenix: Oryx Press.
Macy, Beth. 1999. "The Scarlet P: Why Pell Grant Holders Aren't Slackers." *Chronicle of Higher Education,* 15 January, A56.
McDonough, Patricia. 1997. *Choosing Colleges: How Social Class and Schools Structure Opportunity.* Albany: State University of New York Press.

McPherson, Michael S., and Morton Owen Schapiro. 1998. *The Student Aid Game: Meeting Need and Rewarding Talent in American Higher Education.* Princeton, N.J.: Princeton University Press.

Redd, Kenneth E. 1999. "The Changing Characteristics of Undergraduate Borrowers." Pp. 78–97 in *Financing a College Education: How It Works, How It's Changing,* ed. Jacqueline E. King. Phoenix: Oryx Press.

Schmidt, Peter. 2000. "Boom in Merit-based Scholarships Drives 8.8% Rise in State Funds for Student Aid." *Chronicle of Higher Education,* 21 April, A39.

University of Houston–Downtown. 2001. "Return of Title IV Funds Policy." Unpublished policy statement, duplicated.

Wolff, Paula. 2001. "Very Part-Time Students Are Hobbled by Very Little Financial Aid." *Chronicle of Higher Education,* 16 March, B20.

12   The Leper Keepers

Front-Line Workers and the Key to Education for Poor Women

It is through the elusively simple and utterly equal exchange of personal truths and unconditional listening that each of us gathers the wisdom and strength to rewrite her script in her own words.

—Mary Bricker-Jenkins

THE EVENTS in the lives of poor women that shape their paths and destinies are significant, but equally important are the social contexts that affect their lives, including their interactions with the public welfare system. The reform of welfare brought about by the passage of the Personal Responsibility and Work Opportunity Reconciliation Act of 1996 (PRWORA) has been described at length elsewhere in this book. PRWORA replaced Aid to Families with Dependent Children (AFDC) with Temporary Aid to Needy Families (TANF); it also affected benefits to legal immigrants, Supplemental Security Income (SSI) for disabled children, the food-stamp program, child support, and foster care. TANF eliminated any guarantee of support or assistance for poor women and provided increased flexibility to states. The implementation of TANF and its requirements has been monitored for unforeseen problems and consequences for client services and for the jobs of front-line welfare workers. One important change is that implementation of new policy has denied poor women access to resources for education that opened up greater possibilities in their lives and has often made it more difficult to obtain other supportive services.

A concern voiced early in the implementation of TANF is that "under the new welfare law, front-line workers, who serve as the gatekeepers to the nation's welfare programs ... will play critical roles that may involve increased levels of administrative discretion" (Hagen and Owens-Manley 1998, 1). This increased discretion is complicated by the inherent stresses of front-line social work, particularly in regard to the stigma attached to such employment. According to Hugh Crago (1988, 34), the public welfare agency has been characterized at its worst as a "low morale/high burnout" organization and the front-line workers as "the human services equivalent of janitors and lavatory attendants. They cope with society's litter and excrement, as it were, and are paid accordingly." Although Crago is describing the welfare system in Australia, a study of U.S. welfare agencies revealed welfare workers describing themselves as "the leper keepers" and viewing themselves as dealing with an element of society that no one else wants to touch (Hagen and Owens-Manley 1998, 26). The ability, then, to use personal discretion to influence access to employment, job training, education, and other support services has strong implications for the centrality of those personal interactions between poor women and welfare workers as they occur at the front line.

In addition, for many human services organizations today, including public welfare agencies, there is increased accountability, concern with cost, and ambivalence toward the needy. Burton Gummer describes a change in the culture of such organizations beginning in the late 1960s that moved us from a government culture, an environment in which social policy and remediation were promoted for those less well off, to a more businesslike culture. Today, Gummer says, these agencies are more concerned with "growth, productivity, efficiency and rationality" than with service quality or effectiveness (Gummer 1990, 33). The tendency to borrow practices from the corporate world, however, does not respect the important differences between service and corporate organizations. This is both the immediate work environment and the larger societal context in which public welfare workers do their jobs and in which poor women's lives are affected, for better or worse.

Ira Progoff notes that some changes in our lives are created by our own decisions, but others "were forced upon us by the impersonal circumstances of life" (Progoff 1975, 134). The lives of poor women are constructed in larger contexts: contexts of the family, the neighborhood or community, and the part of the world that we occupy, with the opportunities, limitations, possibilities, and constraints that are naturally available. In addition, the distinction between "the personal troubles of milieu" and the "public issues of social structure" is one that C. Wright Mills explains as a key feature of work in the social sciences. Mills stresses that the ordinary individual will not be able to solve troubles caused by what are essentially structural issues imposed on him or her by society (Mills 1959, 6). In a similar vein, Mimi Abramovitz describes "blocked opportunities" in her work on social-welfare policy that begin to constrain and limit possibility in the lives of poor women (Abramovitz 1996, 21). Women who have fewer personal and social resources are more vulnerable to being affected by those structural aspects of society about which Mills speaks and more apt to be constrained in their opportunities.

My life is an example of the impact of both social contexts and constraints. I am the child of a woman who was poor. My mother did not receive welfare benefits, and she was married, but we were nevertheless very poor. My father, who never completed high school, had a low-wage job and a family of five children by the age of twenty-nine. He was an alcoholic at fifteen and continued to drink and gamble his wages from the time he was married at eighteen. In addition, my father was abusive when he drank, primarily to my mother, but also occasionally to his children. Even after their separation when I was seven years old, my mother went to work rather than go on welfare. It would be easy to see this as an American success story. A woman with five children picks up the pieces of her life and goes on, relying on no one but herself, her own intelligence, and her own initiative. But that would not be the whole story. It was the context of my mother's life that enabled her to survive her circumstances in the manner she did. Her choice to work instead of stay home with five rather traumatized children is in itself a questionable one, but it was the path she chose.

My mother lived in a small town in which she was surrounded by a large, extended family. My grandparents bought us food when my father spent his paycheck elsewhere and helped to ensure that we had a place to live. They, as well as aunts and uncles and cousins, provided respite from home, both literally and figuratively, and models of other ways for families to live. I first heard opera music at my uncle's home, and I often spent weekends playing card games with my grandparents at their seaside cottage. My uncles and grandfathers were loving and attentive, and I experienced the consistency of caring and attention from those male relatives that my father's unpredictability could not give me. Even the family doctor was a source of support in this small town, as his was the phone number my mother remembered when she was in imminent danger from my father one night, and the doctor, a reformed alcoholic himself, responded and took my father away. The Catholic nuns from the school we attended lived in a convent at the corner of our street, and the church was just down the street. They were part of the support system that watched over us day and night. We did not live in isolation. My mother's sense of belonging, of being cared for, no doubt enabled her to see herself as valuable and gave her resiliency in the face of hardship.

My mother was academically talented, and she graduated first in her class in high school. As is the case with many poor women, no one ever suggested that she go to college. Even when she was separated, a single parent to five children, no one urged that she receive any kind of advanced training. My mother's route out of poverty was the most common one for women of her generation: another man. She remarried, and we moved eight hundred miles away from all of that extended family, a dramatic turn in the road and one that still left her dependent for economic survival on her choice of partner. Still, it was the social context of my mother's life that supported her through her troubles and left little to chance—family, friends, a faith community and their resources, in addition to my mother's resiliency, acted as her safety net and kept her head above water.

The questions of chance and circumstance are crucial ones for poor women, because they speak to the importance both of understanding what will be successful in helping them through their own obstacle courses and of believing that the investment in human capital and human development is worth the effort and money. The combination of personal resources and social networks enabled my mother to avoid dependence on public welfare for even temporary assistance through a difficult time. For women who lack sufficient personal resources and social networks, it is necessary to turn to government assistance in the form of public welfare. The lives of poor women dependent on public welfare are influenced not just by circumstances and immediate social supports of family and friends, but also by social policies toward the poor and the manner in which those policies are implemented in public welfare agencies. To understand further the influence of context on the lives of poor women, their interactions with welfare agencies and welfare policies must be examined.

THE CONTEXT OF PUBLIC WELFARE

The lives of women on welfare are affected not only by policymakers and regulations but also by how policy is interpreted and implemented at the front line. For instance, education is often the surest route out of poverty, but new regulations set with PRWORA and TANF have established limits on educational benefits and emphasized the work-first strategy. In addition, exemptions from work requirements and time limits for a portion of cases receiving TANF are often determined in practice by front-line workers in welfare offices. There is concern that the fate of thousands of women's opportunities to continue the educational pursuits that will ensure lives of sufficiency is determined in an ad hoc manner when rules and regulations are interpreted in public welfare offices in what could be a very individualized, particularistic, and capricious process. Factors thought to be influencing those decisions are the nature of the public welfare agency itself, including perceptions of front-line workers of their clients as "leprous" and decisions regarding prioritization that are made on a day-to-day basis.

The climate of the public welfare agencies continues to be negative and unsupportive, and workers complain about the physical surroundings, the lack of supervisory support, lack of financial reward, and lack of status or acknowledgement for the work they do (Hagen and Owens-Manley 1998). In an earlier study, Jan Hagen concluded that it is important to "improve the work environment of income maintenance workers, reduce the drain on organizational resources, and enhance the overall quality of public welfare" (Hagen 1989, 62). Hagen, Irene Lurie, and Ling Wang (1993) described other features of the work environment that were problematic, such as the pressure of excessive workloads, paperwork that took time away from clients, and a lack of clarity in roles. Other factors that deserve emphasis are the lack of physical comfort, lack of supervisory support, and lack of support for teamwork and friendship. In a recent study using focus groups, front-line workers said that friendship was actively discouraged, units were "pitted against one another," and co-worker teams that developed were intentionally broken up through relocation (Hagen and Owens-Manley 1998).

Catherine Kingfisher noted in a 1998 Michigan study that front-line welfare workers are generally close to their clients in socioeconomic status. Similarly, a study of front-line workers in upstate New York found that almost one-third of participants in a focus group had used welfare. Many front-line welfare workers reported their own income as inadequate and voiced concern about child-care issues, as well (Hagen and Owens-Manley 1998, 19). In both the Kingfisher study and the study I conducted with Hagen, it is clear that, for the most part, workers do not feel cared for within their organizations and feel overwhelmed by the work that they do (Hagen and Owens-Manley 2002; Kingfisher 1998). In the same vein, an earlier study by Richard Weatherley and colleagues was concerned that "social services staff saw themselves as beleaguered at the bottom of a large insensitive bureaucracy concerned more about accountability to taxpayers than services to clients" (Weatherley et al. 1980, 568).

Qualitative studies of women on welfare also address front-line workers' attitudes toward clients, which to some extent may represent the front-line workers' attempts to deal with the overwhelming aspects of their jobs (Hagen and Owens-Manley 2002; Kingfisher 1998). Attitudes of workers providing social services to poor women often mirrored attitudes of the larger society. Both studies noted tendencies to categorize clients (also noted in Brodkin 1997 and Weatherley et al. 1980). In Kingfisher's study of front-line workers in the Michigan sample, workers labeled their clients "lazy" and as "liars" and, in another example, generalized to encompass all clients as "criminals" (Kingfisher 1998, 128–31). In the sample of upstate New York welfare workers, there was also concern that clients lied to get increased benefits or advantages, and clients were categorized as "short-timers," "cyclers," "program-jumpers," or "lifers" (Hagen and Owens-Manley 1998, 15). Kingfisher notes that departmental policy "requires workers to treat everyone the same, but are in practice contingent upon front-line workers' co-constructions of clients as deserving/undeserving, responsible/irresponsible, and moral/immoral" (Kingfisher 1998, 132).

For women on welfare, these front-line workers make daily decisions about whom to help and how to help (Brodkin 1997; Hagen and Owens-Manley 2002; Kingfisher 1998; Meyers et al. 1998). Kingfisher found that front-line workers were in effect "producing policy," since workers influence "which clients would have access to what and when" (Kingfisher 1998, 129). Examples of the worker discretion Kingfisher noted are induced waiting, either for the client's immediate appointment or by manipulating the "official" processing period; requiring over-verification for some clients or choosing when to refer for fraud; and withholding or providing information about programs or extra services (Kingfisher 1998, 133). Evelyn Brodkin also emphasizes the front-line worker's control over the decision-making process and describes that process as determined more by bureaucratic constraints and demands, or their own biases, than by client need and entitlement (Brodkin 1997, 11).

In a study of focus groups held with eligibility workers in public welfare departments in New York State in late 1997, just before the new TANF regulations were implemented, workers were asked to rank seven case illustrations or vignettes.[1] Almost without exception, the participants found the process of ranking cases difficult to do, and there was little consensus among the participating front-line workers. For most participants, individualizing each client was important, and some participants felt that they had been trained not to prioritize clients according to the directives of the agency. However, in response to one participant's assertion that it was easy to rank by following the rules (strictly procedural), others countered that it was important to focus on the client's need rather than the rules, especially because the rules can always be changed (Hagen and Owens-Manley 1998, 12). Workers in this upstate New York study agreed that they do in fact prioritize clients, mostly in emergency situations and for "good clients." They explained that good clients are those who appear to be motivated to do something for themselves and to be capable of becoming self-supporting. They may also be clients who are more compliant or grateful and not challenging, angry, or aggressive (Hagen and Owens-Manley 1998, 13).

Women who were prioritized to be "helped" in the case illustrations had children whose safety was in question, were in violent relationships themselves, or were trying to do something to help themselves. Of lower priority were clients who demonstrated repeating patterns of relying on welfare and the cyclical pattern of leaving and returning to their abusive partners. Alcohol abuse, too, seemed to be a trigger for lowering the priority, as was having had one's children removed and not living with the parent. Even the workers themselves were distressed at the results of their exercise in prioritizing cases, because their answers varied so much. One worker said, "How are [workers] going to choose? Our lists are so different. That means that anyone coming in might or might not get help, and it all depends on who they happen to see!"[2]

These cases are mirrored in *The Faces of Poverty* (1995), in which Jill Berrick rebuts prevalent myths about women and welfare. Berrick insists that "women on welfare do not fit a single mold. . . . [E]very family has a distinctive story to tell about its own resilience" (Berrick 1995, 21). She tells the stories of five women and their children living on welfare to portray the varied reasons that families turn to public assistance and the ways in which women strive to provide for themselves and their children. The stories illustrate—as do the stories of other women on welfare—that the paths are many and varied through life, that circumstances create junctures in the road, and that diverse needs call for diverse and individualized services.

ON THE FRONT LINE IN THREE NEW YORK STATE PUBLIC WELFARE AGENCIES

The ways that front-line workers influence the lives of their clients can be linked to their perceptions of their clients and welfare recipients in general. These perceptions, then, were specifically assessed in a survey of eligibility workers in New York State in 1999 (Owens-Manley 2000). Workers were given questionnaires with scales constructed for the study that measured their perceptions of welfare clients, perceptions about welfare services, and the use of personal discretion to prioritize and access services.

The study found that, overall, there was greater agreement on negative perceptions of clients than on positive perceptions (see Table 12.1). The average agreement with positive perceptions was 40 percent, and the average agreement with negative perceptions was 53 percent. For instance, nearly three-quarters (71.5 percent) agreed that many welfare recipients come from groups that attach no shame to being on welfare, and more than two-thirds (67 percent) agreed that when people have been on welfare for a long time, many have little desire to improve themselves. More than 40 percent (42.2 percent and 40.7 percent) agreed that if welfare recipients were given more choices about the services they received, they would not use the choices wisely, and that people end up on welfare because they use their opportunities poorly, not because they do not have opportunities (Owens-Manley 2000, 121).

On the more positive perceptions there was less agreement. Fewer than half of the respondents agreed that welfare recipients are hard-

Table 12.1. Front-line workers' perceptions of clients

	Agree	Disagree	Neutral
Positive Perceptions			
If given appropriate help, many welfare recipients would work hard to become self-supporting	46.8%	15.6%	37.6%
When they get jobs, welfare recipients are as hardworking as other employees	46.8%	19.3%	33.9%
Many welfare recipients feel badly about themselves because they are on welfare	34.9%	32.1%	33%
When given the opportunity to work, many recipients feel that having a regular job is an important goal in their lives	32.2%	28.4%	39.4%
Negative Perceptions			
Many welfare recipients come from groups in our society where it is no shame to be on welfare	71.5%	14.7%	13.8%
When people have been on welfare for a long time, many have little desire to improve themselves	67%	8.2%	24.8%
If we give welfare recipients more choices about the services they will receive from welfare, many will not use these choices wisely	42.2%	26.6%	31.2%
People end up on welfare because they use their opportunities poorly, not because they do not have opportunities	40.7%	24.1%	35.2%
Many people who apply for welfare would rather be on welfare than work to support their families	34.9%	26.6%	38.5%

working when they get jobs and that, if given appropriate help, they would work hard to be self-supporting (46.8 percent for each). Fewer than one-third agreed that welfare recipients feel that having a regular job is an important goal in their lives. I found that a little more than one-third (34.9 percent) believed that welfare recipients feel badly about themselves because they are on welfare, and almost as many disagreed (Owens-Manley 2000, 121).

The perceptions of workers regarding welfare services are described in Table 12.2. The study indicated consensus regarding client employability. The front-line workers in this study agreed almost uniformly that not everyone is able to work (86.3 percent) and supported the emphasis on employment and temporary assistance (80.7 percent). I also found that workers were in strong agreement that welfare recipients should not be able to stay on welfare (83.5 percent), even in the face of low-paying, unstable job opportunities. Disagreement was minimal, at 5.5 percent and 8.3 percent, respectively.

A surprising finding was that more than one-half (56.9 percent) of workers believe that clients should have greater opportunity for education and training. Given the discrepancy between acknowledging that work itself may not lead to self-sufficiency and the unwillingness to continue government support, education and training (severely limited under the new policy) become more important than ever. The need to upgrade potential earnings, especially for single-parent households with children, indicates the importance of higher education as a viable route out of poverty. These statements create a conflict that is not easily resolved, as it acknowledges that gaps will exist in how "everyone" is able to meet the new requirements but insists that they should cease to receive welfare benefits anyway (Owens-Manley 2000, 122).

Another aspect of the study assessed the role of individual front-line workers in the consistent delivery of services. Marcia Meyers and colleagues characterized workers' interventions in an observational study of public welfare in 1998 as those that routinized, particularized, or individualized their work with clients. Routinized services were those that followed the rule book; particularizing services might mean altering the

TABLE 12.2. Front-line workers' perceptions of welfare services

	Agree	Disagree	Neutral
Not everyone will be able to work, and not all work will lead to self-sufficiency	86.3%	5.5%	8.3%
Because of the low pay and instability of the jobs that are available to them, it is acceptable for welfare recipients to stay on welfare (reverse)	6.4%	83.5%	10.1%
I agree with my agency's emphasis on employment and temporary assistance	80.7%	8.3%	11%
Opportunities for more education and training should be made more available to clients	56.9%	18.3%	24.8%
Our government should ensure that the poor are taken care of	37.6%	17.4%	45%

Table 12.3. Personal discretion of front-line workers

	Agree	Disagree	Neutral
INDIVIDUALIZE			
I try to get all the information I can about clients to take all of their needs into account	71.5%	6.4%	22%
I adapt my explanation of opportunities and benefits to clients' individual situations	69.7%	1.8%	28.4%
I try to assess each client's needs individually to determine the services she or he needs	67%	9.2%	23.8%
PARTICULARIZE			
I make special exceptions for "good" clients— the ones who really try	25.7%	39.4%	34.9%
I do the bare minimum for difficult clients— ones who give me a hard time or do not really try	8.3%	66.1%	25.7%
ROUTINIZE			
I try not to individualize, because in my job that is not called for	32.1%	40.4%	27.5%
I try to stay out of personal conversations, as a client's personal circumstances are not part of my job or a part that I have time for	33.3%	36.1%	30.6%
I pretty much follow the same rule book with all of my clients	57.4%	14.8%	27.8%

interventions for "good" or "bad" clients; services were considered individualized when they were tailored to the client's situation (Meyers et al. 1998). The summary of responses of front-line workers responding to my 1999 survey about their own interventions are shown in Table 12.3.

A strong majority of respondents agreed with statements indicating that they attempt to individualize services to clients, and relatively few disagreed. Almost three-quarters agreed they tried to take all of a client's needs into account (71.5 percent), that they adapted their explanation of opportunities and benefits to clients' individual situations (69.7 percent), and that they tried to assess each client's needs individually (67 percent). A little more than one-quarter (25.7 percent) acknowledged making special exceptions for "good" clients. About two-thirds said that they would not do just the bare minimum for difficult clients (66.1

percent). Thus, in a survey format, most workers indicated that they do not particularize services. This is in direct opposition to the findings from the observational studies by Kingfisher (1999) and Meyers and colleagues (1998), who found that workers had a strong tendency to particularize their interventions.

Statements that were characterized as routinizing services indicated strong agreement in some cases and differing opinions in others. More than half of the workers agreed that they would follow the same rule book with all clients (57.4 percent). One-third recognized that clients' personal circumstances are not part of their job or a part for which they have time, and almost one-third agreed that they try not to individualize (32.1 percent). It is still perhaps encouraging that 40.4 percent disagreed with the last statement, and that more than one-third (36.1 percent) disagreed that the clients' personal lives were not part of their job, indicating an interest in individualizing their responses.

This study verifies again that there is a great deal of variation in the way front-line public welfare workers view clients. Only three statements provoked a majority agreement, and they are significant in that they are all negative views and negative stereotypes about welfare clients. The majority of these workers, then, believe that welfare clients come from certain "groups" in society, that they do not really need to be on welfare, and that they have little desire to get off welfare.

As welfare recipients join the ranks of the employed in strong economic periods, those left on the welfare rolls are going to present even greater challenges to workers to move beyond discouragement and stereotyped judgments. In addition, unstable, low-wage jobs and any movement toward recession may mean periods of return to dependence on public welfare. Careful and persistent assessments that continue to look for barriers to long-term self-sufficiency that exist not only in the individual but also in the social environment will be useful. Front-line workers can provide key information about what their clients need and how communities can make it possible for all members to have a subsistence level of living, at a minimum.

Workers had ambiguous views of welfare services, views that may result in conflict about their own roles with their clients. The area of personal discretion may be the most difficult for front-line workers, as shown in other studies (Hagen and Owens-Manley 2002; Kingfisher 1998; Meyers et al. 1998). Whenever personal discretion is exercised, particularly as it affects other people's lives, professional assessment and judgment is needed. With the advent of welfare reform, front-line workers appear to play even more critical roles as gatekeepers to welfare programs and services, with increased levels of administrative discretion. Without clear guidelines, training, and sufficient information, decisions will be unpredictable and arbitrary and driven by considerations of time and feelings of the moment. In the presence of negative bias and beliefs held toward particular clients, the potential for manipulation of information and access to services is very high. In two recent studies of directly observed behaviors of front-line workers in public welfare, manipulation, or selective emphasis and interpretation, was very much in evidence (Kingfisher 1998; Meyers et al. 1998).

Do these discrepancies represent conflicting feelings within workers or diverse responses among workers? To address the difficulty workers had in making decisions in a previous research study (Hagen and Owens-Manley 2002), and the discretionary behaviors described by Meyers and colleagues (1998) and Kingfisher (1998), two things are proposed. First, self-reporting may differ considerably from firsthand observation. Second, there may be a great deal of conflict in how to manage personal feelings and reactions, lack of clarity in role and job duties, and considerable pressure when making decisions that affect people's lives. The area of personal discretion is one in which workers participating in the survey in New York State seemed to strive for the "right" answer (Owens-Manley 2000). Further research is needed to understand how personal discretion is exercised and what would most appropriately support professionally driven, assessment-based decisions on client services. The alternative is to have considerable variability in the provision of client services that depends not only on state and local policy, but also on the luck of the draw that matches clients with workers.

CHANCE AND CIRCUMSTANCE FOR POOR WOMEN

My story followed my mother's in the sense that I had better personal and social-network resources than many women, but they were strained by the circumstances of a very early marriage, at eighteen, and a subsequent divorce and marriage to a man with drug and alcohol problems. We were poor because I cut short my education, he failed to attend college or prepare himself for a vocation, and we made a very passive decision to have children before we were financially ready. He was recently out of the armed services, and we lived near both of our families. They provided assistance for us to buy a home—one that was inexpensive but still one that we owned, a luxury that many low-income families do not have.

Before my marriage, education was always a positive force in my life. I graduated fourth in my class and was consistently in the top ten in school. Yet by my senior year of high school, no one was planning a college career with me or for me. My social-network resources were inadequate at this point in my life to prepare me for the next stage. My parents may not have known much about how to plan for college, and two family relocations in a row had deprived the entire family of school support, close family friends, and neighborhood or community support. I did begin college, at a hastily chosen school, but with halfhearted financial support and a depleted social-support system. Not surprisingly, I dropped out of college after a semester, lacking direction and feeling strained financially, but I continued over the next ten years in a part-time, on-again-off-again fashion to obtain my bachelor's degree. Education was like a beacon in my life, which was often filled with personal turmoil. I had married and divorced twice by age twenty-seven, and I was a single parent of two young children. I remained consistent to my goal, and in truth, getting an education was always something taken for granted in my vision, unlike that of many poor women. It was a surprise to be finished, but the outcome was an expected one.

My first degree helped me to get a job that I not only loved, but one in which I was treated as a social-work professional. It also helped me to leave a marriage that was increasingly strained and abusive. My job was supported by the Comprehensive Employment and Training Act (CETA). I was paid barely a minimum wage, so I also received public support in the form of rental assistance and food stamps. There were many helping hands and community supports to assist me in landing on my feet, and I have no illusions that I did it entirely on my own. I had the necessary self-esteem, socialization, and work skills to excel in such a position and establish myself for future advancement, but the initial lack of an opportunity could have resulted in a much different life path. Those eighteen months of my first professional job were not easy. For one thing, my children and I experienced serious illnesses. At the same time that I scheduled major surgery, I was informed that my CETA job was ending, and there were no funds to hire me permanently.

I am a resilient person in large part because of my strong family support system and as a result of educational opportunities. These networks and opportunities supported my determination, perhaps more an inner assumption of success, which pushed forward. The reality for many single mothers is that following a routine with young children day after day and working full time for wages that do not raise their families out of poverty takes every bit of energy they have, and the grind wears them down. I have always had a life filled with people: a mother who came along at just the right moments, even if she did not agree, to shore up the defenses; wonderful sisters who could listen and empathize; and good, close friends. I also had—which I consider to be key—grandparents, aunts, uncles, and cousins living at a distance but solidly behind me. In them I had a support system many poor women do not have. I believed that I was loved and supported in life always, by many and by those who had sufficient resources themselves to lend support. That belief, I think, is central in a life trajectory that pushes ahead, without a sense of fragility and uncertainty, bent on success not out of desperation but out of a certainty of getting there eventually.

The decision I had to make while fresh out of a job was a difficult one. I could have looked for another job, but I was recovering from major surgery and had two young children, and I had an idea that I should go to graduate school. My plans this time met with considerable opposition, at first from my parents, who thought the safe and stable thing to do would be to continue working at something just to bring in consistent money. My first job had helped me acquire a picture of what I could accomplish with a master's degree, and my financial sense was that, with two children to support, I needed to pursue this goal. I have never been sorry. But I have been reflective about the element of chance and circumstance in my life and the lives of others, and very conscious of the importance of social contexts—the social supports needed to succeed.

The social context of our lives is important for the tangible benefits and assistance we receive as interventions in the paths of our life stories. The context of public welfare is a critical one for women who do not have sufficient personal resources and social networks and require assistance as a result. It also provides important feedback from another juncture in women's lives: feedback about their current positions; their chances of "making it" to another level in their lives; their ability to succeed in jobs, job training, or school; and their inherent worth as human beings. The perception of at least some front-line workers was one in which society wants poor women shut away and for them to "go away," because poor women are perceived as social problems. Individual perceptions of welfare workers continue to be important in establishing useful and respectful partnerships to empower clients. Negative stereotyping and judgmental decisions about clients' behavior get in the way of providing needed information and direction to enable clients to move most powerfully through and away from the welfare system.

Children are the other group to consider when the lives of women on welfare are assessed. A short-term vision is one that computes the immediate cost–benefit ratio of sending a woman to school or even providing the sort of training for work that will elevate the family above the poverty line. A more visionary consideration is one of long-term costs and benefits, not only for the woman herself, but also for her children. Berrick writes, "Sadly, while these women are living in poverty, the opportunities for their children to grasp the American dream diminish considerably" (Berrick 1995, 147). There is concern, noted recently by Hagen, that TANF may have harmful effects for the well-being of children and that monitoring mechanisms that have been put in place are inadequate for tracing increases in child poverty (Hagen 1999). A recent youth-development project in Sacramento, California, advertises a vision for their community in which children grow up healthy by choice, not by chance. It is just this aspect of chance in the lives of poor women and children that has the power to both intrigue and horrify.

By the time my children were old enough to notice, life was sufficiently comfortable. They talk about my educational achievements with pride, and they assume that education is their right and the automatic path in life, the one they will take. In an age of scarce resources, it is hardly true that the opportunity to claim higher education as a right and an automatic pathway is open to all children—if anything, it is becoming less so. The life stories of all of our children should not be unalterably established at a young age so as to preclude the opportunities that education could present in their lives. There is a chance to intervene in the context of social-service provision with social and financial support for education and training when poor women are asking for that opportunity.

The lives of poor women and their children are buffeted by the circumstances of their lives and are often not supported by either informal or formal systems of care. Many clients who turn to the support offered by public welfare lack those systems of care and have, in addition to the ordinary stresses of insufficient income, family histories of abuse and neglect (see Albeda 1995; Brooks and Bruckner 1996). The impact of those stressful life events in a life trajectory cannot be ignored, and those responsible for social policies, social-service agencies, and the actions of front-line workers interacting with poor women need to be aware of the impact left by events and the difference support can make.

Recent changes in social policies typified by the Personal Responsibility and Work Reconciliation Act have set the stage for decreased support for women and children, and front-line workers have an important role to play in providing access to opportunities and supportive services for poor women, including access to higher education. Workers' perceptions of their clients and of their jobs, together with the exercise of personal discretion, may have the ability to tip the scale for some women who are struggling to achieve personal and financial stability that elevates themselves and their children above the poverty level. With the shortsighted policies and practices that instead are increasingly in place, women will struggle with ever more limited paths to alter a life course of poverty.

We know now that increased education makes a critical difference in employability and increased wages for all women (Kates 1995; Seavey 1996; Spalther-Roth et al. 1995). Education has power in women's lives to pull upward, to influence toward success, and to create stories of success and well-being. These benefits have been seen to accrue in the lives of women themselves and for the lives of their children into the future. Women and children will thrive in a society that does not look on the poor as "lepers" and the front-line workers who interact with them as "leper keepers" but, rather, sees their potential and invests in that vision through education and training. With the support of social policies, social structures, and common human decency in service interactions, women can be empowered to pursue life-altering choices in their lives.

NOTES

Epigraph: Bricker-Jenkins (1991, 2).

1. The number 1 represented the highest priority for exemption, and 7 represented the lowest. Based on Kendall's coefficient of concordance (0 equals no agreement; 1 equals complete agreement), the overall agreement of rankings by participants was .173, or very little agreement.

2. These responses are drawn from conversations with front-line workers in public welfare agencies who participated in focus groups with the author and Jan Hagen in upstate New York, 9 and 16 November 1997.

REFERENCES

Abramovitz, Mimi. 1996. *Regulating the Lives of Women: Social Welfare Policy from Colonial Times to the Present.* Boston: South End Press.

Albelda, Randy Pearl. 1995. *An Economic Profile of Women in Massachusetts.* Boston: Center for Women in Politics, John W. McCormack Institute of Public Affairs, University of Massachusetts.

Berrick, Jill D. 1995. *Faces of Poverty: Portraits of Women and Children on Welfare.* New York: Oxford University Press.

Bricker-Jenkins, Mary. 1991. "Introduction." Pp. 1–13 in *Feminist Social Work Practice in Clinical Settings,* ed. Mary Bricker-Jenkins, Nancy R. Hooyman, and Naomi Gottlieb. Newbury Park, Calif.: Sage Publications.

Brodkin, Evelyn. 1997. "Inside the Welfare Contract: Discretion and Accountability in State Welfare Administration." *Social Service Review* 71: 1–33.

Brooks, Margaret, and J. Bruckner. 1996. "Work and Welfare: Job Histories, Barriers to Employment, and Predictors of Work among Low-Income Single Mothers." *American Journal of Orthopsychiatry* 66, no. 4: 526–37.

Crago, Hugh. 1988. "Programmed for Despair? The Dynamics of Low Morale/High Burnout Welfare Organizations." *Australian Social Work* 41, no. 2: 31–35.

Gummer, Burton. 1990. *The Politics of Social Administration: Managing Organizational Politics in Social Agencies.* Englewood Cliffs, N.J.: Prentice-Hall.

Hagen, Jan. 1989. "Income Maintenance Workers: Burned-out, Dissatisfied, and Leaving." *Journal of Social Service Research* 13, no. 1: 47–63.

———. 1999. "Time Limits under Temporary Assistance to Needy Families: A Look at the Welfare Cliff." *Affilia* 14, no. 3: 294–314.

Hagen, Jan, and Judith Owens-Manley. 1998. *Front-Line Workers Discuss Implementing TANF.* Report submitted to Albany and Oneida County (N.Y.) Departments of Social Services.

———. 2002. "Issues in Implementing TANF in New York: The Perspective of Frontline Workers." *Social Work* 47, no. 2: 171–82.

Hagen, Jan, Irene Lurie, and Ling Wang. 1993. *Implementing JOBS: The Perspective of Front-Line Workers.* Albany, N.Y.: Rockefeller Institute of Government.

Kates, Erika. 1995. *Escaping Poverty: The Promise of Higher Education.* Ann Arbor, Mich.: Society for Research in Child Development.

Kingfisher, Catherine P. 1998. "How Providers Make Policy: An Analysis of Everyday Conversation in a Welfare Office." *Journal of Community and Applied Social Psychology* 8: 119–36.

Meyers, Marcia K., Bonnie Glaser, and Karin MacDonald. 1998. "On the Front Lines of Welfare Delivery: Are Workers Implementing Policy Reforms?" *Journal of Policy Analysis and Management* 17, no. 1: 1–22.

Mills, C. Wright. 1959. *The Sociological Imagination.* New York: Oxford University Press.

Owens-Manley, Judith. 2000. "Individual and Organizational Factors Affecting Service Delivery in Public Welfare Agencies." Ph.D. diss., State University of New York, Albany.

Progoff, Ira. 1975. *At a Journal Workshop: The Basic Text and Guide for Using the Intensive Journal.* New York: Dialogue House Library.

Seavey, Dorie K. 1996. *Back to Basics: Women's Poverty and Welfare Reform.* Wellesley, Mass.: Center for Research on Women.

Spalther-Roth, Roberta, Beverly Burr, Heidi Hartmann, and Lois Shaw. 1995. *Welfare That Works: The Working Lives of AFDC Recipients.* Washington, D. C.: Institute for Women's Policy Research.

Weatherley, Richard, Claudia B. Kottwitz, Denise Lishner, Kelley Reid, Grant Roset, and Karen Wong. 1980. "Accountability of Social Services Workers at the Front Line." *Social Service Review* 54, no. 4: 556–71.

LISA D. BRUSH

13   "That's Why I'm on Prozac"

Battered Women, Traumatic Stress, and Education in the Context of Welfare Reform

THIS CHAPTER explores the connections among poverty, education, and battering in the context of welfare reform. Welfare is generally the last refuge of mothers unable to make ends meet (Edin and Lein 1997). Cash assistance; food stamps; subsidies for child care, housing, and transportation; and health-care coverage can enable women of all social classes to escape battering. That is, welfare provides women with an alternative to physical violence and economic and emotional abuse by people they have loved and trusted (their current and former husbands and boyfriends, for instance). Welfare benefits mean that battered women can try to escape abusers, even if miserly cash assistance means they are destitute. Welfare enables battered women to leave, even if they must abandon their jobs (Davis 1999) or their homes (Roofless Women 1996). Welfare benefits can help women get away, get back on their feet, or complete the education or training they need to get themselves and their children out of poverty and out of danger. Battered women are most likely to be killed when they try to leave, and they often leave only when they are convinced that they or their children are in mortal peril (Dobash and Dobash 1998; Hoff 1990). Welfare can be the difference between life and death.

Just as welfare can save the lives of battered women, education can help battered women, especially the more resilient, to recover their dignity and achieve safety and solvency. It takes great courage to learn and work in order to escape poverty and battering, especially when every step toward solvency and safety triggers abuse. My research shows that although education alone cannot protect women on welfare from battering, support for women's educational efforts is crucial to women's escaping poverty and abuse. Ironically, better-educated women—who generally have higher earning capacity than their less-educated sisters—

may find themselves fending off particularly persistent exploitative or abusive men. Women trying to increase their options through education and job training may be stymied by boyfriends or husbands who are threatened by their increased earnings, social networks, or self-confidence. The costs of doing nothing, of letting battered women fend for themselves, of requiring women on welfare to meet strict eligibility standards that endanger them, and of letting battered women fall through the cracks of our education and welfare systems far outweigh the costs of supportive services. My findings suggest that welfare reformers, program staff, and educators who ignore the relationships among education, waged work, and battering are jeopardizing the safety, dignity, and success of poor mothers.

Reforms that shred the welfare safety net push women to depend on a set of sexist social institutions—school, work, and marriage. At school, girls and women may be tracked into "traditional" courses of study or vocational training, ignored in the classroom, and denied funding and mentoring (Sadker and Sadker 1994; Weis and Fine 1993). On the job, women face discrimination in hiring, pay, and promotion and harassment that can threaten their health and circumscribe their opportunities (Hesse-Biber and Carter 2000; Stein 1999). Dependence on marriage is especially risky. Anti-poverty and anti-violence advocates alike fear that welfare reform will punish women unless they affiliate with men in order to legitimate their sexuality and their fertility. Unfortunately, such affiliations often compromise women's well-being, solvency, safety, and dignity. According to National Crime Victimization Survey estimates, the average annual rate of rape, sexual assault, robbery, and physical assault by an intimate is 9.3 per 1,000 U.S. women age twelve or older (Bachman and Saltzman 1995). Surveys of participants in local and state welfare and job-training programs suggest that between 22 and 80 percent of welfare recipients and welfare-to-work program participants report current episodes of battering. Between 26 and 51 percent report that they are past victims (for summaries, see GAO 1998; Raphael 1997).

Anti-violence advocates fear that welfare reform will force battered women into further compromising their safety. Women may stay with abusive men, or feel compelled to renew contact with them, to avoid sanctions (Roberts 1999). Teenage mothers and their children are especially vulnerable to physical and sexual abuse, often perpetrated by the men (fathers and stepfathers, for example) with whom welfare reforms force them to live (Boyer 1999). Women's compliance with work requirements and conformity to "family values" may put them at risk. If abusers feel threatened, they may sabotage battered women's newly developed social networks, education and skills, self-esteem, or financial resources (Raphael 1999).

Both the abuse and the synergy between battering and public policy can obstruct women's safety, education and development, and transition from welfare to work (Brush 2000; James and Harris 1996; Raphael 1997, 1999). Although poverty may keep women trapped in battering relationships, battering keeps them trapped in poverty (Raphael 2000). Welfare reform exacerbates the trap by punishing women for being unable to escape from either and by invalidating education as a "work-related activity" (Brandwein 1999; Raphael 1996b). Welfare-rights advocates are also concerned because battering potentially obstructs the welfare-to-work transition—including education and training—through short-term crises, deliberate destruction, and long-term damage.

Battering creates crises—emergencies of health, safety, housing, and child custody. Battered women are often injured, distraught, and distracted. The dilemmas that poor, battered women face make it hard to comply with the demands of welfare, work, or school. For example, battered women find themselves making absurd choices between abuse and homelessness when the only way to escape a batterer is to leave "his" household (see Malos and Hague 1997; Roofless Women 1996). Battered women of all classes may also end up torn between obligations to themselves and to their children and risk losing custody if they cannot protect themselves and their children from abuse (Atkins and Whitelaw 1996; Roberts 1999). Poor women have even fewer resources for dealing with these conflicting obligations and are even more vulnerable to the demands of child-protective services. Poor, battered women also find themselves in a bind because child-protection agencies require domestic vigilance from mothers, while welfare agencies require waged work (Pearce 1999; this is a long-standing problem, as explained in Gordon 1988). The chaos, pain, and humiliation of recent or ongoing abuse make it extremely difficult for any battered woman to attend school or training programs, to concentrate on her studies, and to learn the skills and content on which to build a future. For women on welfare, the trouble battering adds to survival in poverty can be overwhelming.

Batterers sabotage women's success in school, job training, and waged work. Abusers undermine women with "physical violence, emotional coercion, destruction of books and homework assignments, and harassment ... [and by] turning off alarm clocks and fail[ing] to show up to drive their partners to important job interviews or the general equivalency diploma (GED) examination" (Raphael 1996b, 187; see also Raphael 1996a; Stevens 1996). The sabotage may be subtle or blatant, and it can run the gamut from racking up debts (for instance, when the man makes repeated expensive long-distance calls on a telephone billed in the woman's name; see James and Harris 1996), to coercive involvement in illegal activities (Richie 1996). Either way, in the intermediate term, abusive men can easily derail women's progress in education, job training, and other prerequisites for family-supporting employment (Brandwein 1999; Raphael 1999). Attendance requirements and time limits that fail to acknowledge the myriad ways men thwart women's efforts to learn and develop will simply abuse women all over again.

The long-term consequences of battering can include debilitating injuries; disrupted education; and cognitive and emotional barriers to learning and education, training, and work performance. In particular, some battered women may need time and services to recover from physical injuries and mental-health problems that can linger long after abuse has stopped. Battering and its consequences may make it particularly difficult for some currently or formerly battered women to concentrate, attend to specific learning tasks, plan coursework or training, contain anxiety, interact in high-pressure settings, respond appropriately to criticism, avoid depression in the face of adversity, and conform to the professional or "good student" culture of school and training programs. Issues of control (over self, circumstances, and others), connection (with self and others), and meaning (in language and life) are central to the violation of battering and can make learning in general, and literacy-oriented learning in particular, a challenge (Horsman 2000).

Persistent physical, mental, and emotional abuse can cause symptoms of traumatic stress in women who have been battered or raped. (The classic feminist source is Walker 1988; see also Dutton 1992; Foa and Rothbaum 1998; Herman 1992.) Traumatic stress symptoms can be acute or chronic, and they can develop immediately or some time after the trauma is over (Herman 1992; Rigley 1985; Root 1992). Post-traumatic stress disorder (PTSD) is the clinical diagnostic name for a cluster of symptoms originally diagnosed in combat veterans. PTSD symptoms include intrusive memories (flashbacks, nightmares), flattened affect (depression, hopelessness), and hyperarousal (insomnia, nervousness, angry outbursts; see APA 1994). Trauma has multiple, cumulative, interactive effects on battered women's cognition, affective regulation and belief systems (Friedman 1997). Traumatized battered women report these symptoms, plus feelings of worthlessness and profound doubt in the orderliness and trustworthiness of reality. (For a non-technical summary and review, see Murphy 1993.)

Without support or time and space for healing, some battered women may find that their survival strategies inadvertently obstruct their progress at school or work. For instance, battered women may dissociate or "check out" mentally and emotionally or imagine that the abuse is happening to someone else (Breslau et al. 1997; Friedman 1997). They may become habituated to being arbitrarily controlled and terrorized by an external force and adopt a stance of "learned helplessness" in the face of abuse that carries over into educational and vocational settings (Lefcourt 1976; Peterson et al. 1993; Seligman 1975). The experience of being violated by someone at least formerly trusted and loved may generate a level of cognitive dissonance that interferes with making other rational decisions, planning for safety, and setting goals (Blackman 1989). The women may use alcohol or other drugs to manage physical and emotional pain, a strategy that distorts perception, undermines motivation, and inhibits cognition and regulation of emotions. Battering and its symptomatic consequences can spill over from the private realm of the family and mental health and derail women's progress in public settings such as school and work, thus thwarting women's achievements and aspirations (Murphy 1993, 1997).

To the extent that they fail to recognize battering and its effects, time limits on benefits that restrict support for poor women's recovery are likely to undermine some battered welfare recipients' use of education to support their transition from welfare to work. Work requirements, time limits, and the rigidly punitive rhetoric of welfare reform may moreover retraumatize women by reproducing the feelings of stress, failure, and lack of control that are at the heart of abuse (Horsman 2000). Welfare reforms that focus exclusively on work and foreclose education as a route out of poverty and battering deny women important support for achieving safety and solvency.

Post-Traumatic Stress Disorder and Its Discontents

The psychiatric model of PTSD provides a tangible marker and credible measure of the harm of battering to women. It specifies strict diagnostic grounds on which welfare recipients might successfully petition for exemption from the work requirements and time limits imposed by welfare reform. A psychiatric diagnosis of PTSD can legitimate the difficulties some welfare recipients face in going to work or succeeding in school. Viewing PTSD as a rare, clearly diagnosable clinical category assuages welfare administrators' concerns about fraud and malingering (Brush 1999). Psychiatric diagnosis provides legal grounds for women with a history or crisis of abuse and related distress to receive referrals for vocational rehabilitation, occupational therapy, and supplementary income (Murphy 1993). The medical model of PTSD is also a useful heuristic device for helping women understand and recover from battering and its physical, emotional, educational, and vocational consequences (Murphy 1997).

Of particular interest in the case of education and welfare reform, the medical model of PTSD holds that poor women are not stupid, lazy, or immoral. Rather, they may suffer from a set of symptoms that may interfere with learning, training, and program compliance. Research on the physical and functional effects of trauma show a robust connection between PTSD and cognition, specifically through diminished hippocampal volume. The hippocampus is a part of the brain that is considered a key site of memory and learning. Traumatic stress affects learning capacity in part through this mechanism (Yehuda and McFarlane 1997; but see also Agartz et al. 1999). Moreover, adult survivors of childhood sexual abuse with PTSD show selective recall deficits that suggest problems in learning neutral or positive items not related to trauma (Jenkins et al. 1998; McNally et al. 1998).

Post-traumatic stress symptoms can obstruct education, work, and compliance with welfare-reform requirements. Intrusive memories, sleep disruptions, selective attention, emotional numbing, and dissociation all interfere with concentration, and hence with education (Bryant and Harvey 1997; Litz et al. 1997; Yehuda and McFarlane 1997). The inability to regulate affect—for example, raging in the face of small frustrations or experiencing panic attacks in unfamiliar or triggering situations—can make education fraught for both student and teacher. The hopelessness, depression, and profound sense of violation and loss of control produced by battering can limit aspirations, motivation, and achievement in an educational setting. Students who are unable to plan a course of study, defer gratification until graduation, or imagine a better future are unlikely to succeed and may attract only negative attention from teachers and advisers who do not understand battering and its consequences. The PTSD diagnosis acknowledges the devastating effects of trauma on women's bodies, minds, spirits, well-being, and prospects. Formal diagnosis opens the door to acknowledgement and treatment of symptoms, and potentially to recognizing and preventing recurrences of the abuse that caused them. Efforts to recognize and treat PTSD can draw attention to battering and its consequences for women's achievements and ambitions at school, at work, and at home. Diagnosis can win women the supportive services and resources they need to heal and escape the traps of poverty and abuse.

For all the advantages of the medical model of trauma, however, there are also significant problems. Psychiatric models that focus on individual traits too easily slide into punitive models that stigmatize poor women and their children. Adding a claim to physical and mental-health problems from battering may strike welfare reformers as special pleading on behalf of poor women who are, in their view, unfit for either motherhood or first-class citizenship. Further, the medical model empowers psychiatric experts rather than battered women (Dobash and Dobash 1992; Gondolf 1998). As it did for antiwar veterans from the Vietnam era to whom it was first applied, a psychiatric diagnosis of PTSD reframes battered women's suffering and potential political analysis of social injustice into a pathology requiring expert therapy (Lembcke 1998; see also Barker 2002). Also, the supposedly gender-blind medical model nevertheless imposes masculinist notions of "normal" that make some feminists deeply suspicious of the PTSD category. For instance, the diagnostic criteria for PTSD require that the trauma be "generally outside the range of usual human experience." This is a problem, given that far too many women are battered for the experience to be considered "unusual," unless the category of humans includes only men (Horsman 2000). The medical model recognizes harm to women—a momentous accomplishment given the backlash against "victim feminism" (Brush 1997a; Larson 1993). But it does so at the risk of increased levels of surveillance and stigma of welfare recipients, who wind up measured, classified, treated, and sanctioned as gendered clients of the state (Brush 1997b; Fraser 1989).

In stressful, low-paid, long-hours jobs, "service with a smile" can seem hard for even the most cheerful and motivated worker. For a worker concerned about her safety or coping with post-traumatic stress, being "job ready" or "professional" can be a daunting standard. In the classroom, expectations and assumptions about comportment, commitment, cognition, and communication all shape teaching and learning. Educational aspirations and attainment can be disrupted by battering and its physical, social, economic, emotional, and mental consequences.

At the same time, waged work, safety, solvency, social networks, and solidarities formed at school or work, and educational and vocational development can rehabilitate battered women, at least if conducted in a safe and supportive rather than punitive context (Stevens 1996). For a woman facing a safety crisis at home, or suffering from nightmares about past abuse, school or work can be an escape and a route to becoming a "mother hero" (Withorn 1996; see also Brush 2000; Kates 1996). However, for a battered woman, work or school can be just another place where there is no room for her as a human being with feelings. The expert "discovery" and medical model of battering and trauma generates more intrusive interviews, bureaucratic red tape, and prescription-pill popping instead of more talking back and fighting back by welfare recipients.

POLICY ISSUES AND RESPONSE

The contradictions of a PTSD diagnosis aside, some battered women are likely to be among those welfare recipients whose education, training, and transition from welfare to work will be most difficult. Unless programs can recognize and address these obstacles, some battered women on welfare may be especially vulnerable to incurring sanctions. Moreover, their failure to comply with program requirements can count against the performance criteria welfare reformers set for states' drawing down their block grants.

To protect poor, battered women from such penalties, and to motivate states to serve rather than sanction battered welfare recipients, advocates lobbied for an amendment to the welfare-reform legislation.

The Family Violence Option (FVO) allows states to screen for battering, make referrals, provide services, and temporarily waive work requirements and time limits. The FVO makes it possible for states to meet the needs of battered women on welfare without jeopardizing block-grant funds. The FVO also makes it possible to waive work requirements and time limits without counting battered women against the 20 percent of the welfare caseload eligible for "hardship exemption" under welfare reform (Pollack and Davis 1997). Thus, the FVO is an important tool for political organizing. The FVO short-circuits attempts to pit battered welfare recipients against other poor women who may have trouble making a smooth, quick transition from welfare to work. FVO also goes a long way toward getting the interests of welfare administrators and battered welfare recipients lined up with each other instead of clashing over how to respond to the imperatives of reform.

TWO STUDIES: STAFF AND ENROLLEES ON BATTERING AND TRAUMATIC STRESS SYMPTOMS

To increase our empirical understanding of the relationships among battering, traumatic stress, education, and welfare-to-work transition, I conducted a pair of studies in an urban county in a state that adopted the FVO. I met with and surveyed 120 staff at fifteen employment-training sites, and I interviewed a cohort of 122 welfare recipients who were enrolled in a short-term "work-first" program at six of those same sites. I wanted to document rates of battering and traumatic-stress symptoms. I also wanted to know whether the women who disclosed a history of battering or traumatic stress were more likely to drop out of the program than the rest of the women (Brush 2000). I looked for differences in battering and program outcome for women with different levels of educational achievement. Finally, I compared the estimates staff members made of the proportion of their clients who were battered with the actual reports by the women at these job-readiness sites (Brush 1999).

ENROLLEE DATA

Table 13.1 summarizes some of the characteristics of the 122 enrollees, the rates of abuse and traumatic-stress symptoms, and program outcome. Table 13.1 also allows comparisons by level of educational attainment.

TABLE 13.1. Participant characteristics, abuse and consequences, and program outcome by educational attainment (rates in percent; N = 122)

Characteristics and obstacles		Preva-lence	Less than high school (N = 29)	High school or equivalent (N = 40)	Some post-secondary (N = 38)	Technical-school graduate (N = 12)	College graduate (N = 3)
					Educational attainment		
Educational level			24	33	31	10	2
Co-resident with father of child(ren)[a]	Yes	21	5	21	36	11	50
	No	79	95	79	64	89	50
First birth under age 18	Yes	30	41	38	18	25	0
	No	70	59	62	82	75	100
Worked less than one month last year	Yes	50	62	45	47	50	33
	No	50	38	55	53	50	67
Did your current or most recent partner:							
Hit, kick, or throw something at you	Yes	38	35	38	42	33	33
	No	62	65	62	58	67	67
Force or coerce sex	Yes	18	14	15	18	33	33
	No	82	86	85	82	67	67
Cut, bruise, choke, or seriously injure you	Yes	27	21	30	32	17	33
	No	73	79	70	68	83	67
Tell you, "Working women are bad mothers"	Yes	12	7	12	13	25	0
	No	88	93	88	87	75	100
Tell you, "Must keep up with housework"	Yes	8	7	12	5	8	0
	No	92	93	88	95	92	100
Threaten to withdraw or withhold if you worked	Yes	6	7	5	3	17	0
	No	94	93	95	97	83	100

Pick fights with you	Yes	47	38	52	45	50	67
	No	53	62	48	55	50	33
Put you down verbally	Yes	32	31	35	34	17	33
	No	68	69	65	66	83	67
Threaten or harass you at work	Yes	21	10	17	26	25	67
	No	79	90	82	74	75	33
Show jealousy that you might meet someone at work[b]	Yes	46	17	50	63	42	67
	No	54	82	50	37	58	33
Traumatic-stress–related symptoms							
Trouble concentrating	Yes	43	56	38	44	27	33
	No	57	44	62	56	73	67
Intrusive memories	Yes	58	63	68	42	64	67
	No	42	37	32	58	36	33
Depressed	Yes	54	56	56	61	27	0
	No	46	44	44	39	73	100
No energy	Yes	28	33	27	25	36	0
	No	72	67	73	75	64	100
Angry	Yes	51	48	59	47	45	67
	No	49	52	41	53	55	33
Easily startled	Yes	34	30	29	47	18	33
	No	66	70	71	53	82	67
Post-traumatic stress symptomology	Yes	52	48	53	56	36	100
	No	48	52	47	44	64	0
Court appearance for protective order	Yes	24	14	22	32	25	33
	No	76	86	78	68	75	67
Program participation outcome	Drop out	11	17	5	16	8	0
	Get job	16	10	20	13	25	0

[a]$p \leq .05$.   [b]$p \leq .01$.

The majority of women had at least a high-school diploma or the equivalent (33 percent) or more education, and 12 percent were technical-school graduates. Not surprising in a group of current welfare recipients, only 2 percent were college graduates. This confirms the fact that higher education is incredibly important in helping women avoid poverty, and investments in education are likely to have large payoffs for women's safety and solvency. Nearly one-quarter (24 percent) of the enrollees I studied had less than a high-school level of education. Increased education is strongly associated with postponing first birth (Jones et al. 1986), and teenage mothers frequently have lower educational attainment than their non-parenting peers (An et al. 1993; Ribar 1999). However, among the women I studied, educational level did not have a statistically significant effect on teen births, recent work experience, or program-participation outcome. In addition, school-dropout rates, teen births, marital status, and labor-force–participation rates did not significantly affect program outcome (Brush 2000). In short, moralistic factors related to the work ethic or conformity to "family values" are not necessarily the most important obstacles to program compliance.

What *does* significantly obstruct program compliance is battering, which was widespread among the women I interviewed. Nearly four in ten (38 percent) reported that a current or former husband boyfriend had hit, kicked, or thrown something at them. One in four (27 percent) had been cut, bruised, strangled, or seriously injured when physically abused by an intimate. Eighteen percent of program enrollees were forced or coerced into sex by their partners. Other controlling behavior was even more common. Just under half reported their partner picking fights with them (47 percent) and being jealous about their meeting someone new at work (46 percent). One in five (21 percent) was threatened or harassed while at work (through unauthorized visits or phone calls, for example). One-third (32 percent) were told by their intimate partners that they would never be able to succeed at work or school. Three abusive control items, all related directly to threatening or controlling women about work, were rare. Between 6 and 12 percent of enrollees reported their partners' threatening to withdraw or withhold resources if they worked, or telling them they could only work if they kept up with the housework, or telling them that working mothers are bad mothers. Although rare, these controlling factors had considerable impact on program participation, increasing dropout rates significantly (Brush 2000).

Welfare was originally designed to replace the income of a male breadwinner, and both the U.S. Census and the regulations of welfare assumed—indeed, enforced—poor mothers living without a "man in the house" (Brush 1997b; Gordon 1994). However, administrators of job-training program have noted that many welfare recipients "are, in fact, living with or are intimately involved with a male" (Raphael 1996a, 202–203). Although for opposite reasons, both moralistic welfare reformers and battered women's advocates are particularly concerned with poor mothers' affiliations with men. Moralistic welfare reformers claim that education and marriage are important antipoverty strategies and argue that women should stay in school and stay married (even to abusive men) to avoid depending on welfare (Magnet 1993). Advocates for battered women claim that education can help women escape the dual trap of poverty and abuse. Welfare benefits and education or credentials can increase women's capacity for safe, solvent household formation. Women's capacity for safety and solvency threatens conservatives, who apparently fear that women (especially mothers) will not marry unless coerced by economic necessity (Mead 1986, 1992). In contrast, women's ability to avoid both poverty and abuse through a combination of education, waged work, and welfare benefits heartens feminists who seek to increase women's safety and well-being by redressing inequality in the workplace and stopping violence and abuse.

In the group I studied, about one-fifth (21 percent) of the eighty-four women who had contact with their children's father currently lived with him. In addition, co-residence with the father was one of the few characteristics that varied significantly by educational level. Only one in twenty enrollees with less than a high-school education lived with the father of her children. In sharp contrast, one in five high-school graduates, one in three with some post-secondary education, and half of the college graduates resided with the father of their children.

High co-residency rates suggest that neither welfare receipt nor increased education make mothers truly independent. It is true that in the aggregate, marriage and remarriage rates decline with increases in women's employment and earnings. However, at the individual level, increases in women's education and earnings raise the probability of marriage, especially for poor women (for a review and analysis, see Edin 2000). Contrary to the hopes of feminist advocates and fears of conservative reformers, many poor women—especially those with education beyond high school—maintain considerable contact with the fathers of their children. Jody Raphael (1996a, 203) is surely close to the truth when she observes that, "because they cannot live on the welfare check alone, many women become dependent on a man who helps to support the family." No matter their educational level, the wage gap means that many mothers depend on access to a man's earnings to help them avoid poverty. Presumably, some of these single mothers are also heterosexual women who do not want poverty to preclude the possibility of intimate relationships. More educated women also make more attractive partners to some men, a factor that could also contribute to the relatively high co-residency rates of women with more education.

In short, some women may be dependent on men by necessity; some may be affiliated by choice; and some may simply be more preferable partners for men seeking relationships with women who can support them. Either way, it would appear that the independence effects of welfare receipt and education are probably overstated by both conservative and feminist analysts. Education alone obviously will not eradicate battering or poverty. But education is an important prerequisite for living-wage employment in the contemporary economy, and living-wage employment can take women a life-saving step away from poverty and abuse.

Only one of the battering items varied by educational level. Women who had less than a high-school diploma or its equivalent reported significantly lower rates of work-related jealousy than those with at least minimal educational credentials (17 percent versus 55 percent; difference significant at the .001 level). That is, the more education an enrollee had, the more likely she was to report that her intimate partner viewed her work or training as threatening the relationship because she might meet someone new at work. Evidence of increased jealousy of men partnered with more educated women confirms the apprehensions of advocates for battered women that education and training may have unforeseen effects on women's welfare-to-work transition. Progressing toward safety and solvency through education could precipitate or aggravate jealousy, abuse, and control. The direct proportional relationship between education and work-related jealousy, moreover, is consistent with the co-residency finding. That is, there is evidence in this study that some abusive men seek to affiliate with—and control—women who have more education and earning capacity. What women in such situations need is support as they strive to escape poverty and battering. The last thing they need is the additional stigma or burden of sanctions that punish them simply because their lives are complicated by abuse. Educators and welfare reformers who fail to understand these dynamics of men's efforts to control women's earnings, aspirations, and achievements are unlikely to help poor battered women lead safer lives or make progress toward solvency and safety.

Traumatic-stress symptoms and self-protective actions related to battering were also in some cases widespread. One-third (34 percent) of enrollees had at least one symptom from all three symptom categories (intrusion, constriction, and hyperarousal) required for clinical diagnosis of PTSD. One in four had appeared in court to seek a Protection from Abuse (PFA) order. One-quarter had tried to avoid places (such as work or school) where their batterers might find them. Forty-three percent had sought counseling. Rates of reporting of traumatic-stress symptoms were almost uniform across demographic groups, including education, although the small group of college students seldom reported symptoms.

Two traumatic-stress–symptom items made a statistically significant difference in program-participation outcomes. Women who said they had trouble concentrating (an intrusion symptom) had similar dropout rates but significantly higher job-placement rates than women who did not report that symptom. Women who reported angry outbursts—a symptom of hyperarousal—dropped out significantly more frequently than those who did not. One interviewee responded to a question about intrusive memories of abuse by saying, "That's why I'm on Prozac." She was being treated with a prescription antidepressant for post-traumatic stress following battering, but she had been offered no safety planning, no other treatment, no referrals or supportive services, and no temporary FVO exemption from the work requirement or time limits imposed by welfare reform. It is because of women like her that advocates fear the FVO response to trauma in battered welfare recipients will be a clinical one that largely benefits the drug companies and employers who want zombie workers. These findings suggest that while some battered welfare recipients may have trouble complying with welfare-reform mandates because of traumatic-stress symptoms, others may find that education or employment ameliorates their symptoms. In both cases— that is, women whose symptoms undermine their efforts and women for whom school or work ameliorates their symptoms—supportive services and resources to help women escape poverty and abuse may avert costly injuries or work disruptions at a later point in time.

In sum, the effects of battering and traumatic stress on program-participation outcomes are complicated. Women whose intimate partners try to control them by invoking traditional duties of motherhood and housewifery are especially vulnerable to dropping out. Physically battered women, sexually coerced women, and women specifically threatened with desertion or denial of resources if they work more frequently find jobs. Angry women drop out. Women whose symptoms include intrusive memories find that work gets them out of the house and thinking about something else. Education may put women more at risk for jealous behavior and may also increase the stakes in men's control over women's accomplishments, earnings, social networks, and compliance with welfare requirements.

The evidence supports the claims of advocates that abuse shapes welfare recipients' transition to waged work. It suggests that battering is an important obstacle to safety and solvency. The bad news is that a safety crisis severe enough to merit a court appearance to seek a PFA nearly triples dropout rates. The hopeful news is that battered welfare recipients, even those with symptoms of traumatic stress, struggle to use training to comply with program requirements, establish economic autonomy, and possibly distract themselves from their symptoms. These findings further suggest that the FVO could help a substantial proportion of welfare recipients. Poor battered women could avoid sanctions, take the time they need to deal with both the short- and long-term consequences of abuse, and eventually succeed at school, training, and waged work. This positive outcome is likely only if battered women's experiences are taken seriously and they are offered appropriate opportunities and supportive services.

STAFF SURVEY

Unfortunately, the findings of my survey of program staff indicate that battered welfare recipients often receive opprobrium rather than opportunities, and scorn rather than supportive services. In the fall of 1997, I attended a meeting on welfare-reform–related research that brought together campus researchers and state and country officials eager to pool their knowledge of the policy changes and their likely impact on single mothers. I mentioned that advocates were worried that poor battered women might have trouble meeting work requirements and time limits. The director of the county public-assistance office responded with the story of a welfare recipient who was about to complete a computer-repair program when her boyfriend threatened to break her fingers if she finished the training. Obviously, battered women were on the radar screen of the highest welfare administrator in the county. Through my survey and conversations, I found that job-training staff and administrators make relatively accurate estimates of how many of their clients are abused. They overwhelmingly perceive battering as a problem for some clients. However, they perceive most abusive behavior as extremely rare and are especially reluctant to give estimates about physical abuse (Brush 1999). Why?

One reason for low staff estimates is that staff rely on direct observations but seldom talk about abuse with welfare recipients. They are more likely to give estimates—and not to be so far from the rates reported by enrollees—for items they can see for themselves (such as missing training because of a mandatory court appearance; Brush 1999). Unfortunately, some staff hear about problems only when their clients make excuses. In addition, staff may attribute clients' troubles (including battering) to negative stereotypes about poor people and their troubled relationships. Others are skeptical of battered women's claims and think that clients are trying to use battering as an excuse for laziness and poor judgment. While some staff worry about fraudulent excuses by clients, others, for whom the excuses are credible, nevertheless see abuse as resulting from poor individual choices. They may not understand the dynamics of battering and abuse and, as a consequence, blame women for the violence and control or for not leaving.

Finally, in a context of uncertainty about implementing the FVO and general ignorance about battering and its consequences, reports of battering have become politicized in ways that compromise candor. Without a strong sense of how to intervene in battering situations, staff can passively acknowledge abuse but still follow strong organizational disincentives to grant exemptions or actively serve battered women. The same organizational disincentives and individual stereotypes and suspicions that characterize work-first programs such as the one I studied also characterize many educational settings (Horsman 2000). They are formidable obstacles to battered women's learning and staying in school and to their receiving adequate advising, suitable supportive services, and appropriate opportunities.

Given the suspicions and biases of people in general, and of employment-training–program staff in particular, battered welfare recipients have good reason to hide abuse. They may be reluctant to admit that someone they love or trust has hurt them. They may fear losing housing or custody of their children if they admit they cannot keep themselves safe. Moreover, job-readiness programs train women to be "professional," which means leaving personal problems at home. In fact, work, education, and family are intimately connected for battered women, whose educational and vocational development are often held hostage to the abusive and controlling demands of men in the "private" realm of home and family. Battered welfare recipients are trapped between sanctions (if they do not disclose the abuse or are in a state that has not adopted the FVO) and abuse that may escalate as they gain more skills, confidence, and connections outside their homes.

If staff downplay or ignore battering, they invalidate poor women's experiences and may increase abused women's disorientation and trauma and shatter their fragile trust in the helpfulness of outsiders. If staff view poor women's complaints about battering as fraudulent attempts to win exemptions, battered women wind up disbelieved, controlled, and punished for being abused. If staff simply use FVO exemptions to make battered welfare recipients someone else's problem, they push battered women back into the trap of poverty and abuse. These observations apply to administrators, faculty, and staff in educational settings, just as they do to front-line workers and supervisors in welfare offices and employment-training programs.

CONCLUSION

Poverty renders women vulnerable to abuse. Abuse can trap women in poverty and obstruct women's transition from welfare to work. Battered welfare recipients have strong incentives to increase their safety and solvency through education and employment. They may not have much hope of doing so, especially without substantial support and resources. Welfare has historically provided poor mothers with a small measure of financial security, child care, transportation, and health insurance. They may be paltry, but the resources of welfare mean battered women have a high stake in complying with program requirements so they can maintain eligibility. Now that welfare is no longer an entitlement, the resources available to poor women are even more scanty and unreliable. Women's needs render them vulnerable to threats from abusive partners and to sanctions from an increasingly punitive welfare system.

Supporting women's educational efforts—even if they need extra money, time, patience, or services because they are battered—is a vital investment in women's well-being. Women, of course, are half our citizens and nearly half of the U.S. labor force. Investing in women's education, safety, and solvency is a vital investment in labor-force development and in democracy. Welfare reforms systematically disinvest in women's education and put more women at increased risk of poverty and abuse. The problem is not that battered women are less likely to succeed at school or work, and therefore that the extra effort required to meet their needs as students or workers represents a poor investment. On the contrary. As a nation, the United States cannot afford education and welfare policies that leave women trapped by poverty and trapped by abuse. Unfortunately, welfare reform undercuts long-term solutions to poverty—including education—by imposing sanctions, work requirements, and time limits.

Female workers face segregated labor markets and a substantial wage gap (Hesse-Biber and Carter 2000). Family-friendly workplaces are still a utopian dream for most mothers (and fathers, too). The United States lags far behind the other industrial democracies when it comes to helping people combine waged work and family-care responsibilities through affordable day care and health care, paid family leave, and flexible work schedules (Lewis 1993; McFate et al. 1995). All of these structural realities put women at risk for both poverty and battering. They force women to depend on access to a man's earnings. Admittedly, education is an individualistic strategy that does not stop discrimination or change the rules of the game. Nevertheless, education is an important prerequisite for women's safety and solvency. Indeed, education remains the best route for people to try to escape poverty and abuse through family-supporting work. Education helps women—one woman at a time—to gain the skills, confidence, and social networks they need to be productive workers and thoughtful citizens. Education empowers women—one woman at a time—to see safety and solvency as lofty but attainable goals that are in fact fundamental human rights. Education fits into the great American dream of pulling ourselves up by the boot-straps. Struggling for better educational opportunities for women has a long and illustrious history. Those struggles form a legacy that can inspire contemporary educators as we work with poor and battered women.

Educators dedicated to mitigating the damaging effects of welfare reform would do well to include issues of battering in life-skills education, in financial-aid advising, and in assessment, advising, and placement. Education advocates can help battered women on welfare by resisting work requirements and time limits that may short-circuit women's safety and efforts on their own behalf. Education advocates can educate themselves and one another about battering, poverty, and welfare reform and the threats they pose to women's safety, integrity, cognition, and initiative. They can increase poor battered women's ability to use school and employment training to move from welfare to work. Educators can create coalitions with anti-violence programs to include information about battering in the curriculum, provide referrals and support to battered women, and help in safety planning. Educators can question the concept of "normal" and make it clear in work with learners and administrators alike that, although violence is commonplace in women's lives, it is not acceptable. Educators can make battering visible through anti-violence posters in literacy programs, through posted referral information, through class and in-service presentations by local activists, and through assignments involving self-defense success stories (Caignon and Groves 1987; Horsman 2000). Allies in education can make classrooms and campuses safer and more responsive to battered women, even as they deliver tailored educational and training materials to battered women in shelters and other off-campus settings.

The temporary waivers from work requirements and time limits allowed under the FVO may increase the safety and successful outcomes for some battered welfare recipients. My findings certainly recommend against sanctioning battered women for not complying with program-attendance requirements. But waivers are not the whole answer. The evidence from my research also confirms the notion that education and employment are important routes to solvency, safety, and self-respect for women. Women's healing from the physical, economic, and emotional damage of battering may include rehabilitation through school, job training, waged work, and incorporation into the common life. Exemptions should never be another way of pushing women out of school or training programs, denying them services, or meeting performance mandates at the expense of dealing with seemingly intractable social problems or difficult-to-manage individuals.

Moralistic welfare reformers assume that poor women need to learn that "self-sufficiency" has its rewards. This lesson, even if cast in the most benign light, may well be lost on many welfare recipients, especially those who are battered. Indeed, sanctions may rob poor women of resources and control in ways that simply aggravate the trauma of battering. The complications of real women's real lives make it important to think clearly and carefully about the connections among work, school, motherhood, and relationships. Reforms must not impose a one-size-fits-all solution on women who have very different needs. Educators and welfare administrators and staff have to respect welfare recipients, and policy has to be built on the realities of women's lives, not just stereotypes. Thinking clearly about complicated social problems and working on a case-by-case basis with poor women takes time, money, and effort. However, we cannot afford to do any less. The United States cannot afford a welfare and education system that sanctions poor women for taking a beating.

REFERENCES

Agartz, Ingrid, Reza Momenan, Robert R. Rawlings, Michael J. Kerich, and Daniel W. Hommer. 1999. "Hippocampal Volume in Patients with Alcohol Dependence." *Archives of General Psychiatry* 56: 356–63.

An, Chang-Bum, Robert Haveman, and Barbara Wolfe. 1993. "Teen Out-of-Wedlock Births and Welfare Receipt: The Role of Childhood Events and Economic Circumstances." *Review of Economics and Statistics* 75: 195–208.

American Psychiatric Association (APA). 1994. *Diagnostic and Statistical Manual of Mental Disorders (DSM-IV)*. Washington, D.C.: American Psychiatric Association.

Atkins, David G., and John S. Whitelaw. 1996. "Turning the Tables on Women: Removal of Children from Victims of Domestic Violence." *Clearinghouse Review* 30: 261–72.

Bachman, Robert, and Linda E. Saltzman. 1995. "Violence against Women: Estimates from the Redesigned Survey." Special report NCJ-154348. Washington, D.C.: U.S. Department of Justice, Bureau of Justice Statistics.

Baker, Kristin. 2002. "Self-Help Literature and the Making of an Illness Identity: The Case of Fibromyalgia Syndrome (FMS)." *Social Problems* 49: 279–300.

Blackman, Julie 1989. *Intimate Violence: A Study of Injustice.* New York: Columbia University Press.

Boyer, Debra. 1999. "Childhood Sexual Abuse: The Forgotten Issue in Adolescent Pregnancy and Welfare Reform." Pp. 131–43 in *Battered Women, Children, and Welfare Reform: The Ties That Bind,* ed. Ruth A. Brandwein. Thousand Oaks, Calif.: Sage Publications.

Brandwein, Ruth, ed. 1999. *Battered Women, Children, and Welfare Reform: The Ties That Bind.* Thousand Oaks, Calif.: Sage Publications.

Breslau, Naomi, Glenn C. Davis, Edward L. Peterson, and Lonni R. Schultz. 1997. "Psychiatric Sequelae of Post-Traumatic Stress Disorder in Women." *Archives of General Psychiatry* 54: 81–87.

Brush, Lisa D. 1997a. "Harm, Moralism, and the Struggle for the Soul of Feminism." *Violence against Women* 3: 237–56.

———. 1997b. "Worthy Widows, Welfare Cheats: Proper Womanhood in Expert Needs Talk about Single Mothers in the United States, 1900 to 1988." *Gender and Society* 11: 720–46.

———. 1999. "Woman Battering and Welfare Reform: The View from a Welfare-to-Work Program." *Journal of Sociology and Social Welfare* 26: 49–60.

———. 2000. "Battering, Traumatic Stress, and Welfare-to-Work Transition." *Violence against Women* (September–October): 1039–65.

Bryant, Richard A., and Allison G. Harvey. 1997. "Attentional Bias in Post-Traumatic Stress Disorder." *Journal of Traumatic Stress* 10: 635–44.

Caignon, Denise, and Gail Groves. 1987. *Her Wits About Her: Self-Defense Success Stories by Women.* New York: Harper and Row.

Davis, Martha F. 1999. "The Economics of Abuse: How Violence Perpetuates Women's Poverty." Pp. 17–30 in *Battered Women, Children, and Welfare Reform: The Ties That Bind,* ed. Ruth A. Brandwein. Thousand Oaks, Calif.: Sage Publications.

Dobash, R. Emerson, and Russell P. Dobash. 1992. *Women, Violence, and Social Change.* New York: Routledge.

Dobash, R. Emerson, and Russell P. Dobash, eds. 1998. *Rethinking Violence against Women.* Thousand Oaks, Calif.: Sage Publications.

Dutton, Mary Ann. 1992. *Empowering and Healing the Battered Woman: A Model for Assessment and Intervention.* New York: Springer Publishing.

Edin, Kathryn. 2000. "What Do Low-Income Single Mothers Say about Marriage?" *Social Problems* 47: 112–33.

Edin, Kathryn, and Laura Lein. 1997. "Work, Welfare, and Single Mothers' Economic Strategies." *American Sociological Review* 62: 253–66.

Foa, Edna B., and Barbara Olasar Rothbaum. 1998. *Treating the Trauma of Rape: Cognitive-Behavioral Therapy for PTSD.* New York: Guilford Press.

Fraser, Nancy. 1989. *Unruly Practices: Power, Discourse, and Gender in Contemporary Social Theory.* Minneapolis: University of Minnesota Press.

Friedman, Matthew J. 1997. "Post-Traumatic Stress Disorder." *Journal of Clinical Psychiatry* 58, supp. 9: 33–36.

General Accounting Office (GAO). 1998. *Domestic Violence: Prevalence and Implications for Employment among Welfare Recipients.* Report no. GAO/HEHS-99-12. Washington, D.C.: Government Printing Office.

Gondolf, Edward W. 1998. *Assessing Woman Battering in Mental Health Services.* Thousand Oaks, Calif.: Sage Publications.

Gordon, Linda 1988. *Heroes of Their Own Lives: The Politics and History of Family Violence.* New York: Viking.

———. 1994. *Pitied but Not Entitled: Single Mothers and the History of Welfare, 1890–1935.* New York: Free Press.

Herman, Judith Lewis. 1992. *Trauma and Recovery: The Aftermath of Violence from Domestic Abuse to Political Terror.* New York: Basic Books.

Hesse-Biber, Sharlene, and Gregg Lee Carter. 2000. *Working Women in America: Split Dreams.* New York: Oxford University Press.

Hoff, Lee Ann. 1990. *Battered Women as Survivors.* New York: Routledge.

Horsman, Jenny. 2000. *Too Scared to Learn: Women, Violence, and Education.* Mahway, N.J.: L. Erlbaum Associates.

James, Susan, and Beth Harris. 1996. "Gimme Shelter: Battering and Poverty." Pp. 57–66 in *For Crying Out Loud: Women's Poverty in the United States,* ed. Diane Dujon and Ann Withorn. Boston: South End Press.

Jenkins, Melissa A., Philip J. Langlais, Dean Delis, and Ronald Choen. 1998. "Learning and Memory in Rape Victims with Post-Traumatic Stress Disorder." *American Journal of Psychiatry* 155: 278–79.

Jones, Elsie F., Jacqueline Darroch Forrest, Noreen Goldman, Stanley Henshaw, Richard Lincoln, Jeannie I. Rosoff, Charles F. Westoff, and Deidre Wulf. 1986. *Teenage Pregnancy in Industrialized Countries.* New York: Alan Guttmacher Institute.

Kates, Erika. 1996. "Colleges Can Help Women in Poverty." Pp. 341–48 in *For Crying Out Loud: Women's Poverty in the United States,* ed. Diane Dujon and Ann Withorn. Boston: South End Press.

Larson, Jane E. 1993. "'Imagine Her Satisfaction': The Transformative Task of Feminist Tort Work." *Washburn Law Journal* 33: 56–75.

Lefcourt, Herbert M. 1976. *Locus of Control: Current Trends in Theory and Research.* Hillsdale, N.J.: L. Erlbaum Associates.

Lembcke, Jerry. 1998. *The Spitting Image: Myth, Memory, and the Legacy of Vietnam.* New York: New York University Press.

Lewis, Jane, ed. 1993. *Women and Social Policies in Europe: Work, Family and the State.* Brookfield, Vt.: Edward Elgar Publishing.

Litz, Brett T., William E. Schlenger, Frank W. Weathers, Juesta M. Caddell, John A. Fairbank, and Lisa M. LaVange. 1997. "Predictors of Emotional Numbing in Post-Traumatic Stress Disorder." *Journal of Traumatic Stress* 10: 607–18.

Magnet, Myron. 1993. *The Dream and the Nightmare: The Sixties' Legacy to the Underclass.* New York: William Morrow.

Malos, Ellen, and Gill Hague. 1997. "Women, Housing, Homelessness and Domestic Violence." *Women's Studies International Forum* 20: 397–409.

McFate, Katherine, Roger Lawson, and William J. Wilson, eds. 1995. *Poverty, Inequality, and the Future of Social Policy: Western States in the New World Order.* New York: Russell Sage Foundation.

McNally, Richard F., Linda J. Metzger, Natasha B. Lasko, Susan A. Clancy, and Roger K. Pitman. 1998. "Directed Forgetting of Trauma Cues in Adult Survivors of Childhood Sexual Abuse with and without Post-Traumatic Stress Disorder." *Journal of Abnormal Psychology* 107: 596–601.

Mead, Lawrence M., ed. 1986. *Beyond Entitlement: The Social Obligations of Citizenship.* New York: Free Press.

———. 1992. *The New Politics of Poverty: The Non-working Poor in America.* New York: Basic Books.

Murphy, Patricia A. 1993. *Making the Connections: Women, Work, and Abuse.* Orlando, Fla.: PMD Press.

———. 1997. "Recovering from the Effects of Domestic Violence: Implications for Welfare Reform Policy." *Law and Policy* 19: 169–82.

Pearce, Diane M. 1999. "Doing the Triple Combination: Negotiating the Domestic Violence, Child Welfare, and Welfare Systems." Pp. 109–20 in *Battered Women, Children, and Welfare Reform: The Ties That Bind,* ed. Ruth A. Brandwein. Thousand Oaks, Calif.: Sage Publications.

Peterson, Christopher, Steven F. Maier, and Martin E. P. Seligman. 1993. *Learned Helplessness: A Theory for the Age of Personal Control.* New York: Oxford University Press.

Pollack, Wendy, and Martha F. Davis. 1997. "The Family Violence Option of the Personal Responsibility and Work Opportunity Reconciliation Act of 1996: Interpretation and Implementation." *Clearinghouse Review* 31: 1079–1100.

Raphael, Jody. 1996a. "Domestic Violence and Welfare Receipt: Toward a New Feminist Theory of Welfare Dependency." *Harvard Women's Law Journal* 19: 201–27.

———. 1996b. "Prisoners of Abuse: Policy Implications of the Relationship between Domestic Violence and Welfare Receipt." *Clearinghouse Review* 30: 186–94.

———. 1997. "Welfare Reform: Prescription for Abuse? A Report on New Research Studies Documenting the Relationship of Domestic Violence and Welfare." *Law and Policy* 19: 123–37.

———. 1999. "Keeping Women Poor: How Domestic Violence Prevents Women from Leaving Welfare and Entering the World of Work." Pp. 31–43 in *Battered Women, Children, and Welfare Reform: The Ties That Bind,* ed. Ruth A. Brandwein. Thousand Oaks, Calif.: Sage Publications.

Ribar, David C. 1999. "The Socioeconomic Consequences of Young Women's Childbearing: Reconciling Disparate Evidence." *Journal of Population Economics* 12: 547–65.

Richie, Beth 1996. *Compelled to Crime: The Gender Entrapment of Battered Black Women.* New York: Routledge.

Rigley, Charles R., ed. 1985. *Trauma and Its Wake.* New York: Brunner/Mazel.

Roberts, Paula. 1999. "Pursuing Child Support for Victims of Domestic Violence." Pp. 59–78 in *Battered Women, Children, and Welfare Reform: The Ties That Bind,* ed. Ruth A. Brandwein. Thousand Oaks, Calif.: Sage Publications.

Roofless Women, with Marie Kennedy. 1996. "A Hole in My Soul: Experiences of Homeless Women." Pp. 41–56 in *For Crying Out Loud: Women's Poverty in the United States,* ed. Diane Dujon and Ann Withorn. Boston: South End Press.

Root, Maria P. P. 1992. "Reconstructing the Impact of Trauma on Personality." Pp. 229–65 in *Personality and Psychopathology: Feminist Reappraisals,* ed. Laura S. Brown and Mary Ballou. New York: Guilford Press.

Sadker, Myra, and David Sadker. 1994. *Failing at Fairness: How American Schools Cheat Girls.* New York: Charles Scribner and Sons.

Seligman, Martin. E. P. 1975. *Helplessness: On Depression, Development, and Death.* San Francisco: W. H. Freeman.

Stein, Laura W. 1999. *Sexual Harassment in America: A Documentary History.* Westport, Conn.: Greenwood Press.

Stevens, Dottie. 1996. "Welfare Rights Organizing Saved My Life." Pp. 313–25 in *For Crying Out Loud: Women's Poverty in the United States,* ed. D. Dujon and A. Withorn. Boston: South End Press.

Walker, Lenore E. 1988. "The Battered Woman Syndrome." Pp. 139–49 in *Family Abuse and Its Consequences: New Directions in Research,* ed. Gerald T. Hotaling, David Finkelhor, John T. Kirkpatrick, and Murray A. Straus. Newbury Park, Calif.: Sage Publications.

Weis, Lois, and Michelle Fine, eds. 1993. *Beyond Silenced Voices: Class, Race, and Gender in United States Schools.* Albany: State University of New York Press.

Withorn, Ann. 1996. "Recognizing Mother Heroes." Pp. 327–36 in *For Crying Out Loud: Women's Poverty in the United States,* ed. Diane Dujon and Ann Withorn. Boston: South End Press.

Yehuda, Rachel, and Alexander C. McFarlane, eds. 1997. *Psychobiology of Post Traumatic Stress Disorder.* New York: New York Academy of Sciences.

Vivyan C. Adair

14   Fulfilling the Promise of
Higher Education

I GREW UP amid poverty, violence, and despair. Even though my young mother, the single parent of four, dedicated her life to bringing order, grace, and dignity to our lives, my siblings and I were often touched by hunger, lack of medical and dental attention, and fear. Growing up, I had little reason to believe that my life would be any different. And indeed, unable to acquire an education and without a sense of worth, I eventually had a child and became involved with a man who violated and abused me, leaving me hurt, frustrated, despondent, and profoundly impoverished.

I know all too well the desperation and hopelessness that shape and patrol the lives of poor women in the United States today. Yet I was fortunate enough to have been involved with a pre-reform welfare system, with superb educational institutions, and with instructors who enabled me to positively transform my life and that of my daughter.[1] When I had absolutely no one to turn to, no resources, and almost no hope, welfare was a safety net. Because I received welfare benefits, I was able to feed, clothe, and house my daughter without being forced to go back to the man who had torn our lives apart so destructively. Crucially, I was able to return to school so that eventually I could enter the workforce as a capable and committed worker able to support and nurture my family.

In 1987, I joined almost half a million welfare recipients who enrolled in institutions of higher education as a route out of poverty (Greenberg et al. 1999). As a result, today I have a Ph.D. and am productively employed as a professor at a private liberal-arts college in central New York State. I have the great fortune of working with supportive and brilliant colleagues, bright and earnest students, and friends who embrace, support, and nurture me. My healthy and happy sixteen-year-old daughter and I are also very active in the community, engaging in volunteer work and political activism. We strive to be conscientious citizens and contributing members of the college community, New York State, and the nation.

Certainly, access to post-secondary education permanently changed my economic status; my self-esteem; my capacity to think clearly, critically, and creatively; my ability to care for my child; my commitment to citizenship; and my authority and value in the world. Recently, one of my former students wrote to me about her own transformative experience. Now in her final year of law school, she reflected:

> It is difficult sometimes for me to fathom just how greatly my experience at the university changed my life and that of my children. One moment I was just one more poor, black woman, living in a broken-down car with my sons, trying to recover from the years of beatings that had left all of us so shell-shocked. And, the next moment I was happy to be living among other poor single-parent students in university housing, learning about philosophy and literature and law, supporting one another, going to concerts and lectures, thinking about our futures with hope and foresight. Rather than just reacting to my horrible situation on a moment-by-moment basis, I started planning my future, consciously marking out my contribution to the world and to my boys. The other day my oldest son, now ten, earnestly asked me whether I thought he should study to be a lawyer or an engineer when he goes to college. I broke down and wept for joy.[2]

In "Together We Are Getting Freedom," Noemy Vides recalls that her life as a poor immigrant welfare mother began anew when she was encouraged to seek an education. She tells us, "It is here I was born as a new woman with visions, dreams, hopes, opportunities, and fulfillment" (Vides and Steinitz 1996, 304). Vides and her coauthor, Victoria Steinitz, agree that a college education is "the key ingredient in poor women's struggles to survive" (Vides and Steinitz 1996, 304). In addition to changing women's lives economically, they claim that education

> builds self-worth; it provides concrete evidence that one has strengths and is a person of value. Beyond these economic and psychological benefits, a critical education that challenges dominant explanations can be transformative. Such an education provokes awareness that the labels— ignorant peasant, abandoned woman, broken-English speaker, welfare cheat—have nothing to do with who one really is, but serve to keep

women subjugated and divided. A critical education gives women tools
to understand the uses of power; it emboldens us to move beyond the
imposed shame that silences, to speak out and join together in a common
liberatory struggle. (Vides and Steinitz 1996, 305)

Before welfare reform in 1996, tens of thousands of poor single mothers quietly accessed post-secondary education to become teachers,
lawyers, social-service providers, business and civic leaders, and medical professionals. In addition to becoming valued members of their communities, these women changed how they interpreted their value and
authority as they reconceptualized their personal and familial goals. Their
experiences reflect the findings of Marilyn Gittell, Margaret Schehl, and
Camille Fareri (1990, 14), who observe that, "in addition to the economic
benefits of graduation, [low-income single mothers] reported improved
lifestyles, better standards of living and greater self esteem, and most said
they planned to encourage their children to attend college."

The process of earning post-secondary undergraduate and graduate
degrees can and does break otherwise inviolate cycles of intergenerational poverty. Becoming college educated transforms how poor single
mothers think, write, speak, act, work, parent, befriend, and love. Education is important to all citizens; it is absolutely essential to those who
must go on to face continued obstacles of racism, classism, and sexism,
to those who have been distanced and disenfranchised from the U.S.
mainstream culture, and to those who have suffered lifetimes of oppression and marginalization.[3]

Today, unfortunately, the opportunity for low-income single mothers to better their lives through education, and the pivotal supports necessary to do so, are simply not adequately available in the United States.[4]
The passage of punishing and restrictive welfare-reform legislation in
1996, coupled with a failure on the part of educators to respond to the
unique needs, challenges, and strengths of this population, has forced
poor single-mother students from colleges and universities in droves
(Center for Law and Social Policy 1999; Greenberg et al. 1999; Strawn
1998). As a result, they are prevented from gaining access to the knowledge, skills, and credentials that would otherwise allow them to lift
their families out of poverty on a productive and permanent basis.

I argue that, as educators committed to fostering social and economic
equity through education, we must challenge ourselves to understand
how crucial post-secondary education is to low-income single mothers,

to recognize that this student population is increasingly "at risk," and to work against legislation that at best discourages, and at worst prohibits, these students from entering and successfully completing post-secondary–degree programs. Further, we must begin to understand, critique, and creatively redress traditional, allegedly "neutral" pedagogical practices that can act as barriers to this population's academic success. By creating pathways of entry and support for low-income single mothers in our institutions, we begin to work toward ensuring that education remains a fair and equitable process that gives all students the opportunity to transform their lives, abilities, values, and places in the world.

KEEPING THE POOR POOR

Since the implementation of welfare reform in 1996, politicians, policy analysts, and political pundits have unabashedly celebrated a reduction in the "welfare rolls" as evidence that the United States is "renewing its democratic principles and foundational work ethic" (see Clinton 1997). As President Bill Clinton boasted in his 1997 State of the Union address, "Over the last few years, we have successfully renewed those values and moved millions out of poverty and into work" (Clinton 1997). Yet, as many recent studies indicate, moving people off of welfare is not tantamount to moving them out of poverty (Bazie and Kayatin 1998; Institute for Women's Policy Research 1998; Loprest 1999; Strawn 1998; U.S. Bureau of the Census 1999). Indeed, as a result of welfare reform, the poor in our country have become poorer. In a study for the Center on Budget and Policy Priorities, M. Bazie and T. Kayatin (1998, 3) found that "the average income for the most destitute single mother households fell from $8,624 in 1995 to $8,047 in 1997, largely because of the 1996 welfare reform law designed to get people off of the public dole."

According to Jane Ollenburger and Helen Moore,

> Families maintained by single women are one of the fastest growing economic units in America, and in 1995, 32.4% of those families lived in poverty. This compares with fewer than 5.6% in poverty for those families that have two heads of household and 10% for those that are single male headed. (Ollenburger and Moore 1998, 102)

The U.S. Bureau of the Census indicated that the mean annual income for households headed by single mothers in 1998 was $22,163.[5]

A full one-third of these single-mother families had $10,000 or less a year to live on, and 3.4 percent of them lived on less than $5,000 per year (U.S. Bureau of the Census 1999). Laura Lein and Katherine Edin also found that poor single mothers and their children experience hardship at many levels, including going without food, lacking medical and dental care, experiencing multiple utility shutoffs, living in unsafe homes or being homeless, becoming the victims of crime, and lacking sufficient winter clothing (Lein and Edin 1996; see also Loprest 1999; Nightengale et al. 1999). According to Jody Raphael (2000) of the Taylor Institute, poor women also have five times the risk of experiencing domestic violence. These stark statistics, coupled with our emerging awareness of the epidemic of abuse and neglect experienced by poor children whose mothers are forced to work long hours in low-paying jobs, paint a frightening picture of the lives of the poor in the United States (Burt et al. 2000).

Families remain poor, despite the fact that poor single mothers work. As Randy Albelda and Chris Tilly remind us:

> Not only do they do the unpaid work of raising children, they also average the same number of hours in the paid labor force as other mothers do—about 1,000 hours a year (a full-time, year-round job is about 2,000 hours a year) ... most welfare mothers cycle between relying on families, work and [welfare] benefits to get or keep their families afloat. That means that for many single mothers, [welfare] serves the same function as unemployment insurance does for higher-paid, full time workers. (Albelda and Tilly 1998, 369)

Race, class and gender work with marital and maternal status to determine an individual's chance of being and staying poor in the United States (U.S. Bureau of the Census 1998, 1999). Although too little tracking has been done since the implementation of welfare reform in 1996 to definitively assess its ramifications on the lives of poor women and their children, it is clear that, three years after the devolution of welfare, single mothers who have made the transition from welfare to work remain on the lowest rungs of the economic ladder. For example, the Urban Institute found that in 1997, the most employable of the welfare recipients who initially left the welfare rolls did so for jobs that paid an average of $6.60 per hour, a wage that simply cannot support a family (Nightengale et al. 1999).[6] Pamela Loprest finds that "hourly wages, monthly earnings, and job characteristics all indicate that [welfare] leavers are entering the low end of the labor market where they are working in much the same circumstances as near-poor and low income mothers" (Loprest 1999, 1). She also notes that "nearly one third of those who left welfare [for work] returned to welfare within one year" (Loprest 1999, 2). Research from the Institute for Women's Policy Research (IWPR) supports these findings and disabuses us of the notion that job-training programs make a long-term difference in lifting poor women out of poverty.[7] After considering the impact of welfare-to-work job-training programs across the nation, the institute found:

> Although job training increased the likelihood of working by nearly 28%, those with job training earned only three cents per hour more than those without job training. Both groups earned hourly wages that, even if earned full-time, year round, would not lift a family out of poverty. (Institute for Women's Policy Research 1998, 20)

The widening chasm between the economically stable and the poor is a gap most often predicated on the distinction between those who have an education and those who do not. Anthony Carnevale, an economist with the Educational Testing Service, posits that since the 1980s access to college has determined the side of the gulf on which a person will land. On one side of that gap are heads of households who must somehow survive and support their families in dead-end jobs with few benefits and little hope of advancement. In a recent report delivered at the National Conference on Welfare Reform and the College Option, Carnevale reminded attendees that the most undereducated are positioned to engage in work with no career ladders, no training, and often no way out. In a telling calculation, Carnevale emphasized that the sentiment "any job is a good job," which underwrites much contemporary welfare-reform policy, is based on fallacious logic. This rhetoric rests on the notion that starting at entry-level positions eventually will lead to sustainable employment. Carnevale countered this logic by illustrating that a single mother with two young children who begins a job that pays $13,000 per year today (which is much higher than the average reported by the Center for Urban Studies) and who is able (against all odds) actually to keep that job will earn only $17,000 after ten years of steady cost-of-living adjustments. At $17,000, the income of her family of three will still fall well below the poverty threshold. The theory that she will "rise above" this position is unfounded unless she has access to training and

Median earnings (thousands of dollars)

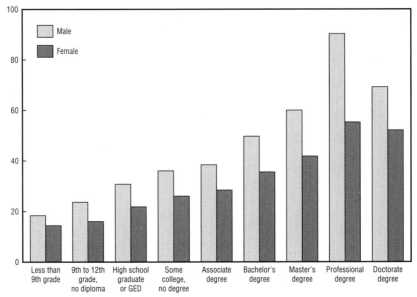

FIGURE 14.1. Median earnings by sex and educational attainment: 1998, full-time, year-round workers, age 25 and older. *Source:* U.S. Census Bureau, Current Population Survey, March 1999.

education. Carnevale further argued that the same single mother could earn $28,000 to $32,000 a year after only two years in a post-secondary educational program. Carnevale's findings are clear and convincing: Only training, support, and education will provide the poor with access to jobs that will enable them to support their families (Carnevale 1999). Figure 14.1 from the U.S. Census Bureau illustrates Carnevale's theory that educational attainment is directly related to the ability to earn family-sustaining incomes.

Post-secondary education can unlock the door to economic opportunity and thus enable disadvantaged women to live lives of dignity, supporting and nurturing their children. As Leslie Wolfe and Marilyn Gittell (1997, 2) say, "A college education has always been a route for people to lift themselves out of poverty—and women on welfare are no different." Indeed, countless studies have exposed a strong correlation between education and the ability to exit poverty successfully and permanently (Wolfe and Tucker 1998; Day and Curry 1998; Karier 1998; Spalter-Roth et al. 1997). A study by the Center for Women's Policy Studies (Wolfe and Tucker 1998) shows that women who attend college for just one year are more likely to exit and stay off public assistance than are those who try to leave public assistance by working without education. According to the 1997 Census Bureau Population Survey, among families headed by white women, the poverty rate declines from 22 percent to 13 percent when those women have at least one year of post-secondary education. The statistics are even more dramatic for women of color. For African American women, the poverty rate declines from 51 percent to 21 percent, and for Latinas the poverty rate drops from 41 percent to 18.5 percent (Day and Curry 1998).

In another compelling study sponsored by the Jerome Levy Economics Institute, Thomas Karier researched outcomes of 253 welfare recipients who graduated from Eastern Washington University during a two-year period from 1994 to 1996. Of those graduates, 85 percent earned $8 per hour, 50 percent earned $11 or more per hour, and 12 percent earned $18 per hour or more. As of November 1997, approximately 94 percent of the 1995 graduates and 85 percent of the 1996 graduates were not receiving welfare benefits. Karier concludes that "the returns of a college degree for welfare recipients are sufficiently high to make postsecondary education a particularly promising avenue to financial independence" (Karier 1998, 1).

Finally, a study by the Institute for Women's Policy Research found, in its analysis of data on 4,500 working mothers participating in the Survey of Income and Program Participation (SIPP), that a college degree is worth an additional $3.65 per hour (in 1997 dollars) for working mothers, relative to the wages of high-school graduates. In comparison, the return in hourly wages for one year of work experience is ten cents per hour in 1997 dollars (Spalter-Roth et al. 1997). If we truly want to assist the poor in pulling their families out of poverty on a permanent basis, we must invest in human capital. Rather than vilifying and punishing the victims of poverty, we must allow those who are willing and able to educate or train themselves to become productive and well-supported citizens and members of the workforce. My own research suggests that students experience dramatic and enduring benefits from completing college degrees and that the opportunity and support required to do so is increasingly limited.

POVERTY AND THE FRAGILE PROMISE OF EDUCATION

Despite numerous studies confirming the relationship between higher education and increased earnings, in 1996 Congress enacted the Personal Responsibility and Work Opportunity and Reconciliation Act (PRWORA) as part of welfare reform. Composed of a broad tangle of legislation, the act "devolved" the responsibility for assistance to the poor from the federal to the state level, and through a range of block grants, sanctions, and rewards, it encouraged states to reduce their welfare rolls by developing work requirements, imposing strict time limits, discouraging "illegitimacy," and reducing the numbers of applicants eligible for services. The act also allowed for the development of programs and requirements that had the effect of discouraging welfare recipients from engaging in educational programs, mandating instead that they engage in "work first." Specifically, the Temporary Assistance for Needy Families (TANF) program's work requirements, part of the 1996 PRWORA, drastically limited poor women's opportunities to participate in post-secondary–education programs while receiving state support. Unlike previous laws governing Aid to Families with Dependent Children (AFDC) and JOBS education and training programs, the new TANF restrictions did not allow higher education to be counted as "work" and required a larger proportion of welfare recipients to engage in recognized work activities. This work-first philosophy emphasized rapid entry into the labor force and penalized states for allowing long-term access to education and training. Since the passage of PRWORA in 1996, colleges and universities have seen dramatic declines in enrollment among welfare recipients (Greenberg et al. 1999; Pastore 1999; Strawn 1998).

Since Congress enacted its sweeping overhaul of welfare policy, recipient students have been forced to leave college for low-wage jobs. Even as our nation passionately embraces the conviction that access to education is the pathway to social and economic mobility, poor women are denied access to education that could positively alter the course of their lives. This sad irony is not lost on Karen Kahn, who notes that:

> "Providing the best quality education to all of America's children" is a popular campaign slogan. . . . In the face of this passion to educate America, it is a bit ironic to realize that at least one group of citizens has been deemed undeserving of the fruits of education. Although all the evidence

points to the need for high quality education beyond high school level to succeed in today's job market, women receiving public assistance are being driven from higher education programs. (Kahn 1998, 31)

Welfare scholar, activist, and educator Luisa Deprez agrees, noting:

Newly proposed educational policies offering tax incentives and tax credits stand in stark contrast to the welfare law which dramatically limited the number of recipients who can participate in education and threatened states with fiscal consequences when access is granted. The double message that "yes" education and training is critical to the future of the individual and the nation state but "no" it not be available to those who need it most, women on welfare, is deeply distressing.[8]

According to the Center on Budget and Policy Priorities, in the first year of welfare reform, tens of thousands of poor women were forced to drop out of school; across the nation, the decrease in enrollments among welfare recipients ranged from 29 percent to 82 percent (Bazie and Kayatin 1998). As Wolfe and Gittell (1997, 5) proclaim, "The work requirement of the new federal welfare law is causing thousands of low-income women to drop out of college to take dead end jobs with low pay and no future. This exodus of welfare recipients from the classroom must stop."

In 1998, the Center for Law and Social Policy (CLASP) conducted a preliminary survey of key policy advocates in the fifty states and Washington, D.C., regarding welfare recipients' abilities to engage in postsecondary education. Their study found that welfare recipients are "generally unable to count post-secondary education as a work activity, or may only do so on a very limited basis" (Strawn 1998, 28). The CLASP study reported that, "although the TANF plans in many states allow some access to postsecondary education, many local welfare administrators are nevertheless limiting participation in postsecondary education programs" (Strawn 1998, 32). CLASP data indicate that, as a result, the number of families reported as participating in activities that would lead to a post-secondary degree was cut in half by 1998. In 1995, almost 648,763 students across the nation were receiving AFDC benefits while enrolled in full-time educational programs; by the 1998–99 school year, that figure had dropped by 47.6 percent, to fewer than 340,000 students (Greenberg et al. 1999).

I began to see a drop in the enrollment of welfare recipients in my own classes in late 1996. In 1998 and 1999, I conducted a survey to

TABLE 14.1. Welfare-recipient students' responses to PROWRA legislation
($N = 75$)

Outcome	Number of students (%)
Exited the university to fulfill TANF work requirements	29 (38%)
Exited the university after trying to fulfill TANF requirements by working, attending school full time, and caring for children	20 (26%)
Dropped off welfare rolls to attend school full time	10 (13%)
Attended school full time or part time while fulfilling TANF requirements (working thirty hours per week while attending school, studying, and caring for children)	16 (23%)

Source: Adair (1998, 1999).

measure the impact of the 1996 welfare-reform legislation—particularly
the Personal Responsibility and Work Opportunity Reconciliation Act—
on the lives of welfare-recipient students at a large state university on
the West Coast, where I was employed as a postdoctoral instructor. My
goal was to measure students' ability to remain in school and to determine their strategies for finishing their degrees in the face of this new
legislation. I sent surveys to more than two hundred students who had
been enrolled at the state university in the previous year. Seventy-five
surveys were returned. I followed those surveys up with forty-five–
minute taped interviews with twenty former-student respondents. I
found that, of seventy-five students originally on welfare, only sixteen
were able to remain in school after signing a Personal Responsibility
Plan with the state (Adair 1999) (see Table 14.1).

Forty-nine of these seventy-five students—including pre-nursing
majors, business majors, and sociology majors—were forced to abandon
school and the dream of education and economic stability for low-wage,
dead-end jobs. The prospects for these students, a few years later, is
dismal. One survey respondent, a twenty-five-year-old student with a
ten-year-old son, now works full time earning $6.10 per hour. In re-
sponse to a question asking her to describe changes in her family's quality of life as a result of the 1996 welfare reform, she wrote:

> Things are so much harder now. We can barely pay our rent. My son is
> alone all the time when I work. I just don't see a future anymore. With
> school there was hope. I was on my way to making a decent living for us.

Now it is just impossible to survive day to day. Usually I can't pay my rent. They are hounding me to repay school loans and I don't have enough for food. Did you know that you can't even bankrupt student loans? I don't have a cent saved for emergencies. I don't know what I'm gonna do. (Adair 1998)

A second student who was a gifted and dedicated education major has temporarily returned to welfare after losing several minimum-wage jobs because she could not afford reliable child care and was denied child-care assistance from the state. She described the nightmare of losing job after minimum-wage job in order to care for her child, emphasizing that this was "a choice no mother should be forced to make." She added:

It came down to, if I want to keep this job at Burger King I have to leave my three year-old daughter alone or maybe with a senile neighbor. And I couldn't even really afford that! Or we could go back to her dad who is a drunk. If I don't do that we could both end up hungry and homeless. The choice they are making me make is to either abandon or hurt my daughter, and for what? (Adair 1999)

A third student was forced to allow her neglectful ex-husband to raise her three children so she could work two jobs. She hopes to save enough money to return to school someday, where she will finish a degree in social work. In the meantime, she and her children suffer. She reflected:

In just two short years, my kids have gone from being solid "A" students to failing. We used to study together each evening. Now they are on their own, barely hanging on. They're miserable and I just hope they don't make permanent mistakes. I tell them to hang on until we can pull ourselves out of this mess. (Adair 1998)

The experiences of these students who had worked diligently to become responsible workers, taxpayers, and parents capable of providing their families with financial security, and who are now forced to live in poverty, illustrates one startling failure of 1996 "welfare reform." Certainly, not all low-income single mothers are able or willing to go to school. However, to prevent those who can do so from completing postsecondary degrees is shortsighted and fiscally irresponsible.[9] Citizens, educators, and legislators are beginning to recognize the flaws in a system set up to punish rather than to support hardworking single mothers with dreams of education.

The Promise of Education

Welfare-reform pundits are beginning to recognize the contradiction in policy restrictions and the alleged goals of welfare reform concerning access to higher education. Douglas Howard, director of the Iowa Department of Human Services, for example, asserted that his department finds a contradiction between "the requirements of government and the promises of education: government requires that 30 percent of the TANF recipients be working by a certain date, yet statistics show that the more education a person has, the higher his or her earnings will be" (Howard 1998, 15). Brian Wing (1999), commissioner of New York State's Department of Temporary and Disability Assistance, has similarly reflected that "in order to improve career opportunities for welfare recipients we must begin to include innovative educational programs." Wing continued that, in a state with a twenty- to thirty-hour-a-week TANF work requirement, "difficult challenges must be met by a broad spectrum of community initiatives" (Wing 1999).

A small but growing number of colleges and universities have responded to this neglect of a struggling population by implementing mechanisms designed to assist poor single-mother students in their efforts to negotiate punitive TANF restrictions and gain access to education. Across the nation, these forward-thinking private and public institutions are assisting poor single mothers who must overcome seemingly insurmountable barriers to enter and complete the post-secondary programs that will allow them to raise and nurture their children productively while challenging them to reach their own potential in the world.

California, Maine, Massachusetts, Minnesota, New York, and Wyoming are but a few of the states with creative and successful programs designed to address this pressing issue. Maine's touchstone Parents as Scholars program at the University of Maine; Wyoming's POWER program; New York's ACCESS Project at Hamilton College, Welfare Rights Initiative Project at Hunter College, and COPE Program at the City University of New York (CUNY); California's CARE program; Massachusetts's Ada Comstock Scholars Program at Smith College; and the University of Minnesota's Student Parent HELP Center are all examples of these programs (Greene 1998). These schools—large and small, private and public, colleges and universities—have programs that cover a wide range of services. For example, Maine's Parents as Scholars program offers low-income student-parents academic and social support that includes child-care, health-care, and transportation allowances; the Welfare Reform Network at Hunter College encourages welfare students to mobilize and organize for political change. Wyoming's Power Program offers academic support but little social-service coordination throughout a large public university and college system, while the ACCESS Project at Hamilton College offers a comprehensive set of academic, social, career, and family supports at a private liberal-arts institution. What all of these programs have in common is a dedication to moving impoverished single mothers from welfare to meaningful and sustaining employment through the pathway of post-secondary education.

Educators can have a significant impact on the lives of poor single mothers attempting to gain access to post-secondary education by challenging our institutions to advocate for individual poor women and for programs that are designed to address their needs. Ann Withorn reminds us that educators across the country can

> lobby directly for programs that support women on welfare when they try to attend college and to oppose any reform that doesn't allow women to go to college to earn whatever level of degree they can attain. When this happens as it has in Massachusetts, the debate and policy outcomes are shifted. It is also possible to create state or citywide groups of academics to lobby, coordinate research efforts, and support each other in paying attention to the welfare issue. (Withorn 1996, 327)

Erika Kates concurs:

> I have seen a number of colleges put into practice strategies that work: Faculty have formed groups to fight against poverty; women college presidents have conducted research into AFDC recipients experiences in their own institutions and advocated for better access, students have formed low-income student organizations, lobbied against benefit reductions and for more childcare, and participated in discussion shaping state financial aid policy. (Kates 1998, 343)

Other educators and post-secondary educational administrators are working with state legislators and local welfare offices to advocate for policies that encourage qualified and committed poor single mothers in their efforts to attend college, lobbying to extend the amount of time recipients can receive educational training beyond most states' twelve-month enrollment limit, and encouraging colleges to work with state and local officials to provide employment opportunities that are aligned with academic schedules and that allow students to stay in school and to complete academic degrees. Dedicated educators are also working for economic parity by attempting to amend the Higher Education Act so that financial aid offices can count the costs associated with dependent children in the needs analysis for federal financial aid, so that student financial aid can be exempted as income when calculating welfare eligibility, and to increase Pell Grants to cover dependent care allowances.

Recent legislation in New York State is a good example of the kind of projects that academics have worked on collectively to support poor single mothers in their efforts to change their lives through education. In the early fall of 2000, educators from Hunter College, CUNY, and Hamilton College worked with state legislators to support passage of a bill that would allow welfare recipients to count college and university internships and work–study positions toward their mandated work requirement. According to Maureen Lane of the Welfare Rights Initiative at Hunter College, this policy came to fruition after legislators heard from New York State college administrators and faculty and "spoke with students who bring a wealth of firsthand expertise to a vision of true welfare reform" (Lane 2000, 1). The Work–Study and Internship Bill (A08475), signed into effect in September 2000, represents an important step in increasing poor women's access to and support for post-secondary education.[10]

Collaborations between policymakers and post-secondary institutions are crucial to efforts to ensure that poor single mothers are able to gain access to post-secondary education and its rewards. Yet these are only the first steps. Access to post-secondary education alone may not be sufficient to allow low-income single mothers to escape the cycle of poverty by completing college degrees.

HELPING RATHER THAN HINDERING WELFARE-RECIPIENT STUDENTS

Many obstacles—financial, material, familial, cultural, and pedagogical—can impede otherwise capable low-income single-mother college students from succeeding in academe in the United States. Even programs that have developed innovative pathways of entry for this at-risk population often rely on the ability of recipient students to patch together their own academic, financial, family, and social-service "safety nets." As a result, many poor single mothers are forced eventually to relinquish their goals of acquiring an education and to engage in work that does not adequately or permanently allow them to care for themselves or their families.

An absence of comprehensive social, academic, personal, family, and career services in many programs means that poor single mothers often must face insurmountable barriers to their education when they are most vulnerable. In a 1993 study of 420 graduates of fourteen two-year and ten four-year state-supported colleges and universities in the South, Joanne Thompson (1993) identified factors that affect low-income, first-generation, college-educated single mothers' enrollment, retention, and graduation from undergraduate programs. Thompson found that the majority of respondents cited their own perseverance and their desire to get a job as central to the completion of their degrees. The study also found, however, that factors such as the availability of responsive financial aid, access to affordable and reliable child care and transportation, faculty support, the presence of affirming and informed role models and mentors, and a strong academic and personal support system had an even greater impact on these students' abilities to complete degree programs successfully.

Thompson makes several recommendations that are germane to educators and administrators interested in supporting this population of students. She emphasizes the importance of: 1) familiarizing welfare caseworkers with opportunities for higher education; 2) securing needed familial support for low-income student-parents; 3) developing coursework that recognizes and values the experiences that these students bring with them; and 4) promoting the success stories of poor women who have achieved economic security through post-secondary education. Thompson believes that the dissemination of these success narratives can mitigate rampant stereotyping and the concomitant alienation that injures and impairs poor women both in and out of the academy.

Thompson's study reveals that low-income student-mothers coming to the academy, many for the first time, require additional academic, social, intellectual, cultural, emotional, and familial supports. Claude Steele (1999) provides intriguing pedagogical strategies for addressing the intellectual and psychological needs of those who have traditionally been excluded from the academy. He reminds us that the threat of being read and judged through rampant and demeaning stereotypes, or fearing that one's own actions will result in the perpetuation of these stereotypes, affects students' ability to thrive—indeed, to survive—in the post-secondary academy. Steele's work confirms that negative stereotypes directed even implicitly toward students have a bearing on their academic life. Steele refers to the threat of being viewed through the lens of a negative stereotype and its concomitant performance reduction as "stereotype threat." He clarifies:

> "Stereotype threat" involves being in a situation where a negative stereotype about your group could apply. This threat and the prospect of confirming a stereotype or of being seen that way was distracting enough, upsetting enough, to undermine a person's [academic] performance. It happens whenever these students are in the domain where the stereotype is applicable. So with any kind of intellectual performance or interacting with professors or in a classroom this stereotype is relevant and constitutes pressure on those behaviors. (Steele 1999, 45)

Steele adds that when students experience prolonged "stereotype threat" they respond by "divesting [themselves] from the domain. That is making it less a basis of one's self esteem and self regard" (Steele 1999, 46). Steele calls this process of ceasing to identify with the part of life in which pain occurs "disidentification." He explains, "But [disidentification] and not caring can mean not being motivated. And this can have real costs. When stereotype threat affects school life, disidentification is a high price that groups contending with powerful negative stereotypes about their abilities too often pay" (Steele 1999, 45).

Steele's work specifically focuses on the ways that negative stereotypes impair the academic performance of capable and engaged black students in the post-secondary academy. Yet he also extends his theories to apply to many other groups who are negatively stereotyped in academic venues. Certainly, low-income, first-generation-college-educated single mothers, often still "on welfare," are multiply marked by myriad and intersecting codes of race, class, gender, age, sexuality, nationality, and physical difference. As they are bombarded with public and overt, as well as more subtle, forms of negative stereotyping on a daily basis, they are at even greater risk for suffering stereotype threat as "self-fulfilling prophecy"—that is, as internalized negative images—

resulting in diminished academic performance and in reductions in the completion of courses, programs, and degrees.

Steele's policy recommendations for combating the negative impact of stereotype threat are applicable but in some cases difficult to implement for welfare-recipient students. He suggests that one of the most effective strategies is to "use high standards, sending the student a signal that we have high expectations for them and are not viewing them through the lens of the stereotypes ... [and] that we believe that they can meet those standards" (Steele 1999, 53). This certainly makes sense for populations of poor single-mother students, but only when programs ensure that students' social-service needs are met. Holding students to a high standard while failing to address their need for support in areas such as child care, transportation, housing, and family maintenance results in students being hindered rather than supported in their efforts to earn educational degrees.

Steele's second suggestion is that "if the leadership of the university expresses a value in diversity, and an acknowledgment that people from different backgrounds bring things to campuses that are of value to everybody here, that sends a clear message that the things about my group will not result in negative judgements, but will be valued in this environment" (Steele 1999, 54). This recommendation rests on the presumption that universities are willing to position low-income single mothers as a population that enhances rather than detracts from campus learning. This presumption is far from the norm on college campuses today.

Finally, Steele counsels that faculty support and positive role modeling helps to mitigate stereotype threat. He claims, "Even though the stereotypes held by the larger society may be difficult to change, it is possible to create niches in which negative stereotypes are not felt to apply. In specific classrooms, within specific programs, even in the climate of entire schools, it is possible to weaken a group's sense of being threatened by negative stereotypes" (Steele 1999, 54). Again, this is a viable remedy, but one that rests on the assumption that there are faculty willing to be identified as former welfare recipients. Given the devaluation of other than middle-class values in the academy, the pressure for working-class and poverty-class professors to "pass" as members of the privileged and elite class, and the general lack of acknowledgment of the workings of class in America today, this recommendation, although potentially effective, may be difficult to achieve.

A study I conducted in 1999 and 2000 with my colleagues Erol Balkan and Sharon Gormley in central New York State provides additional analysis regarding the inability of some welfare recipient students to earn college degrees. Our research provides support for and expands on Thompson's and Steele's theories. Analyzing survey responses and narrative interviews with eighty-five former welfare-recipient post-secondary students, we found that poor single mothers had indeed often left school even when they had been successful with their studies because they could not manage child-care, transportation, and work responsibilities (Adair et al. 2000).[11] Respondents also reflected Steele's concerns about disidentification, making clear that they often ended their studies because they felt demoralized, misunderstood, and misrepresented in the academy. Table 14.2 presents a breakdown of the former students' responses to the query, "What were the main reasons that you felt that you should leave school? Please list as many reasons as you feel accurately reflect your decisionmaking process at the time." As Table 14.2 shows, only 17 (20 percent) of the respondents noted that failing grades were the reason they left school. Supporting Thompson's claims, a far greater number reported that one of the reasons they left school was a lack of sufficient social-service support, such as child care, transportation, family support, and financial aid. However, a substantial number of responses also indicated that welfare-recipient students left academic programs because of the way that they had been made to feel "shamed," "erased," and "blamed" throughout their educational experiences.

Underscoring Steele's theory of the detrimental impact of negative stereotyping and disidentification, these respondents made it clear that they had suffered as a result of negative views of the group that they had been positioned to represent. These stereotypes were expressed both covertly and overtly. As one former student reflected, "I left to protect myself. Rather than feeling better about who I was, teachers' actions and words told me that I was a problem, that I was selfish, that welfare women were lazy, stupid, and bad. I just don't care about it any more. In a way, I can't afford to" (Adair et al. 2000).

Our work reflects the fact that, for some poor single mothers, the academy becomes a place of fear and diminished value rather than a site of

TABLE 14.2. Reasons cited most often for failing to complete at least two consecutive terms in an undergraduate program, Oneida County, New York ($N = 85$ students)

Reason given by student	Number of students (%)[a]
Inability to juggle demands of work, family, and school	62 (73%)
Inadequate child care or insufficient child-care funds	58 (69%)
Lack of academic support	55 (65%)
Felt unsupported/misunderstood or undervalued in class	51 (60%)
Parent or children's physical or emotional health problem	51 (60%)
Lack of reliable or affordable transportation	47 (55%)
Felt alone, ostracized, or alienated by other students	42 (50%)
Could not afford tuition; financial aid not sufficient	28 (33%)
Failing grades or lack of academic preparation	17 (20%)
Educational debt too high or growing too quickly	13 (15%)

[a]The percentages do not add up to 100 because of multiple responses from participants.
Source: Adair et al. (2000).

empowerment. For it is here that a culture that often "others" poor single mothers is represented and legitimized by those who profess authority over their lives. These low-income single-mother students often experienced profound and debilitating terror, shame, humiliation, and objectification, even in classrooms meant to foster independent scholarship and critical thinking. Students reported having felt alienated and inferior in ways that often reflected the language and sentiments found in the PRWORA, an act that includes the goal of "end[ing] the dependence of needy parents on government benefits by promoting job preparedness, work and marriage" (Loprest 1999, 2). For example, several students were told by caseworkers, professors, and even fellow students that if they were responsible parents they would be working rather than attending college, that they had made "bad choices" and should now live with the consequences, and that they were unworthy and incapable of being productive students. One respondent astutely reflected:

> With the passage of welfare reform, poor single moms were deemed unfit and suitable only to flip burgers and take out garbage. Layers of citizens

from welfare officials right on down to other students internalized this value system often questioning why I was in school rather than working full-time, as they felt free to judge me and to say that by attending college I was somehow wasting my (and by implication their) time and money. One caseworker actually told me, "You can't stay in school. Why don't you try to be a good parent to your kids and either find a husband or get off your [behind] and go to work? We won't let you waste your time with school." (Adair et al. 2000)

Students also referred to feeling as though they were "'stupid' even when [they] had studied and were prepared for class." Some reported "having [their] professors represent their experiences of poverty in ways that they felt mocked and humiliated them." Still others reported "missing more than two classes per month because of feelings of alienation and fear." One former student with a B+/A− average confided:

I would actually feel sick to my stomach when I would enter the Sociology of Poverty class that I had enrolled in so that I could understand the social conditions of my own experience. I was made to feel as though I had nothing of value to say, that my experiences and evaluations of class readings were worthless, and even that I was a worthless student who was doomed to failure. This was with a professor that everyone else loved so much and one who won awards—I was alone in my frustration. I quit school after I had missed too much school in this class. I don't think I will ever be able to return. I still feel sick. (Adair et al. 2000)

These personal narratives reflect the debilitating experiences of low-income single-parent students who have little support, few role models, and a severe sense of dislocation, disidentification, and class anxiety. These experiences need to be recognized, validated, and addressed if this population is to survive in the post-secondary academy. It is essential that colleges and universities develop programs that include innovative, responsive, and challenging curricula and a range of academic, cultural, and family supports. In addition, it is important that educators design coursework that draws on the strengths and experiences of low-income single parents while challenging and supporting them as they move beyond their knowledge of the world. We must support rather than hinder these students. In the process, we will aid them in their efforts to embrace the lifetime challenge of becoming fully engaged and responsible thinkers, citizens, workers, and community members and to improve their economic status for generations to come.

Extensive research illustrates that education is a necessary step in moving poor single mothers permanently out of poverty (Carnevale 1999; Gittell et al. 1990; Karier 1998; Wolfe and Gittell 1997). Certainly, post-secondary education had an impact on my life and the lives of countless numbers of friends, students, and colleagues in profound and enduring ways. As Leslie Wolfe and Marilyn Gittell (1997, 6) point out, policymakers and educators must remember that "the goal of welfare reform is not simply to 'end welfare as we know it' but also to help low-income women to become self-sufficient. By providing women the opportunity to go to college, states will reap the economic benefits of a skilled workforce. And tens of thousands of low income women and their families will walk the path toward economic security and social mobility." Deprez put it this way:

> If the current restrictions on higher education are not minimized or elim-inated, the lives of millions of poor women will be in extreme jeopardy as we enter a technology-based future.... It is imperative that institu-tions of higher education and organizations affiliated with them be at the forefront of a movement to secure postsecondary education for our most vulnerable citizens, otherwise the avowed objective of welfare reform ... "to lift welfare recipients out of poverty by moving them into paid employment" reveals only dismal prospects for the future.[12]

We stand at a critical juncture. If we challenge ourselves to champion and support this vulnerable population in their attempt to negotiate punitive PRWORA restrictions to earn college degrees, we will take a step toward ensuring that education remains a truly democratic project that has the potential to enact social change and foster economic equity. By failing to act, we acquiesce to the production of a two-tiered educa-tional and economic system that increasingly widens the gulf between educated, and thus economically viable, and undereducated, and thus economically underprivileged, citizens.

NOTES

1. I am particularly indebted to the faculty at North Seattle Community Col-lege in Seattle, Washington, for supporting and nurturing me in ways that changed my life and that of my entire family.

2. Letter to the author, 10 June 1999.

3. The most prominent scholars researching and writing about the connec-tion between access to post-secondary education and the ability of poor women

to exit poverty permanently are Gittell et al. (1990); Greenberg et al. (1999); Kahn (1998); Karier (1998); Kates (1998); Lein and Edin (1996); Loprest (1999); Spalter-Roth et al. (1997); Thompson (1993); Withorn (1996); and Wolfe and Gittell (1997).

4. Throughout this article, I use "welfare recipients," "low-income single parents," and "working poor" interchangeably because, as a recent Urban Institute study makes clear, these terms refer to the same population (Loprest 1999). I also focus on low-income single mothers as a population that is increasingly at risk. Although low-income single fathers do face some of the same barriers, they are not subject to gender bias, nor are they as threatened by social stereotypes as are low-income single mothers.

5. In addition, the median income in 1998 for families maintained by a husband with no wife present was $35,681; the median income for families maintained by married couples in the same year was $54,180 (U.S. Bureau of the Census 1999).

6. In *Making Ends Meet* (1996), Lein and Edin found that average monthly expenses of 165 low-wage workers averaged from $1,330 (net) in Charleston, South Carolina, to $1,383 (net) in Boston. Assuming that a single mother was able to work a forty-hour work week (which is often not possible) to generate this income, she would have to earn $9–$10 per hour.

7. Under PRWORA, welfare recipients are limited in their ability to enter vocational programs and almost prohibited from entering accredited educational programs. According to the National Governors Association (1996), the act mandates that, in any given state, "not more than 20 percent of families may count toward the work rate by participating in vocational education" (National Governors Association 1996, 2). Although "the bill provides no definition of vocational educational training," in most states this kind of training must be shorter than six months in duration; must be directly related to job skills; and cannot lead to a degree (National Governors Association 1996, 4). There are no allowances for recipients interested in starting longer-term academic programs; in most states, this activity simply does not count as a "work activity."

8. Luisa Deprez to the author, e-mail communication, 21 November 1999.

9. Jillyn Stevens has effectively argued that supporting low-income women who are earning college degrees makes fiscal sense: "My three years on AFDC cost the state and federal government around $15,800 in monthly checks and Food Stamps. To date the government has realized [through payment of federal and state income taxes,] at minimum, a $42,000 profit from investing in me while I pursued my education—a 266 percent return rate. If I maintain my current income over twenty years, I will pay a minimum of $200,000 in additional federal and state taxes. The bottom line is that society stands to earn a net gain of at least 1533 percent on its investment in my education" (Stevens 1997, 15–16).

10. Part of the language of New York State Assembly Bill A08475 reads: "Public Assistance recipients must be allowed to educate themselves and gain work experiences. Working your way through college has provided many individuals the means to better themselves through hard work and education simul-

taneously. Federal work–study programs, internships and other work placements provide the exact remedy to help people move toward self-sufficiency through work and education. Such work activities should be countable toward the participation rates and districts should not impose additional or conflicting work requirements beyond those needed to meet the participation rate" (Center for Law and Social Policy 1999).

11. In 1999 and 2000, we conducted research into the phenomena of intergenerational poverty, education as a pathway out of poverty, and the barriers that poor women face in trying to gain access to education. For the study, we surveyed eighty-five college students who had received AFDC and TANF, then followed our surveys with twenty-eight interviews with participants who were able and agreed to meet with us for one hour. The results of the survey were collected, assessed, and used to design Hamilton College's ACCESS Project.

12. Deprez, e-mail.

REFERENCES

Adair, Vivyan. 1998. Unpublished survey. Seattle, Wash. June.
———. 1999. Unpublished survey. Clinton, N.Y., and Utica, N.Y. December.
Adair, Vivyan, Erol Balkan, and Sharon Gormely. 2000. Unpublished survey. Clinton, N.Y.
Albelda, Randy and Chris Tilly. 1998. "It's a Family Affair: Women, Poverty and Welfare." In *Race, Class and Gender: An Anthology*, ed. Margaret L. Andersen and Patricia Hill Collins. Belmont, Calif.: Wadsworth Publishing.
Bazie, Michelle, and Toni Kayatin. 1998. *Average Incomes of Very Poor Families Fell during Early Years of Welfare Reform, Study Finds*. Washington, D.C.: Center on Budget and Policy Priorities.
Burt, Martha, Kathryn Schlichter, and Janine Zweig. 2000. "Strategies for Addressing the Needs of Domestic Violence Victims with the TANF Program," Urban Institute, Washington, D.C. (online). Available at: <http://www.urban.org>.
Carnevale, Anthony. 1999. "Poverty and Education." Paper presented at the National Conference on Welfare Reform and the College Option, Gallaudet University, Washington, D.C., 25–27 September.
Center for Law and Social Policy. 1999. *Welfare Update*, newsletter, 31 July, 16.
Clinton, William J. 1997. "State of the Union Address." *USA Today*, 5 February, A12.
Day, J., and A. Curry. 1998. "Educational Attainment in the United States." In *Annual Population Report*. Washington, D.C.: Government Printing Office.
Gittell, Marilyn, Margaret Schehl, and Camille Fareri. 1990. *From Welfare to Independence: The College Option*. New York: Ford Foundation.
Greenberg, Mark, Julie Strawn, and Lisa Plimpton. 1999. *How State Welfare Laws Treat Post-Secondary Education*. Washington, D.C.: Center for Law and Social Policy.

Greene, J. 1998. *Model College Programs.* New York: Howard Samuels State Management and Policy Center, City University of New York.

Howard, Douglas. 1998. Untitled. In *Proceedings of the Heartland Symposium on the Future of the Welfare State.* Madison: University of Wisconsin.

Institute for Women's Policy Research. 1998. Education and job training under welfare reform. *IWPR Welfare Reform Network News* 9/10: 1–15.

Kahn, Karen. 1998. Workfare forces single mothers to abandon college education. *Sojourner: The Woman's Forum* 24(2): 31–33.

Karier, Thomas. 1998. Welfare graduates: College and financial independence. In *Public Policy Notes* 1.

Kates, Erika. 1998. College can help women in poverty. In *For Crying Out Loud: Women's Poverty in the United States,* edited by Diane Dujon and Ann Withorn, 341-348. Boston: South End Press.

Lane, Maureen. 2000. Passage of work-study and internship bill. Welfare Rights Initiative, list-serve policy note, Hunter College, New York.

Lein, Laura and Katherine Edin. 1996. *Making Ends Meet: How Single Mothers Survive Welfare and Low-wage Work.* New York: West End Press.

Loprest, Pamela. 1999. *Families Who Left Welfare: Who Are They and How Are They Doing?* Washington, D.C.: Urban Institute.

National Governors Association and National Conference of State Legislatures. 1996. *TANF Provisions in Welfare Reform.* Available from: <http://aphsa.org/reform/analysis.htm>.

Nightengale, D., J. Trutko, and B. Barnow. 1999. *Status of the Welfare to Work Grants Program after One Year.* Washington, D.C.: Urban Institute.

Ollenburger, Jane C., and Helen A. Moore. 1998. *A Sociology of Women: The Intersection of Patriarchy, Capitalism and Colonization.* Upper Saddle River, N.J.: Prentice-Hall.

Pastore, C. 1999. "Threatened with Lawsuit, State Overhauls Policies for Student Welfare Recipients: Deadline Approaches." Equal Rights Advocates Web site, 11 August. Available from: <http://www.equalrights.org>.

Raphael, Jody. 2001. "Saving Bernice: Women, Welfare and Domestic Violence." Paper presented at Hamilton College, Clinton, N.Y., 4 April.

Spalter-Roth, R., B. Burr, H. Hartmann, and L. Shaw. 1997. *Welfare That Works: The Working Lives of AFDC Recipients.* Washington, D.C.: Institute for Women's Policy Research.

Steele, Claude. 1999. "Thin Ice: 'Stereotype Threat' and Black College Students." *Atlantic Monthly,* vol. 284 (August), 44–54.

Stevens, Jillyn. 1997. "Investing in the Future." *Women's Review of Books* 14, no. 5: 15–17.

Strawn, Julie. 1998. *Beyond Job Search or Basic Education: Rethinking the Role of Skills in Welfare Reform.* Washington, D.C.: Center for the Law and Social Policy.

Thompson, Joanne. 1993. Women, welfare and college: The impact of higher education on economic well being. *Affilia* 8: 425–441.

U.S. Bureau of the Census. 1998. *Population Survey: Selected Characteristics of Households by Total Money Income in 1997.* Washington, D.C.: Government Printing Office.

———. 1999. "Money Income in the United States: 1998." Pp. 60–206 in *Current Population Reports.* Washington, D.C.: Government Printing Office.

Vides, Noemy, and Victoria Steinitz. 1996. "Together We Are Getting Freedom." Pp. 295–306 in *For Crying Out Loud: Women's Poverty in the United States,* ed. Diane Dujon and Ann Withorn. Boston: South End Press.

Wing, Brian. 1999. Untitled paper presented to the From Welfare to Meaningful Work through Education Conference, Hamilton College, Clinton, N.Y., 15–16 October.

Withorn, Ann. 1996. "Recognizing Mother Heroes." Pp. 327–36 in *For Crying Out Loud: Women's Poverty in the United States,* ed. Diane Dujon and Ann Withorn. Boston: South End Press.

Wolfe, L., and Marilyn Gittell. 1997. *College Education Is a Route out of Poverty for Women on Welfare.* Washington, D.C.: Center for Women's Policy Studies.

Wolfe, Leslie, and Jennifer Tucker. 1998. *Getting Smart about Welfare: Action Kit for State Legislators.* Washington, D.C.: Center for Women's Policy Studies.

About the Contributors

VIVYAN C. ADAIR is an assistant professor of women's studies at Hamilton College in Clinton, New York. She also directs the ACCESS Project at Hamilton College, with the mission of supporting TANF-eligible low-income parents in their efforts to exit intergenerational poverty through the pathway of higher education. She is the author of *From Good Ma to Welfare Queen: A Genealogy of the Poor Woman in American Literature, Photography and Culture* (1999), and her articles have appeared in *Harvard Educational Review, Signs: Journal of Women in Culture and Society, Pedagogy,* and *Public Voices.*

LETICIA ALMANZA earned her B.A. from the University of Houston–Downtown and teaches English at Spring Woods High School in Houston, Texas, a school in which the majority of students are defined as "at risk" due to economic disadvantage and race. She is currently pursuing a master's degree in Educational Administration under a cohort corporate school. She dedicates her time and energy to promoting the idea that all children can learn, in spite of their socioeconomic backgrounds. Almanza is also a single mother with two girls, Kristina and Allyson.

LISA D. BRUSH is an associate professor and director of Graduate Studies in the Sociology Department at the University of Pittsburgh, where she founded and directs the Family Violence and Self-Sufficiency Project. Her most recent articles in the *Journal of Sociology and Social Welfare, Violence Against Women,* and *Violence and Victims* reflect her research interests in battered women, poverty, and welfare-to-work transition. Another current project is a book that views state and social policies through a gender lens and focuses on the importance of including both safety and solvency in definitions of "welfare."

SANDRA L. DAHLBERG is an associate professor at the University of Houston–Downtown, where she teaches courses in American literature, including Mexican American literature and literary representations of poverty. She is the author of articles published in *Multilingual America,* *Recovering the U.S. Hispanic Literary Heritage, Pedagogy,* and *Public Voices.*

ANDREA S. HARRIS is a law-school student at the University of Washington. Her interest in law stems from her experiences with the legal system as a homeless youth and later with the family-law court system. She hopes to practice family or criminal law, specifically advocating for the poor, women and children of minority backgrounds, and homeless youth.

SANDY SMITH MADSEN is a doctoral student at Emory University's Institute for Women's Studies, where her research focuses on the impact of public policy on people marginalized by race, class, and gender, with particular emphasis on the pauperization of motherhood. Madsen is also the founder and executive director of the Mother's Project, a nonprofit organization that works to promote public policy of support and respect for care labor, especially for low-income and minority communities.

DEBORAH MEGIVERN is a postdoctoral researcher at the Center for Mental Health Services Research, Washington University School of Social Work. In 2003, she will become an assistant professor with the School of Social Work at Washington University in Saint Louis. Her research is focused on the intersection of poverty, mental health, and higher education as she studies how access to and retention in higher education for poor people with serious mental illness may prevent dependence on social-welfare programs.

TONYA MITCHELL, forced out of college by welfare reform, hopes to continue her pursuit of a nursing degree. She is currently a nurse's aide in a convalescent home. Mitchell is the single mother of twin daughters for whom she works to provide the opportunities she did not have as a poor child.

JOYCELYN K. MOODY is an associate professor at the University of Washington in Seattle, where she teaches courses in American autobiography, African American literature and culture, and women's literature. She is the author of *Sentimental Confessions: Spiritual Narratives of 19th-Century African America Women* and has published articles in *Black American Literature Forum* and *Religion and Literature.*

JUDITH OWENS-MANLEY is the associate director of community research at the Arthur Levitt Public Affairs Center at Hamilton College; she also maintains a practice as a psychotherapist. She earned her Ph.D. from the School of Social Welfare at the State University of New York, Albany. Owens-Manley has published articles that address human-services issues such as welfare and domestic violence and is currently working on a book about refugees in upstate New York.

NELL SULLIVAN received a B.A. from Vanderbilt University and a Ph.D. from Rice University. She is an associate professor of English at the University of Houston–Downtown, where she teaches American literature, literary theory, and Southern literature. Her publications include essays on William Faulkner, Nella Larson, Eavan Boland, and Cormac McCarthy. She is currently at work on a book that examines representations of gender in McCarthy's fiction.

LAURA SULLIVAN-HACKLEY holds a bachelor's in journalism and English from Western Kentucky University. Her work has appeared in *The Iowa Review, Press, Kalliope,* and other publications. She is a self-employed graphic designer inTallahassee, Florida.

LISA K. WALDNER is an associate professor of sociology at the University of St. Thomas in Saint Paul, Minnesota. She has published work on a variety of issues including lesbian/gay political activism, sexual coercion, violence in same-sex relationships, and identity issues of gay/lesbian adolescents. Her articles have appeared in the *Journal of Homosexuality, Archives of Sexual Behavior,* and *Aggression and Violence.* Waldner is a member of the editorial board of the journal *Violence and Victims* and associate editor of *Research in Political Sociology.* She is currently working on an examination of bias in crimes based on sexual orientation and attitudes toward lesbian/gay political activism held by heterosexual African Americans and Hispanics.